CARAVAN CITIES

By

M. ROSTOVTZEFF

Translated by

D. *and* T. TALBOT RICE

OXFORD
AT THE CLARENDON PRESS
1932

OXFORD UNIVERSITY PRESS
AMEN HOUSE, E.C. 4
LONDON EDINBURGH GLASGOW
LEIPZIG NEWYORK TORONTO
MELBOURNE CAPETOWN BOMBAY
CALCUTTA MADRAS SHANGHAI
HUMPHREY MILFORD
PUBLISHER TO THE
UNIVERSITY

PRINTED IN GREAT BRITAIN AT THE UNIVERSITY PRESS, OXFORD
BY JOHN JOHNSON, PRINTER TO THE UNIVERSITY

PREFACE

THIS book is really the outcome of a series of travel sketches written in 1928 while the impressions of my journey to Syria, Arabia, and Palestine in the early part of that year were still fresh in my mind. These sketches first appeared in two Russian newspapers published at Berlin and at Paris, *The Helm* and *Resurrection*, and they were reprinted later in the Russian magazine *Contemporary Notes* (Paris), this time with certain alterations and with the addition of several new sketches. Finally, they appeared in book form at Paris in 1931 under the title *O Blijnem Vostoke*. Then the Clarendon Press offered to produce an English edition, but as I was on the point of undertaking another and more ambitious journey to the Near East, I decided to postpone revision for the English edition until my return. It was my intention to revisit the sites which form the subjects of my sketches and also to include lower Mesopotamia, the modern Iraq, in my travels.

The new and vivid impressions with which I returned from this journey, and the opportunity that it gave me of examining the ruins in detail and of appreciating the enormous advance made by archaeology in the study of these sites, led me to form so many fresh conclusions that I have found myself obliged not merely to revise my text, but even in part to rewrite it. In doing so, I have omitted the last two sketches of the Russian volume, since they dealt with Rhodes, Cyprus, and Mycenaean Greece and not with caravan cities.

Whilst on these travels I was able to collect the material with which this book is illustrated. I am indebted for it partly to my wife, partly to the 'Service des Antiquités' of Syria and the Lebanon and to its director H. Seyrig, and partly to the field-directors of the Jerash and Dura excavations, Dr. C. Fisher, M. M. Pillet, and Prof. C. Hopkins. I take this opportunity of expressing my sincere thanks for assistance so readily accorded.

I cannot claim to have produced in this volume a final and complete picture either of caravan trade in general or of the life of certain caravan cities in particular. The consideration of caravan trade in general raises innumerable problems, of economics, of geography, of climate, and of history, which have never been fully dealt with, and which no scholar has ever attempted to study in this connexion. Consequently, the section that I have devoted to the history of caravan trade in the Near East is no more than a sketch; the outline of a larger work which some one else will fill in in the future.

The sections which deal with the caravan cities are equally imperfect. My choice of these cities is accidental. It is not based on the historical importance of towns concerned but on the amount of information available; or, to be more precise, on the state of preservation of the ruins. It is obvious that in Syria, for example, such a town as Damascus has a far longer and far more instructive history as a caravan city than Palmyra, while in Transjordania Amman is larger and more important than Jerash. In northern Syria, again, the history of Aleppo through the centuries would be more instructive than that of Dura. But so little of the history of these important towns has survived and the little that has survived is of so fragmentary a nature, that the picture we can form of them is necessarily incomplete. In Damascus, for instance, traces of the caravan route, the temple, and the caravanserais are still recognizable, but the old is so much overlaid by the new that the topography of the ancient city only becomes intelligible when it is studied in connexion with Petra and Palmyra. Amman, again, is a modern city which is continually growing and can never, therefore, be thoroughly excavated. The topography of Aleppo, which till now has never been studied, is even more difficult to reconstruct. It was considerations such as these that determined my choice; it is for the reader to decide whether I have done wisely.

Finally I must say a few words about my treatment of the separate cities. Syria, Palestine, and Arabia are now entering upon a period of systematic, historical, and archaeological exploration, and it is probable that this will soon throw fresh light on the caravan cities which are considered in this book. Why then, the critic may ask, do I hasten to set down my conclusions? Why do I not wait until more facts are available and a less problematic reconstruction can be made? Such a question is legitimate: yet in archaeological research it is often the general outlines of the evolution of a given site which are of primary importance. For the search to be as simple and as satisfactory as possible, it is essential to realize the exact objects of one's search. I do not for a moment suppose that I have given an exhaustive account of the historical problems to which I have referred in these pages, but I am confident that the line of research that I have indicated is the right one, and that the historical importance of many Syrian towns will only be properly appreciated when it has been recognized that they are towns of a peculiar type and when their development as caravan cities has been fully acknowledged.

One word more on the bibliographical Appendix. It is my principle never to publish a book without acknowledging my indebtedness to those who have previously dealt with any particular problem. I am sorry that I have not been able to refer to all the ancient sources and all the modern books and articles which I have used. To have done so would have changed completely the character of the book. I have therefore confined myself to mentioning those books and articles in which the reader will find the sources quoted or published in full and which contain a detailed and up-to-date bibliography.

M. R.

CONTENTS

LIST OF ILLUSTRATIONS	xi
I. CARAVAN TRADE. AN HISTORICAL SURVEY	1
II. PETRA	37
III. JERASH	55
IV. PALMYRA AND DURA	91
V. THE RUINS OF PALMYRA	120
VI. THE RUINS OF DURA	153
BIBLIOGRAPHY	220
INDEX	227

LIST OF ILLUSTRATIONS
PLATES
facing page

I. MODERN CARAVANS: 1. Part of Mr. Warren's caravan in the Gobi desert (*by courtesy of Mr. Warren*); 2. Part of M. N. Roerich's caravan in Central Asia (*by courtesy of Roerich Museum Press*); 3. Caravan leaving Petra for Egypt (*by courtesy of Miss A. E. Conway*) 16

II. ASSYRIAN AND PERSIAN CAMELS: 1. Dromedaries of the Arabian desert (*British Museum*); 2. Camels of Central Asia (*from a cast in the British Museum*) 17

III. MEN AND CAMELS OF SOUTH ARABIA: 1. Funeral stele (*Louvre, Paris*. 'Corpus Inscriptionum Semiticarum', IV. 2, No. 445); 2. Funeral stele (*Bombay Museum*. 'Corpus Inscriptionum Semiticarum', IV. 2, No. 698); 3. Bronze camel (*British Museum, hitherto unpublished*); 4. Bronze horse (*Ottoman Museum, Constantinople*. 'Corpus Inscriptionum Semiticarum', IV. 2, No. 507, p. 15) . 24

IV. CAMELS OF THE CHINESE CARAVANS: 1. Camel carrying two camel-bags (*by courtesy of the Pennsylvania University Museum, Philadelphia*); 2, 3. Central Asiatic two-humped camels (*Collection of C. T. Loo, Paris. Hitherto unpublished*) . . 32

V. PETRA: 1, 2. Two views of El-Khasne (*photos. Raad, Jerusalem*) 40

VI. PETRA: 1. The theatre; 2. The archway over the main street (*photos. American Colony, Jerusalem*) 41

VII. PETRA: ROCK-CUT TOMBS. 1. The tomb of the obelisks (*photo. American Colony, Jerusalem*); 2. The Urn-tomb . . 42

VIII. PETRA: 1. Rock-cut sanctuary: 2. The two obelisks (*photos. Raad, Jerusalem*) 43

IX. PETRA: 1. A Spring and the Spring Sanctuary (*photo. Raad, Jerusalem*); 2. Staircase up Jebel en Umer (*photo. Miss A. E. Conway*) 46

X. JERASH: 1. 'Triumphal' arch outside the city; 2. The pear-shaped square 72

XI. JERASH: 1. One of the side fronts of the Temple of Zeus; 2. The seats of the theatre 73

XII. JERASH: 1. The main street; 2. Part of the colonnaded street 78

XIII. JERASH: 1. The Nymphaeum; 2. Entrance to the Church of St. Theodore 79

List of Illustrations

facing page

XIV. JERASH: 1. Monumental Propylaea; 2. Front of the Temple of Artemis 80

XV. JERASH: 1. The big water tank; 2. The little theatre . 88

XVI. PALMYRA: 1. The ruins of Palmyra drawn by Cornelius Loos, 1711 (*University Library, Upsala. By courtesy of Mr. Anderson*); 2. General view of Palmyra (*by courtesy of Mr. Amy*) . . 120

XVII. PALMYRA: 1. Town tombs outside the city; 2. One of the temple tombs 121

XVIII. PALMYRA: 1. Part of the colonnaded street; 2. The interior of the caravanserai 128

XIX. PALMYRA: 1. Front view of the Temple of Bel (*by courtesy of Mr. Cantineau*); 2. Side view of the Temple of Bel (*by courtesy of Mr. Amy*) 129

XX. THE GODS OF PALMYRA: 1. Bel, Yarhibol, and Aglibol. Clay tessera; 2. Bel, Yarhibol, and Aglibol. Clay tessera; 3. Arsu. Tessera (*Cabinet des Médailles, Paris. Photos. Giraudon*) 136

XXI. THE GODS OF PALMYRA: 1. Atargatis (*British Museum. Photo. Giraudon*); 2. Atargatis and Hadad. Clay tessera (*Collection of the Viscountess d'Andurain, Palmyra. Photo. Giraudon*); 3. Allat. Clay tessera (*British Museum. Photo. Giraudon*); 4. Tyche. Clay tessera (*British Museum. Photo. Giraudon*); 5. Tyche or Bel. Bronze tessera (*Cabinet des Médailles, Paris. Photo. Giraudon*) . . 137

XXII. THE GODS OF PALMYRA: 1. Arsu and Azizu. Basrelief (*Damascus Museum. By courtesy of Prof. Ingholt*); 2. Arsu. Clay tessera (*British Museum. Photo. Giraudon*); 3. Arsu (*Collection of the Viscountess d'Andurain, Palmyra*) 138

XXIII. THE PEOPLE OF PALMYRA: 1. Young priest (*Art Museum of Yale University*); 2. Veiled woman (*Art Museum of Yale University*); 3. Schoolboy (*Collection of the Viscountess d'Andurain, Palmyra. Photo. by Mr. Amy*) 144

XXIV. DURA: 1. SE. part of the citadel; 2. NW. gate and tower . 168

XXV. DURA: 1. Hellenistic wall surrounding the redoubt; 2. Entrance to the palace which stood on top of the redoubt . . 169

XXVI. DURA: 1. The main gate; 2. The main gate and the main street 176

XXVII. DURA: 1. The main street in the centre of the city; 2. Central court of the palace-fortress of the citadel . . 177

List of Illustrations   xiii

facing page

XXVIII. DURA: 1. Ruins of the temple of Atargatis; 2. The little theatre 178

XXIX. DURA: 1. The temple of the Palmyrene gods: 2. Court of the sanctuary in the SE. corner of the fortifications . . 182

XXX. DURA. THE GODS: 1. Fragment of a plaster statue of Artemis (*Louvre, Paris. Photo. Giraudon*); 2. Atargatis and Hadad. Bas-relief (*Art Museum of Yale University*) . . . 184

XXXI. DURA. THE GODS: 1. Parthian god (?). Fragment of a bas-relief (*Louvre, Paris. Photo. Giraudon*); 2. Nemesis. Bas-relief (*Art Museum of Yale University*) 192

XXXII. DURA. THE GODS: 1. The god Aphlad. Stele; 2. Temple of Artemis Azzanathkona 193

XXXIII. DURA. The aristocracy of Dura in the Parthian period: 1. Konon and two priests performing a sacrifice. Fresco (*Museum of Damascus. Reproduced from Cumont,* 'Fouilles de Doura-Europos', pl. XXXII); 2. Performance of a sacrifice. Fresco (*reproduced from Cumont,* 'Fouilles de Doura-Europos', pl. LV) . . 200

XXXIV. DURA: Wall-painting of Julius Terentius the Tribune (*Art Museum of Yale University*) 201

XXXV. DURA: Parts of a Sasanian wall-painting from a private house in Dura 214

FIGURES IN THE TEXT

page

1. Deified Parthian King. Graffito (*reproduced from Cumont,* 'Fouilles de Doura-Europos', pl. XCIX, fig. 2) . . . 193

2. Parthian horseman, from a graffito found at Dura (*drawing by Mr. Pillet*) 194

3. Parthian or Persian *clibanarius*, from a graffito found at Dura (*Art Museum of Yale University*) 195

4. General view of the early Sasanian fresco showing a battle between Persians and Romans 211

5. Graffito showing a caravan in Dura (*Art Museum of Yale University*) 212

6. Graffito showing a Euphrates ship (*Art Museum of Yale University*) 213

List of Illustrations

MAPS AND PLANS

		page
1.	The Near-East Trade Routes	2
2.	The City of Petra (*after Wiegand*, 'Petra', fig. 1; *by courtesy of Prof. Th. Wiegand*)	38
3.	Sketch-map of the City of Jerash (*from a drawing by Prof. Clarence Fisher*)	54
4.	The City of Palmyra (*from a map drawn by M. Gabriel.* 'Syria', 1926, pl. XII)	*facing p.* 121
5.	The City of Dura (*from a drawing by Prof. C. Hopkins*)	154

NOTE

The numbers in brackets in the
text refer to the illustrations.

I
CARAVAN TRADE. AN HISTORICAL SURVEY

WHAT do I mean by the term 'caravan cities'? Before answering this question I must recall certain well-known facts, and to begin with I must, at the risk of covering familiar ground, trace the configuration of Syria and Phoenicia, Palestine, Mesopotamia, and Arabia (see map I). The huge quadrilateral of the Arabian peninsula is bounded on the south by the ocean and on the east and west by two of its inlets, the Persian Gulf and the Red Sea. With the exception of a small, fertile strip of land on the south-western coast known as 'Arabia Felix', and of several oases, Arabia is a land of unbroken desert. To the north the uplands and mountains of Palestine, Phoenicia, Syria, Asia Minor, and the Iranian plateau form the boundaries of this desert land, enclosing it in a semicircle. The snows and abundant rains that fall on the Lebanon, on the Taurus, and on the Iranian plateau supply water to a number of rivers large and small, such as the Jordan, Orontes, Euphrates, Khabur, and Tigris, and these in their turn form rich and fertile plains. The fertility caused by the rivers, together with frequent rains and cooling sea-breezes, transforms the coastal fringe of the Mediterranean, that is maritime Palestine, Phoenicia, and Syria, into an almost continuous belt of natural gardens or rich cornfields. Behind the coastal fringe these rivers and rains have wrested from the desert a wide area of watered, or partly watered, country in the shape of a crescent and converted it into

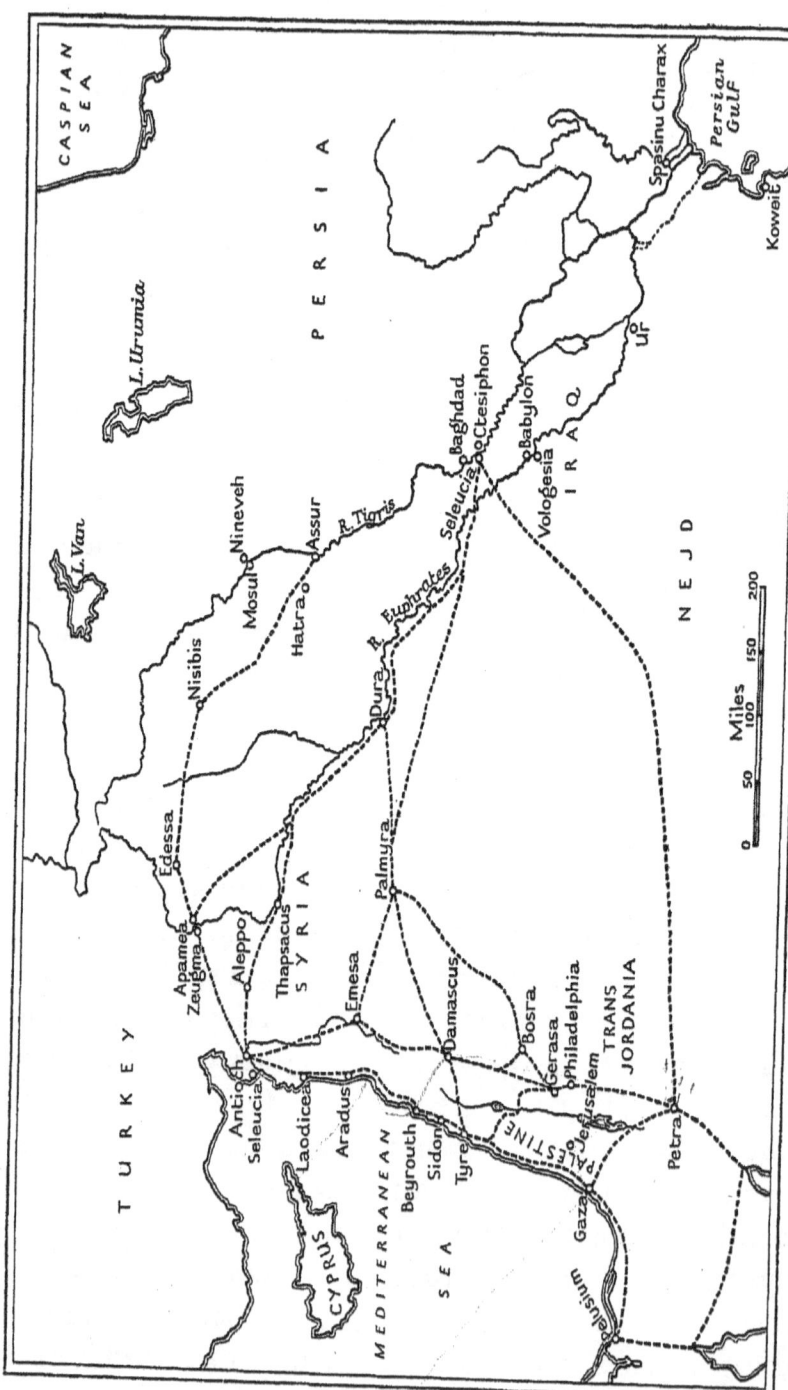
Trade routes of the Near East

fertile grazing land for the nomadic population of the desert and potential arable land for the settled inhabitants. Moreover, the swift waters of the Tigris, the Euphrates, and the Khabur, and their tributaries can be harnessed and used by the local population to irrigate and reclaim from the desert a considerable tract of land on either side of their high banks. Finally the Tigris and the Euphrates have together formed that fertile alluvial delta known as Lower Mesopotamia. If this delta were properly cared for, drained, and irrigated, it could be transformed from desert or marsh into the richest gardens, the most productive cornland, or the most admirable pasture.

Such was the configuration of the Near East in antiquity and such it has remained in its general lines to the present day. An historical study of climatology undertaken mainly by my colleague at Yale, Professor Elsworth Huntington, has, it is true, revealed the fact that in ancient times the band of cultivation along the fringe of the desert varied in size. This so-called 'crescent' of fertile land changed according to the increase or decrease of moisture in the region, so that during the wet periods enormous sections of land became available for agriculture and for cattle-breeding, though they were arid, unproductive desert during the dry periods. During the wet periods the nomadic population of the desert not only increased in numbers but also tended to become settled. But then another period of dryness would ensue, famine would descend upon the flourishing communities of settled inhabitants, ravaging and devastating the work of man and man himself, and when its work of destruction was complete, it would be succeeded yet again by a period of moisture.

Then the process of reconquering and civilizing the desert would begin anew.

In local and particular instances, historical climatology has undoubtedly often proved correct, and such changes as I have described are in general due to climatic conditions. But in the once prosperous land of Mesopotamia it is man rather than nature who is responsible for the utter desolation which now reigns. The same is true of the numerous ruined cities which stand on the banks of the Tigris and Euphrates and of their tributaries, which were at one time so flourishing. In these lands man has lost the habit of continuous and productive labour which it took him centuries of training to acquire, and it is for this reason that we now see only a wilderness where once there flourished gardens, cornfields, and rich pastures. It was man, not nature, who created the canal, the dike, and the irrigation systems, without which no civilization can survive in the valleys which border the larger rivers of the Near East.

These are characteristics which hardly promise a great role in the history of the world for the area of which I am speaking. It is true that certain localities in this area were not only capable of producing sufficient for the inhabitants, but also of providing them with a surplus for export. For this purpose, however, it was not enough for the inhabitants to possess an organized system of agriculture and cattle-breeding; they needed as well a more or less organized system of trade. It is very difficult to determine whether production or barter is the first to make its appearance in a district which is able to export, for we know of no period in the history of mankind when barter was not practised. Barter is, in fact, as old as production, and the existence of a period of completely isolated domestic economy is only an imaginary creation of the brain of the theorizing economist.

The Near East was an ideal region for the development of barter. In its eastern part it is intersected from north to east by two great rivers, the Tigris and the Euphrates, and although they are not especially well suited to navigation and never became carriers of a lively traffic, their banks are so well supplied both with vegetation and water that they form a natural route for trade. To the west, in Egypt, the more placid and more easily navigable Nile, which flows northward from the south, has always been an almost perfect carrier of goods.

Lastly there is the Arabian desert which must not be regarded as a barren waste on the earth's surface nor even as a boundary of civilization. Like the sea, the desert not only divides; it also joins, for it is a thoroughfare open to trade from every side. It has even created the means of transport for this trade, that 'ship of the desert', the camel. On the eastern side of the Arabian desert stretches the favoured plateau of Iran and to the south and east of it, beyond the Persian Gulf, lies the fabulous wealth of India. To the west the Red Sea separates Arabia from, yet at the same time connects it with, another legendary country, central Africa, with its precious and exotic products; while in the north the Isthmus of Suez links the Arabian desert to Egypt, and a number of excellent harbours on the shores of Palestine, Phoenicia, and Syria bring it into close relationship with the Mediterranean lands, Greece, Italy, and Spain.

Caravan Trade. An Historical Survey

As soon as the earliest civilizations known to us were born in the deltas of the Tigris, the Euphrates, and the Nile, and began to prosper and to develop, caravans from all parts began to journey towards Babylonia and Egypt. First came the nearest neighbours: the Arabs of the desert and the dwellers in the Iranian hills. Strings of camels followed in their tracks, shaggy two-humped beasts, the northern brethren of the elegant single-humped dromedaries of Arabia, bringing goods from the mountains of Iran. From the north, from northern Syria and Asia Minor, trains of donkeys, heavily laden, moved down the Euphrates and Tigris valleys. At the same time the first ships began to traverse the sea, putting out from Egypt, and from the shores of the Persian Gulf, from southern Arabia, and from the sea-coast of India.

These ships and caravans were laden with the goods which Babylonia and Egypt lacked, goods which were daily becoming more of a necessity and less of a luxury to civilized man. They carried stone and wood for the erection of temples, palaces, and cities, copper for the manufacture of arms and of agricultural and industrial implements; gold and silver, ivory, rare woods, precious stones, pearls, and incense for the delectation of gods and men; scents and cosmetics ever dear to the Oriental, or spices for use in cookery. In Syria and Cappadocia, on the Iranian plateau and in India, in southern and central Africa such wares abounded and in exchange for them civilized society sent her various new products: specimens of metalwork, especially weapons of the chase and war, elaborate coloured fabrics, glass beads, wine, dates, oil and fine bread were exported, the foodstuffs being especially acceptable to the half-starved Bedouin of the desert. Soon a similar intercourse arose between civilized countries, for it was impossible for them to avoid an exchange of their most recent products. Thus Babylonia would send her latest novelties to Egypt and Egypt hers to Babylonia; India would export her products to Babylonia and Babylonia hers to India.

Recent excavations in Babylonia and Egypt have penetrated to the very lowest levels of inhabited sites and they have brought to light objects from temples and palaces, houses and tombs, which date back to the earliest stages of civilization. Amongst them are some of the earliest written texts in existence. Both the objects and the texts tell us that even at this early date the oldest city-states of Sumer in Mesopotamia were linked to far distant lands by caravans: to Egypt in the west, to Asia Minor in the north, to Turkestan, Seistan, and India in the east and south-east. The discovery of similar seals in India at Harappa and Mohenjo Daro and in Babylonia at Ur, the presence of archaic gold objects of Sumerian type at Astrabad on the Caspian Sea, the similarity in type of the copper arms and utensils of Egypt, Babylonia, Syria, and Iran are further proof of this fact. A number of resemblances, not only in objects of daily use but also in the decorative motifs of Egypt and Babylonia, show the close connexion between these two lands. Even more conclusive evidence of early foreign trade is discoverable from the analysis of finds in the predynastic tombs of Ur and Kish. Beautiful objects of gold, silver, copper, and of different kinds of wood embellished with rare stones have been found here in amazing profusion, and the materials of none of them are indigenous. They were imported from a great distance, and the lion's share in this import business fell to caravan trade.

With the advance of the centuries civilization spread over wider and still wider fields. Sargon and Naramsin, kings of Akkad in Babylonia in the third millennium B.C., were largely responsible for this by their creation of the first extensive empire known to mankind. They formed it by uniting western Asia into a single state—a policy which was followed later by Ur-Nammu of the third dynasty of Ur. This enabled them not only to strengthen the already existing lines of intercourse between various regions within the empire, but also to establish fresh connexions with their neighbours to the north, south, east, and west. The most important result of this policy was, however, the appearance of numerous trading towns in the valleys and fields of the 'fertile crescent' and the development of the maritime settlements of Palestine, Phoenicia, and Syria into important centres of commerce. Cities appeared in Asia Minor also, and a trade was begun with the European coast of the Mediterranean Sea, where a demand upon similar commercial lines was nascent. The use of Indian, Arabian, and African goods steadily increased and commercial relations with Arabia and through Arabia with India and Africa on the one hand and with the Iranian plateau on the other gradually became more binding and led by degrees to a more efficient organization.

Business conventions came into being, trading sagacity was gradually acquired by those who had now become professional traders, and civil and commercial law gradually developed. These were first based upon customs, but at a later date written clauses came into being and we find them in Babylonia at the very dawn of civilization, not only recorded in writing but even codified. We know to-day that Hammurabi's legal code of about the year 1900 B.C. was not the first attempt to systematize criminal and civil law. The third dynasty of Ur, which followed Sargon's imperialistic aim, had already created a code of this type, probably intended for the use of the whole empire, whilst as early as in the year 3000 B.C. there existed thousands of contracts and agreements of the most varied kind, written in the most ancient legal language that we know—Sumerian. The legal essence of, and the formulas used in, these contracts and agreements, which are evident to all who study such documents, remained almost unchanged from the days of Sargon to the time when first Greek and, later, Roman law penetrated the Near East.

In the course of time the territories outside Sumer and Babylonia became accustomed to the rules of law and to intercourse based upon carefully defined rights, as is proved by the recently discovered fragments of an ancient Assyrian legal code, which probably dates back to the fifteenth century B.C. Another code of slightly later date belongs to the great Hittite power of Asia Minor, which grew into a cultured and well-organized state during the first centuries of the second millennium B.C.

Barter is the ancestor of commercial law, but law in return regulates barter, civilizing it and defining its wide limits. The discovery of hundreds of very early private documents of a legal character at Kul Tepe in Cappadocia, in the north-east of Asia Minor, the later

Mazaka, offers an excellent illustration of this. The documents tell of the systematic exploitation of the silver and copper mines of Cappadocia and Cilicia by the combined efforts of the local population and of some immigrants from the south; these may have been enterprising colonists from a province of the Sumerian empire, the early Assyria. These colonists had arrived not later than the first half of the third millennium B.C. and soon became the business leaders of the district. Politically they were at the same time dependent on Assyria and also under the protection of the Sumero-Akkadian empire. The metals which were extracted from these mines of Asia Minor were sent both down the Euphrates to Mesopotamia and along the caravan route to the ports of Phoenicia, and more especially to Byblos. Thence they were conveyed to Egypt in the form of massive rings.

The Cappadocian documents have brought to light numerous facts of interest regarding the organization and development of caravan trade. We cannot here speak of them in detail though we may note that most of the documents formed the archives of important trading and banking houses. These firms equipped and financed the large caravans, generally composed of donkeys, which travelled south and south-west. The tablets tell us of the complicated business enterprises of the period and of the fully developed legal and civil procedure of the time, as well as of the regular and orderly work carried out by special legal bodies. As we read, it becomes evident that these documents must have had behind them hundreds of years of organized barter, and that the law which governed it must also have developed through hundreds of years. Babylonia

Caravan Trade. An Historical Survey

laid the first foundations of this evolution, but as early as the third millennium B.C. we find Asia Minor introducing much which was new and original. The system in fact influenced the whole life of Asia Minor as much as it did that of Syria and of the countries connected with them.

The decay of the empires of Akkad and of Ur led to a period of political anarchy, the result of which was the autonomy of minor powers. This, in turn, was followed by a new union under the leadership of the west-Semitic dynasty of Babylonia, the dynasty of the renowned Hammurabi. During this period the political and economic life of the ancient world became increasingly complicated, though Babylonia still remained the ruling force.

One of the greatest achievements of the Sumero-Babylonian culture in the realm of trade took place at this time, that is to say the later part of the third millennium B.C. This was the introduction of a metal unit of exchange which was partly created by, and partly responsible for, an amazing development in the standard of individual life and an ever-growing complexity in the life of civilized humanity. This metal unit was the direct predecessor of coined currency, which made its first appearance two thousand years later, in the seventh century B.C., in Asia Minor and in Greece. The early unit was based upon the silver 'mina', with its subdivisions into 'shekels'. This innovation was partly the work of private merchants (the earliest banker-tradesmen in history), partly that of the state.

Thus all the events of the time led to a more extensive development and to a more complex organization of caravan trade. The Bedouins of the desert and the highlanders of the Upper Euphrates or the Tigris, the inhabitants of the Iranian plateau and of Asia Minor, all of whom used to be shepherds or highwaymen, now became merchants and business men. The caravan became a definite body, it assumed the character of a complicated and carefully regulated world of its own, and it still remains the same to-day, for railways and motor-cars have not yet put an end to its strangely independent existence.

While the Babylonian kingdom was still powerful and alive, while it still ruled firmly at the mouth of the Tigris and Euphrates, and while its greatest rival, Egypt, far in the west, became ever more strong politically and created an amazingly high civilization, Indian and Arabian goods found an excellent market both in Mesopotamia and the countries which depended on it, and in Egypt.

Indian goods were sometimes dispatched to Babylonia by sea from the Indian ports, straight to the mouths of the Tigris and Euphrates. More usually they arrived at one of the Arabian harbours, often at Gerrha on the western shore of the Persian Gulf, and thence were conducted by nomad Arabs on the backs of camels and donkeys to Babylonia. The goods produced by 'Arabia Felix', and purchased by the south-western Arabs beyond the Bab-el-Mandeb in Africa, either travelled across the desert to the same Gerrha and thence to Babylonia or were brought in ships along the shore either to Gerrha or directly to the mouths of the Tigris and Euphrates.

Another set of important desert-routes led to Egypt. The south-western Arabs would send their own goods, the goods of India, and those of Africa, northwards along the eastern shore of the Red Sea and then across the Sinai peninsula to Egypt. Or the Gerrhaeans would dispatch the same goods and probably some of the goods of Babylonia first to the rich oasis of Tema in the heart of the Arabian desert and from this oasis to one of the stations of the shore-route along the Red Sea to Egypt.

In these early days the land-routes were much more used than the sea. The sea was as yet neither favoured nor trusted and was used only when absolutely necessary. Transport by camels across the desert was reckoned a far safer and more trustworthy method of conveyance than that by ship, and it was mostly by means of caravans that the products of India, of Arabia, and even those of central Africa were dispatched from Arabia to Babylonia, to Syria, to Egypt, or even much farther to north and to west.

It is not surprising that this regular and profitable trade with Babylonia, Egypt, and their dependencies (all civilized powers) led, as it had done formerly in Cappadocia, to the creation of organized states and of an individual, highly developed civilization in Arabia. As yet, our knowledge of the culture of eastern and southern Arabia is scanty. We are but vaguely familiar with the Gerrhaeans in the east, with the inhabitants of Hadramaut, of Catabania, or with those of the kingdoms of the Sabaeans and Minaeans on the south and south-western coast-lands. The last ruled that fertile tract of land which, even in antiquity, bore the name of 'Arabia Felix'. Recently the travels of a number of European scholars in this fabulous land have revealed thousands of inscriptions and have made us familiar with the amazing constructions erected by these peoples, which comprise cities, fortifications, and temples. But here, as in most cases where no systematic excavations have been undertaken, we are still faced by a number of difficult problems, the chief of which is that of chronology. We may, however, conclude with safety that in southern Arabia the beginnings of order and civilization, of writing and of building, date far back into the past, probably to the second millennium B.C.

It seems probable that the earliest cultural development in Arabia is connected with the Gerrhaeans and the Minaeans, that is to say with the peoples who, owing to their geographical position, controlled the one the eastern, the other the western, caravan route. It seems that the Catabanians and the population of the Hadramaut played but a minor part in the history of the world's commerce, whereas the Sabaeans, the neighbours of the Minaeans, outdistanced these rivals at a very early date.

Centuries passed, Hammurabi's Babylonian empire fell and the so-called 'balance of power' was established in the Near East. The culture and trade of Babylonia passed into the hands of the larger and smaller cities and states of the Near East, her successors being the Indo-European Mitanni, the alternately powerful and powerless Assyria, the Aryan Hittite empire, the large trading cities of northern Syria, more especially Aleppo and Damascus, and the towns of the Phoenician coast. Egypt, too, experienced changes and after a temporary subjection to the so-called Hyksos rulers from Syria she created, in the middle of the second millennium B.C., the Egypto-Asiatic empire of the great eighteenth dynasty, which survived just long enough to leave a deep mark upon the future development of cultured and commercial life.

For the first time in the history of civilized man the west was now united with the east in a single kingdom and the Babylonian manner of life was definitely linked up with the Egyptian. For the first time in history commerce flowed in increasing volume between regions lying within the boundaries of a single great empire, the power of which extended not only over the Near East but also over Cyprus and Crete. Thus it is not surprising that caravan trade developed at this time with amazing vigour, and that the different states which upheld the 'balance of power' in the second millennium struggled in an endeavour to surpass one another in the splendour of their life, in the beauty and magnificence of their buildings, and in the high standard of their military equipment. A study of the diplomatic correspondence of the time is a convincing proof of this. It is evident, for example, that Thothmes III, who speaks with such pleasure of the Assyrian tribute of Persian lapis lazuli and its Babylonian equivalent, considered the cultured world of the period as a single, complex organism, closely bound together by commercial ties.

At the beginning of the first millennium the Sumero-Babylonian, the Egyptian, and the short-lived Hittite empires were succeeded by a single empire, that of Assyria, and Assyria, after a short revival of Babylonia, was superseded in its turn by the mighty empire of Persia. Throughout this period trade, and more especially caravan trade, was in process of constant development and was gradually becoming better organized. It was this caravan trade that brought riches and splendour to Aleppo and later to Damascus, the most flourishing cities of the Near East, and it was this caravan trade that put the Phoenician cities of Tyre, Byblos, and Aradus in a position which enabled them to acquire outstanding importance in the development of commerce.

The history of foreign commerce and of the gradual consolidation of caravan trade in the Assyrian and Persian empires has not yet been written, though modern scholars have here and there recorded isolated facts about it. It is, however, clearly evident that Assyria played an immense role in its development. We know that there existed in Assyria special itineraries not only for the army but also for merchants. These itineraries were probably shown upon maps, for maps of a very early date—both pre-Assyrian and Assyrian—have survived to our day, and it was undoubtedly such maps that formed the basis of the Greek science of cartography. Both itineraries and maps of this early date presuppose the existence of a highly developed network of roads, and we know that the Assyrian kings created such a network mainly for military purposes. But the system that is useful to an army is also of use to merchants, who will select for choice the safe and guarded roads across the desert or along mountain ranges. The merchant benefits as much by the establishment and maintenance of wells, and by the regular transmission of news from one part of the empire to the other, as does the soldier.

The development and increased stability of caravan trade under the guardianship of the powerful Assyrian monarchs is illustrated by the fact that new and more

1. Part of Mr. Warren's caravan after a snowstorm in the Gobi desert

2. Part of M. N. Roerich's caravan in Central Asia

3. Caravan leaving Petra for Egypt by S. road, passing the Wady Teighra

I. MODERN CARAVANS

1. Dromedaries from the Arabian desert. Bas-relief of the time of Ashurbanipal

2. Camels of Central Asia. Bas-relief from the palace of Xerxes at Persepolis

II. ASSYRIAN AND PERSIAN CAMELS

Caravan Trade. An Historical Survey

direct roads had now been rendered safe for caravan travel. References to the city of Tadmor, which later became known as Palmyra, appear for the first time in Assyrian documents of this date; we read of it, for instance, in the inscriptions of Tiglath-pileser I and of Ashurbanipal. This shows that by this date, perhaps even earlier, caravans were accustomed to travel from the mouth of the Euphrates across the desert to Damascus, following much the same route as that used by later caravans or by the motor convoys of the present day, which run from Damascus to Baghdad. It is also possible that a direct road from Nineveh to the mouth of the Khabur and thence through Palmyra to Damascus was already in use.

Organized caravan trade was not limited to the confines of the Assyrian empire. Royal inscriptions dating from the time of Tiglath-pileser III and of Sargon and inscriptions and bas-reliefs of Ashurbanipal (from Nineveh) show that a series of campaigns into northern Arabia had enabled the Assyrians to compel the Minaeans and the Sabaeans to obey their dictates. Although these kingdoms never became the vassals of Assyria they did conform to her wishes, and from time to time they would send gifts—an unofficial tribute—to the Assyrian kings.

These gifts were, no doubt, a mere trifle in comparison with the profits which the southern Arabs drew from a safely organized trade with Assyria. From this time we may probably date the dawn of their prosperity which is testified by the ruins of their cities, especially by those of Mariba, the Sabaean capital. Thousands of inscriptions of a most varied character, the earliest of which date back to the seventh, possibly even to the eighth century B.C., show the importance of Arabia at this period, even though they cast but a pale and flickering light on the darkness of our ignorance.

For more precise knowledge we must wait until scientific excavations can be carried out in Arabia. Then only shall we obtain a more or less correct chronological sequence of the southern Arabian inscriptions, architecture, and sculpture. However, in the light of what has already been accomplished we find that the Bible stories of the fabulous wealth of the Sabaeans and of their mighty queen is correct enough, and that the events there recorded were even somewhat prosaic. Thus the Biblical description of the Ishmaelite caravan laden with perfumes which travelled from Gilead across the desert to Egypt no longer seems miraculous or incredible, while the account in the Book of Kings of the sumptuous gift of one hundred and twenty golden talents, of perfumes, and of precious stones sent to Solomon by the Sabaean queen does not seem at all improbable.

If the Assyrians and their successors, the Neo-Babylonians, were to realize their aim of controlling new caravan routes it is obvious that they would require points of vantage which would make them masters of the situation in the Arabian and Syrian deserts. It is therefore not surprising to hear that it was probably the Assyrians who first realized the importance of Tadmor-Palmyra for the Syrian caravan trade, and that the Edomites, the predecessors of the Nabataeans, who ruled in the region known later as Petraea, had to pay a tax to the Assyrian kings. In the light of this policy we can better understand the efforts first of the Assyrian kings and later of Nabonidus, the well-known king of

Caravan Trade. An Historical Survey

the Neo-Babylonian empire, to control not only Gerrha but also Tema, the great centre of the caravan traffic in central Arabia. Nabonidus even made his temporary residence at Tema and sent out from there expeditions against the Amorites and the Edomites.

The mantle of the Assyrian and Neo-Babylonian empire fell on the Persians, and this union of all the cultured states of the East into one powerful and splendidly organized state gave enormous impetus to Persian trade. Persia possessed excellent roads which intersected it from east to west and from north to south and had a firm and stable currency, her 'golden daricus' which penetrated to every corner of the Mediterranean world. Literary references tell of constant commercial intercourse between Persia and the Farther East, India and China, and this is corroborated by the great influence exercised by Persian art on the development of architecture and carving in India and on monumental sculpture in China. I have discussed this influence in greater detail in my recent monograph dealing with a Chinese bronze vessel of the Han period in C. T. Loo's collection.

There is no doubt that Darius and his successors were not satisfied with the narrow scope of their existing trade and that they wished for wider fields of activity. They dreamt of oceanic trade, of direct intercourse between India and Egypt, of a direct sea-route round Arabia to Africa, and of one through the Red Sea, and some sort of Suez canal to the Mediterranean.

Even more extensive was Persia's trade with the west, her intercourse with the city-states of the Greek mainland, with the Black Sea coast, with Italy and Sicily, and with the Phoenician colonies in northern

Africa, and through these channels with the tribes of south-western and northern Europe. It was chiefly the products of caravan trade that were exported to these countries, notably the various kinds of incense essential for religious observances, a number of luxuries such as perfumes, cosmetics, ornaments of ivory, precious woods, or stuffs died in purple and embroidered with gold. The Phoenician cities of the Mediterranean coast and the Greek cities of Asia Minor, especially Miletus, all of them under Persian control, flourished and prospered on account of this trade; the riches of Phrygia, and later of Lydia in Asia Minor during the early period of the Persian monarchy, were the result of the role which these states played as the middlemen between the east and the west; and last, but not least, we must mention the enormous commerce carried on by Greek Naucratis, the predecessor of Alexandria. This city had been founded by Greek traders on the coast of northern Egypt to serve as entrepôt between Egypt and the west. Moreover, the Greek cities of the northern coast of the Black Sea, though they owed much of their prosperity in the sixth and fifth centuries B.C. to their trade with their kinsmen of the Mediterranean, no doubt also profited considerably by a lively commerce with the Persian empire, both by way of the Caucasus and the Black Sea, and by the ancient caravan route across the steppes of south-eastern Russia from Turkestan to the Don and to Panticapaeum. The influence of Persian art in the sixth and fifth centuries B.C. on the Graeco-eastern art of southern Russia has not yet received due recognition in the works of Russian scholars.

In the Near East, that is to say in Arabia, Mesopotamia, and Syria, the caravan trade of the Persian empire differed but little from that of Persia's forerunners, the Sumero-Babylonian and Assyrian powers. Both the eastern and the western trade routes through Arabia were used. We may suggest that, of these two routes, the eastern gained somewhat in importance, while the western which mainly looked towards Egypt, now a province of Persia, showed a certain decline. This accounts for the continuous growth of some of the age-old Semitic cities of the Syrian desert: Aleppo, Damascus, Hamath (modern Hama), Emesa (the present Homs), and many others. Each of these cities was the centre of a fertile strip of land of varying size possessing fully developed agricultural, horticultural, and pastoral occupations. Not one of them was a 'caravan city' in the real sense of the word, that is to say a city brought into existence solely by caravan trade. Yet it was caravan trade that rendered them wealthy and important.

We are poorly informed on the relations between Persia and the Arabs. Some chance references show, however, that they ran upon the same lines as those of the Assyrian era. Thus we hear, for instance, of tribute being paid to Darius by southern Arabs, and we possess a text which speaks of Minaean merchants resident in Egypt. The presence of such merchants in one of the countries which imported south Arabian goods was probably no rare event, yet it was undoubtedly due to the peaceful intercourse between Arabia and Persia, and to the weight of Persian authority, that Arab merchants were able to reside for long periods in the Persian empire and that it was possible to regard such visits as ordinary events. The correspondence of a Jewish trading house in Nippur, carrying on active business with the Chaldaeans, Medians, Aramaeans, Edomites, and Sabaeans, provides further important evidence of the briskness of caravan trade at that time.

It is very probable that another important text proving the regularity of caravan trade between the various countries of the Near East and southern Arabia belongs likewise to the Persian period. I refer to the Minaean inscription of Beragish, the modern Yathil, the second capital of the Minaean kingdom, which is by far the most important Minaean text in existence. It speaks of some buildings and sacrifices dedicated to Athtar-Dhû-Gabdim by some merchants trading with Egypt, Syria, and Assyria. They dedicated these to the god in gratitude for protecting their caravans from the Sabaeans during an important war. This was probably one of the wars between Persia and Egypt, either when the latter country was conquered in the year 535 B.C., or when she was overcome by Artaxerxes Ochus in 343 B.C. Another similar text, this time from Main, the capital city of the Minaeans, unfortunately bears no date. It is probable that the Minaeans carried on their trade with the Persian empire by way of their own military and trading colonies (of which the most important was the modern El-Ela), and that they sent their goods to Egypt, either by land through Gaza or else across the Red Sea from a Minaean port to one of the harbours in Egypt. The latter route may have been frequently adopted in order to avoid paying a tax to the Nabataeans.

The Minaean inscriptions quoted above, as well as certain other facts, point to the appearance of a new and independent centre of caravan trade either during the last years of the Neo-Babylonian or the early days of the Persian empire. I refer to Petra of which more will be said below. Perhaps at this date the Nabataean Arabs first superseded the Edomites in Petra, and became the instruments of Persia for reducing the power of the Sabaeans, who had grown too mighty and too rich to please the rulers of the world.

But the Persian empire fell before the advance of Alexander the Great, and under his followers the centre of affairs gradually shifted from east to west. A similar change occurred in caravan trade, especially in Arabia and Syria. In the organization of his Graeco-eastern power Alexander generally acted in accordance with Persian custom and tradition, but both as an innovator and also as a follower of Darius he wished to go farther than the Persians had gone. Of his intentions before his untimely death one of the few facts which we know is that he wished to establish himself firmly in Arabia and to transform into a vassalage the friendly attitude assumed by the Arabs towards the Persian world-empire. This was the underlying idea of the two expeditions which he sent round Arabia to prepare the way for his army and his fleet. The one directed westward was to have rounded Arabia from the Persian Gulf, whilst the other, directed eastward, was to sail from the Red Sea to the mouth of the Euphrates. Unfortunately death put an end to these daring but quite reasonable schemes.

After Alexander's death his empire was broken up and the east was divided into a number of states, some of them Greek, some semi-Greek, some purely local. The Iranian plateau withdrew from Greek influence and became the seat of the Parthian kings, who followed

Persian traditions; semi-Greek Bactria (Afghanistan) grew and developed independently; India, which had first been a province of Persia and then of Alexander's empire, returned to independence. A powerful, though temporary, empire was even created there, later separated into a number of independent states. The more western states which arose in place of Alexander's mighty empire, in Greece and in the Near East, Syria, Egypt, and Macedon, were constantly in dispute or at war with one another, and at a later date certain minor Asiatic powers such as Pergamum, Bithynia, the Pontus, Cappadocia, and Armenia entered into this keen competition. By no means foreign to Hellenistic culture were some of the older states, ruled by more or less Hellenized kings, who in time became surprisingly similar to their fellow kings in the Near East: such were those of the Cimmerian Bosphorus, of Thrace, and of Nubia. From Egypt Hellenistic influence penetrated in a varying degree both to the northern and southern kingdoms of Arabia.

The growth and development of civilization remained unaffected by this dismemberment of a once mighty empire, and the demand for Indian, Arabian, and African goods became increasingly great. But the route which eastern trade should follow became a sore question in the politics of the Hellenistic world. The monarchs of Syria wished to monopolize it, the kings of Egypt did all that they could do to direct it through their own territories and make Alexandria the greatest of entrepôts. The Arabian desert became a province of the first importance. First Antigonus the One-Eyed and his son Demetrius attempted to get a firm foothold in northern Arabia by taking possession of Petra. Then

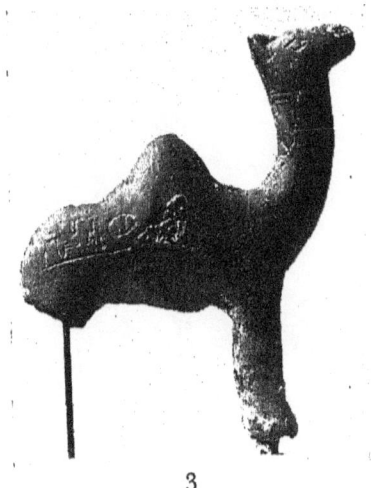

III. THE MEN AND CAMELS OF SOUTH ARABIA

(*for description see p.* 36)

the Seleucids, kings of Syria, and the Ptolemies, rulers of Egypt, both continued to hanker after exclusive control of the Arabian caravan routes.

Neither Alexander nor his followers could conquer Arabia, and even to-day neither the English nor the French, in spite of their aeroplanes and armoured cars, are able to subdue it. But to-day where arms prove of no avail diplomacy is at work. It was the same in Hellenistic times. For whilst the Seleucids of Syria firmly controlled Mesopotamia, and the Ptolemies of Egypt held Phoenicia, Palestine, and Transjordania, something in the nature of an *entente cordiale* was established. As a result of this eastern Arabia and the caravan routes passing through the Iranian plateau fell to the Seleucids and the western road with its African trade to the Ptolemies. In Mesopotamia the Seleucids created Seleucia on the Tigris which, under the influence of caravan trade, developed into one of the largest cities of the world; and in the west, Antioch on the Orontes and her two sea-ports, Laodicea and Seleucia in Pieria, grew no less considerably. The same caravan trade led to the foundation by Seleucus I and by Antiochus I of a number of towns on the road from Seleucia to the land of the Gerrhaeans, and on those from the Tigris to the east. And finally it was commercial considerations that persuaded Antiochus III to make his unsuccessful attempt to conquer the Gerrhaeans. On the other hand, it is to the western road and to its connexion with India and Africa that Alexandria owes its development. To the same influence the creation of few ports on the Arabian, and of many on the Egyptian, shores of the Red Sea is due. To this also must be attributed the attempt of

Ptolemy II Philadelphus to subject, or at any rate to isolate, Petra.

The situation altered somewhat towards the end of the third, and still more during the second and first centuries B.C. Then, after a long and blood-thirsty struggle, the Seleucids found themselves finally obliged to leave the Iranian countries alone and even to cede Mesopotamia to the Parthians. In exchange, however, they obtained the eastern provinces of Palestine and Phoenicia from the now almost powerless Ptolemies. Syrian and Parthian warfare nearly wrecked the caravan trade of the Iranian plateau and of the Persian Gulf, and the Parthian conquest of Mesopotamia dealt it an even severer blow. Parthia obtained the mastery of these routes, but she never became an entirely stable or centralized state. She never ceased to dream of the conquest of the whole of Syria and as a result the struggle round the Euphrates became endemic.

It is therefore not surprising that we find the later Seleucids losing interest in the eastern caravan routes through the Parthian empire and attempting to break free from the Parthians. They endeavoured to direct the trade of India and Arabia as much as possible along other roads. These were not new: from time immemorial they had carried the Indo-Egyptian trade leading both to Egypt and to Palestine and Phoenicia by way of western Arabia. The Seleucids, however, tried to force a new orientation of this trade, directing it exclusively to Phoenicia and Syria instead of allowing it to carry goods to Egypt.

In this they were probably successful, at least for a certain period, as is illustrated by the fact that Antiochus IV Epiphanes was able to show his subjects during some festivities at Antioch as much gold, cosmetics, ivory, and perfumes from India and Arabia, as could his far more powerful ancestors. His display equalled that of the great Ptolemy II Philadelphus or of his own contemporaries in Egypt.

In order to retain as much as possible of their Indian, Arabian, and African trade only one course was open to the Ptolemies, namely, to maintain as much control as possible over Petra, in order to prevent this city from falling completely under Seleucid influence and, more important still, to draw Indian, Arabian, and African goods by sea to Alexandria and to the Egyptian ports of the Red Sea.

Petra, the former centre of the northern Arabian caravan trade, refused to be subjected either by the Seleucids or the Ptolemies. She retained her independent semi-friendly attitude towards both of them, benefiting at the same time by the weakness of both; for she was able to draw more firmly into her own hands the control of the important caravan route leading to the south, to Arabia Felix, which had formerly perhaps been under Ptolemaic direction. She also endeavoured to obtain for herself an outlet to the sea, and was so far successful that some time in the second or first century B.C., Aila, modern Akaba on the Gulf of Akaba, and the White Village (Leuce Come) on the Arabian coast of the Red Sea became her ports. It was about the same time, or perhaps a little earlier, that Petra came into direct contact with Parthia, by way of Gerrha and of that semi-independent vassal of the Parthians, the kingdom of Charax at the mouth of the Tigris.

The later Ptolemies were too weak to renew the aggressive policy of Ptolemy II with regard to Petra, but one thing they still could do, namely, launch a number of naval enterprises which would make their commerce independent of the goodwill of Petra. We thus find them seeking a route to India without any call at Arabian ports. One daring merchant after another tried it. We hear, for example, of two successful voyages of Eudoxus of Cnidus in the late second century B.C., and these were not isolated enterprises. The result was that probably in the first century B.C. one of these merchants, Hipparchus, discovered the monsoons and thus rendered a direct trade between India and Egypt possible.

We know but little of the late Hellenistic period in the Near East or of the gradual solidification of Roman power in Syria, Phoenicia, and Palestine. The chief events of the time were, on the one hand the growing strength of Parthia, and on the other both the gradual advance of the Arabs towards the north and the growing desire for independence evinced by certain sections of the Syrian empire, more especially by Judaea. Independent states ruled by local Arab dynasties of the north sprang into being at Chalkis, Emesa, Edessa, and possibly even Palmyra. Simultaneously the Nabataeans began to penetrate into northern territories, and texts and inscriptions make it seem probable that they controlled, early in the first century B.C., the whole of the caravan route between Petra and Damascus, together with the towns which lay upon it. It is interesting to note that no similar expansion is to be observed in the south, for there the Nabataeans never advanced beyond Nejd. The process of the disintegration of the Seleucid empire was still more emphasized by the emancipation from the central Seleucid power of several of its more important towns, especially those of Phoenicia.

All these events could not fail to affect caravan trade which had also to deal with certain new factors. The most important of these was the fact that the old routes leading up the Euphrates through northern Syria were no longer entirely safe, for they were falling into the hands of greedy and undisciplined local dynasties. Petra, now the chief controller of Arabian caravan trade, was obliged to look for some substitute for the former centres of caravan trade in Syria, and Palmyra's growth as a caravan city may have been partly due to Petra's desire to open a new road from the middle Euphrates to Palmyra, and thence through Bosra to Petra, or straight across the desert to Damascus, which would thus be entirely under her own control.

We know that following upon the period of political anarchy which reigned in the Near East at the end of the second and the beginning of the first centuries B.C., Pompey placed the government of Syria, Palestine, and Phoenicia in Roman hands. This marked the dawn of a new era in the history of caravan trade, for its market could now become the entire *orbis Romanus*. The whole of the Mediterranean and all the countries adjoining it were now open to it. During the long period of internal and external peace which ensued (uninterrupted but for a short spell of civil war during which Antony repartitioned Syria and restored Ptolemaic rule in the greater part of the south), the empire's prosperity steadily increased from the time of Augustus and with it the demand for foreign goods continually developed.

The Romans, like their Hellenistic predecessors,

continued to find Arabian and Indian trade a matter of great importance. They inherited it from the Macedonians in all its complicated aspects. Rivalry between the civilized powers of the west and their constant struggle for the control of the caravan routes was now at an end, but Arabs and Parthians still existed. The Arabs retained all their immemorial anarchical characteristics, whilst the Parthians remained not only unconquered but also unconquerable by the west.

Rome inherited the obligation of organizing eastern caravan trade both from the Seleucids and from the Ptolemies. As regards the Egyptian trade Augustus so frightened the Arabs, first by his expedition into Arabia Felix which, though unsuccessful, was truly awe-inspiring, then by his equally impressive preparations for a second campaign which never took place, that from that day it became easier for Egyptian merchants to arrange for regular maritime journeys to India with calls at Arabian ports when necessary.

In northern Syria the Romans constituted themselves the successors of late Seleucid rather than of the Ptolemaic tradition. It was Pompey who put an end to the Nabataean empire of Petra and brought as a result the northern commercial caravan route of Transjordania under the political and military control of Rome. In the name of Rome he granted autonomy to the Greek cities lying along this route. All the caravan routes which Petra controlled and made safe for merchants remained unchanged, and even Petra's commercial influence seems to have remained unaffected. The change was purely a political one. As a result of a number of campaigns waged against her, Petra, in the latter half of the first century B.C., became the vassal of

Rome and this was all. The cities lying on the caravan roads north of Petra now entered upon a period of much greater prosperity, since the Romans with all their military resources and their administrative skill rendered, for the first time in the history of Syria, movement along these roads absolutely safe. Such was the result in the case of Bosra, Canatha, Philadelphia (Amman), and Gerasa (Jerash). The fact that the last-named city enjoyed at that time a period of prosperity proves that the caravan route leading from Philadelphia to Damascus and from Philadelphia to Palestine via the important city of Skythopolis ran past Jerash; and it is obvious that the Romans protected this route. The Egyptians retained the maritime transport and that section of caravan trade which preferred the Egyptian road leading from Petra to that across Transjordania.

A solution of the eastern problem was even more complicated and difficult. In spite of all her costly efforts, Rome found herself unable to break Parthia. So, for the sake of caravan trade, she resorted to diplomacy and reached a silent, perhaps even a written, agreement with Parthia on the subject. The outcome of this was Palmyra. Originally an insignificant village at one of the desert oases, the Tadmor of the Bible, Palmyra was, in the late Hellenistic period, a rapidly growing centre of caravan trade protected by Petra; it now became not only a strong neutral state but also the most important trading centre between Roman Syria and Parthia. Neither Rome nor Parthia found it easy to control or protect the more northern route of Syria, and hence they agreed to choose the desert-route through Palmyra as a shorter and cheaper alternative. The caravans which came from the lowlands of the Euphrates and from the Iranian plateau henceforth passed through Dura, a strong Parthian fortress. Then, instead of moving farther north along the Euphrates, they took the desert road to Palmyra, whence they travelled through Damascus, Hamath, or Emesa, either to Aleppo or to the cities of Phoenicia and Syria. Later we shall say more about the almost fabulous development of Palmyra and Dura in the first century A.D.

We know but little regarding the history of caravan routes after Augustus and Tiberius had laid the foundations of Roman politics in the Syrian East. We do know, however, that Tiberius' successors, Caligula, Claudius, and Nero, reverted to Pompey's policy, a policy to which Augustus, and more especially Tiberius, had wished to put an end. This policy consisted in ruling the Near East by means of vassal kings. In the light of this policy we can easily understand St. Paul's statement, and an inscription of the year A.D. 93-4 referring to the power exercised over Damascus and its territory by the Nabataean kings. They had probably exercised this power over the whole of the northern caravan route from Petra, past Damascus, right up to the ports of the Syrian and Phoenician coast.

With the Flavians and Trajan the history of Arabia and that of eastern trade enters upon a new period. When the Flavians had given Palestine a lesson by destroying and capturing Jerusalem and when nearly all Syria's vassal states had been converted into Roman provinces, Rome's prestige stood high. It no longer seemed necessary for Rome to continue her policy of compromise, diplomacy, and half-measures. The vassalage of Petra and Palmyra seemed anachronistic.

1. Camel carrying two camel-bags, Chinese, Tang Period
2, 3. Central Asiatic two-humped camels. Two bronze belt plaques, Han dynasty (time of early Roman empire)

IV. THE CAMELS OF THE CHINESE CARAVANS

Caravan Trade. An Historical Survey

Trajan annexed Petra and tightened his hold on Palmyra. An ambitious constructional activity covered Syria and northern Arabia with a network of magnificent paved ways. Wide roads with splendid surfaces connected the Aelanitic gulf with Petra, and Petra with the large trading centres of Syria and Palestine by way of Amman, Jerash, and Bosra. One of these roads running straight and smooth through the wilderness of the Ledja to the very gates of Palmyra is still to be seen to-day.

Rome's Arabian military frontier, as established by Trajan, bristled with armed camps, castellos, or towers large and small which protected the new province against the enemy, and these would be close to the wells (hydreumata) which were guarded by soldiers. Such military posts probably guarded also the caravan road south of Petra which had stood for centuries under the military protection of that city, for only in this way can I account for the votive inscriptions of Roman cavalry-men, especially men of the dromedary corps (the ancient Mearists), which were discovered in the vicinity of El-Ela.

Bosra, once a colony belonging to the Nabataeans of Petra, now enters upon that splendid period of her prosperity during which she became the capital of the province of Arabia, the seat of a provincial governor, and a big, ever-expanding centre of caravan trade. Unfortunately I did not go to Bosra to study her wonderful ruins, and I am therefore unable to describe them at first hand. They represent a curious combination of a Roman military camp with the true characteristics of a caravan city. In the second century A.D. Bosra's buildings were undoubtedly finer than Petra's, and in the following centuries her wealth and importance far exceeded those of Petra. After Trajan's death this city entered upon a period of comparative decline, for the caravan traffic preferred to the road passing through Petra another shorter route which missed it. Gradually her merchants either let the strings of caravan trade slip through their fingers or else emigrated to Bosra.

It seemed as though Trajan and his successors had stabilized Roman policy in the caravan trade and the caravan cities for a considerable time. Petra's turn had come and gone; now it was that of Palmyra and, nominally at least, she in her turn became a city of the Roman empire. This new policy had a favourable effect on the development of caravan cities, and the second and third centuries A.D. mark their greatest prosperity.

Then followed the anarchy of the third century, when war and devastation raged within the empire. Everything in Syria changed. Parthia was superseded by a new Persia, re-established under Sasanian rule, and a period of new wars began on the Euphrates. In Syria anarchy reigned: one emperor succeeded another on the throne; the local sheikhs regained their daring and resumed their former thieving habits. Trade declined, yet no one appeared to revive or to safeguard it. Roman legions, occupied with destroying one another, were powerless against the Persians, the Syrian rebels, or the Arabs. The caravan cities themselves at last came to the rescue. Palmyra, the most independent and the richest and strongest of them all, attempted to transform all the lands which were traversed by caravan routes, and all those which were the carriers of caravan

Caravan Trade. An Historical Survey

trade, into a single state. Palmyra, a caravan city, endeavoured to create a caravan empire and for a short time she succeeded. This policy and its end are connected for us with the names of Odenath and of Zenobia, the famous queen of Palmyra.

The power of Rome was, however, revived and restored by Aurelian and Diocletian and was neither able nor willing to give up its control of the East. Palmyra and her short-lived empire fell, and a new era began in the history of the ancient world. This era was the Byzantine.

Caravan trade survived this crisis and the ensuing change; but its character altered. Certain caravan cities, especially Bosra and to a lesser extent Amman, survived it also, but Petra and Palmyra, together with their dependent towns, disappeared. This is not the place in which to trace the ups and downs of eastern trade and of the fortunes of caravan cities during the late Roman and Byzantine periods. These periods lie outside the scope of this book and I have not the material to deal with them—for information on the subject the reader must turn to Father Lammens's book on Mecca and pre-Islamic Arabia. I know also that Professor R. P. Blake, Director of the Harvard Library, has now on hand a general work on the commerce of the period. In these books the reader will find all the information that he requires. For my purpose—in order to trace the history of caravan trade during the flowering of the ancient world—enough has already been said, for the monuments which I discuss in the following chapters were already falling into ruin in early Byzantine times.

DESCRIPTION OF PLATE III.
THE MEN AND CAMELS OF SOUTH ARABIA

1. Funeral stele of a certain 'Igli son of Sa'dlâti Kurain. The upper part bears the funeral inscription in the Sabaean language. The first register is occupied by the figure of the deceased in the other world, represented as drinking wine and listening to music. The second register shows his exploits: he is represented on horseback wearing, as in the upper scene, a long 'burnous' and the typical head-dress (modern kefiya). His horse is richly caparisoned. He holds a spear in his right hand, and before him is a camel. 'Igli is shown returning from a raid.

2. Funeral stele of a certain Aus'ili son of Zabbayiwita. Sabaeic inscription. The picture shows a Sabaean dromedarius riding his camel on a military expedition.

3. Little bronze camel with Sabaeic inscription: votive offering to the god Wadd.

4. Little bronze horse with Sabaeic inscription dedicated by a certain Lahy'atheti to the solar god Dhât Bacdani.

II

PETRA

SOME nineteen years ago when I first went to Palestine, the starting-point for a visit to Petra, Amman, and Jerash, it was not only a lengthy and difficult, but also a complicated and expensive business to attempt to see these cities, and one which a young professor of St. Petersburg University could ill afford. In those days in order to explore these ruins it was necessary to equip a caravan, to find guards, and to obtain an *iradé* from the Turkish officials. In the Palestine of to-day all this has been altered. The English have appeared, bringing in their wake, like the Romans before them, order and safety, good roads and new means of transport. In Palestine the motor-car has now superseded the camel, whilst the Sultan's *iradé*, the consular kavass, and the Turkish zaptieh have been replaced by Mr. Thomas Cook, by one of his talkative guides, and by the police force of the Transjordanian Emir. At Amman there has appeared an hotel which is, comparatively speaking, clean; a similar establishment is soon to be opened at Jerash, and in the valley of Petra Thomas Cook has already pitched his camp-hotel. Its bedrooms consist of tents or of the rock-tombs, rock-houses, or rock-stables of ancient Petra, and its splendid dining-hall is composed of another and larger tent. Tourists have followed in the wake of these innovations and to-day those who visit Jerash and Petra are no longer to be counted in units as in the past, but in tens and hundreds. Soon no doubt they will come in their thousands.

PLAN OF PETRA

The new rulers of Palestine and Transjordania do their utmost to further the tourist development of the district. The local populace shows neither opposition nor friendliness towards this policy, possibly on account of its own heterogeneous origins. Some of them are town-dwelling Circassians, emigrants from Russia, who were transported to Transjordania by Abdul Hamid; others are Levantines or Palestinian Jews. These are the new settlers and they delight in preying on the foreigner, without violating the law, by selling him minor antiquities or something of the slender produce of the country. The Bedouin from the desert frown on the tourists, and are not averse from relapsing to their old custom of highway robbery. They are, however, made to pay a heavy price for such misdeeds, for at Maan, on the Petra road, stands the camp of the new Transjordanian Legion, which is an English force supplied with aeroplanes, barracks, and sheds for armoured cars. The cavalry section of this force is mounted on horses and camels in much the same way as the Roman troops of old, but instead of being called the dromedary corps this detachment is now called the 'Mearist' corps. The armoured cars and aeroplanes are always in perfect order, ready to pounce upon the Bedouin of the desert and to exact retribution for their incursions or for the kidnapping of foreigners. As a result, European and American ladies run but a very slender chance of being carried off by some wild Arab sheikh and must fall back upon such romantic incidents as may happen in Petra's tents.

Like many another, my wife and I also made use of the prosaic services of Thomas Cook in order to visit Amman, Jerash, and Petra, for although the expense of the journey was heavy, we could find no better way by which to make a thorough examination of Petra. If travellers wish to visit only Amman and Jerash and do not mind missing Petra, it is possible to dispense even with Mr. Cook's services, for they can apply to the office of the Jewish chauffeurs of Palestine at Jerusalem; this is an energetic body of young Zionists, most of them emigrants from Russia. With their aid it is easy to visit Amman and Jerash cheaply, yet not wholly without annoyance. We, however, were bound for Petra, and so after a few days spent in Palestine, we moved on to Transjordania.

Palestine has long been favoured by archaeologists, for even Constantine and Helena, and probably many later visitors, began excavations there. Transjordania, however, is a new country so far as the study of the past is concerned, and until quite recently no excavations have been—nor could they be—conducted in the region. Even at present it is no easy matter to procure a permit to dig at Petra. In fact it was only in the year following my visit that a special society for the study of Petraean archaeology was formed, and got to work there for two months in 1920 on funds generously provided by Mr. Henry Mond. G. Horsfield, director of Transjordanian excavations, and Miss Agnes Conway were placed at the head of the expedition, but work at Petra was suspended in the following year; I do not know whether it will be resumed at a future date. Its results have not yet been fully published, but the most important discovery seems to be that of some very strange ceramics, all of which can be dated. These will probably prove to be of the first importance in the correct dating of the more important buildings and

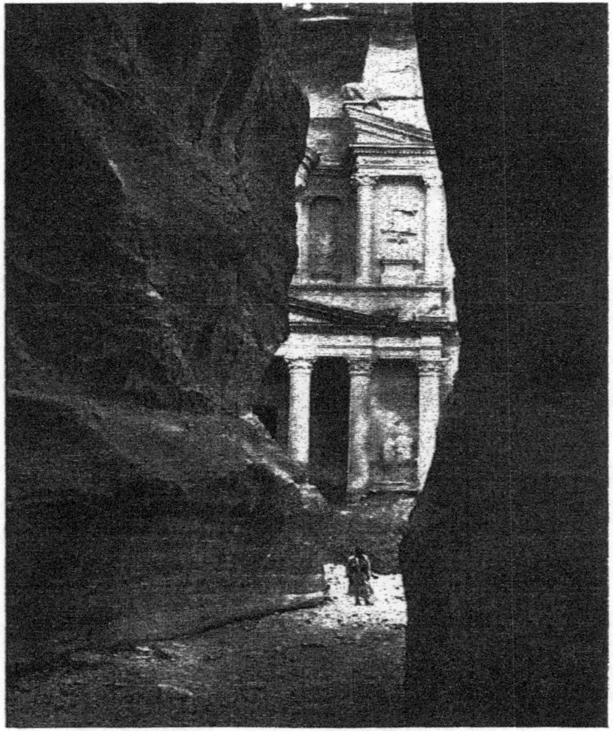

1

2

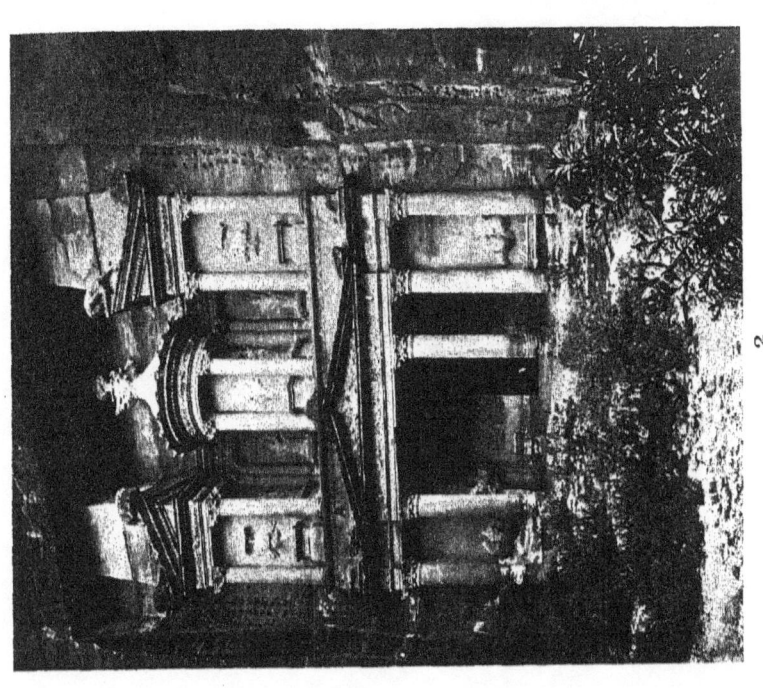

1, 2. Two views of El-Khasne (temple of the Tyche of Petra)

V. PETRA

1. The theatre

2. The archway over the main street

VI. PETRA

tombs at Petra. All the objects discovered by this expedition are at present in the Fitzwilliam Museum at Cambridge.

At Jerash and at Amman excavations were begun some years ago, and the work below the soil succeeded the tabulation of the results of work on the surface. In Amman the Italian scholar Guidi started his excavations high up on the citadel, inside an exceedingly interesting palace, which testifies the short-lived rule of the Sasanian Persians. Now another Italian scholar is at work there, but Amman is a difficult site to dig in, for what was once a modest Caucasian village is rapidly developing into the large but dirty capital of Transjordania, and the new town is spreading all over the site of the ancient one. Little hope now remains of the discovery of the caravan road, which lies beneath the main street of the town. We know, however, that it was partly laid upon vaults spanning the river-bed and was embellished with porticoes, public buildings, and triumphal arches. Along its course stood the great temple and other sanctuaries, the baths, which are still partly preserved, and the caravanserais. The fine ruins of a theatre, practically complete, will alone survive in solitary grandeur above the river, a lasting testimony to the ancient city's wealth and size in Roman times, and a significant reminder of the improvements which will be necessary before the modern town can even slightly resemble ancient Philadelphia.

The cases of Petra and Jerash are entirely different. At Petra the poor Bedouin settlers occupy only some of the rock-cut houses and a few of the tombs in the vast necropolis, so that the centre of the ancient city is uninhabited and the larger part of the ruins are unencumbered. In Jerash the new Caucasian village founded by Abdul Hamid occupies only the poorer quarters of the ancient town, situated on the far side of the river. All the centre of the city, with its streets and public buildings, is a mass of amazing and quite unique ruins, with which only those of Palmyra can be compared in the East, while none, not even those of northern Africa, can be compared in the West.

Much has already been written about Petra and I do not wish to repeat what has already been said. I am tempted almost to liken the city to some wonder from the *Arabian Nights*. When one descends into the valley from the surrounding heights towards the place where the river has cut for itself a passage between the dark-red rocks, one seems to be gazing at some large and fantastic excrescence—a piece of reddish-mauve raw flesh set between the gold of the desert and the green of the hills. It is a most extraordinary sight, which becomes even more extraordinary when the cavalcade slowly descends into the river valley, and the rocky walls of the ever-narrowing gorge tower up to right and left, speckled with red, orange, mauve, grey, and green layers. Wild and beautiful they are, with their contrasts of light and shade; the light blinding, the shadows black. And there is seldom even anything to remind the visitor that this gorge served for centuries as a main road, trodden by camels, mules, and horses, and that along it rode Bedouin merchants who must have felt like ourselves its horror and its mystic fascination. Yet suddenly one may be confronted with the façade of a tomb-tower with dog-tooth design, or with an altar set high up on one of the vertical walls,

1. The tomb of the obelisks

2. The Urn-tomb

VII. PETRA: ROCK-CUT TOMBS

1. Rock-cut sanctuary: in the foreground is the large basin with altar in the centre; behind, to the left, a rock-cut altar and the base for the meteor-stone, the Botylos (Kaaba)

2. The two obelisks (sun-symbols)

VIII. PETRA

bearing a greeting or prayer to some god, inscribed in the Nabataean tongue. Our caravan advanced slowly along the gorge, until an unexpected bend disclosed to us an apparition sparkling pinky-orange in the sun, which must once have been the front of a temple or tomb (v). Elegant columns joined by fascinating pediments and arches form the frames of the niches in which its statues stand. All this rose up before us dressed in a garb of classicism yet in a style new and unexpected even by those well acquainted with antiquity. It was as though the magnificent scenery of some Hellenistic theatre had appeared, as though a Pompeian wall-painting, not of the fourth but of the second period, had been chiselled in the rock. But such parallels spring to the minds of a few travellers only; others may well see in them the pavilions of the palaces and parks of the baroque and rococo periods, and compare the niches set in these palatial walls to those of the façades of houses and churches of those styles. But what is this monument that calls to mind the baroque and rococo? Is it a temple or a tomb? To what period does it belong?

Scholars provide no definite answers to these questions. Generally they refer to this building as a temple of Isis, but I consider this to be erroneous. I agree that the building is a temple and not a mausoleum, but that it was dedicated to the Egyptian goddess and her companions I very much doubt. It was rather the home of a local goddess, of the Tyche, or Fortune, that is to say the Genius of the city of Petra, who represents the Hellenistic equivalent of the Iranian Hvareno and the Semitic Gad, and who at the same time was the mighty deity of the Petraean

Arabs, the moon-goddess Allat. The same goddess appears later on the coins of Petra. With her were worshipped her two male companions of Greek origin, called by the Greeks Dioscuri, both of them being stars, one the morning, the other the evening star. These stars steered the Greeks on their voyages across the sea, whilst they served the Petraean Arabs as true guides across the dark desert. They directed them along the road which conducted to water and prosperity, the road which led to foreign countries, and they escorted them home again on the journey to their native land.

The date of the temple is the next problem, and here again I think that those who suggest the second or third century A.D. are incorrect. The style of the building is so light and elegant, the ornamentation so graceful and yet so spirited, and its relationship with the second Pompeian style so marked, that I feel convinced that the temple was built by Greek artists some time during the late Hellenistic period.

From this point the gorge springs to life; it is peopled by the façades of the houses of the dead which line its sides. Countless tombs border the gorge, covering its rocky walls with their façades (VII). Enormous tower-altars rise to view, with wonderful dog-tooth ornament of Assyrian type, cut in such deep relief that the monuments seem independent of the background of rock; these give place to small yet massive façades of the same type, cut either in low or in high relief. By the side of these façades of indigenous style appear others which are Hellenistic, composed of porticoes and columns topped with capitals of Greek or local type. Sometimes the façade is adorned with a Greek statue.

These Hellenistic façades reach a height of one, two, or even three tiers.

A whole necropolis, a fantastic city of the dead, or better still, the setting for a scene in some gigantic, fairyland theatre stretches ahead. The gorge steadily widens. But here the façades of some of the ancient tombs have been destroyed to make way for an elegant theatre (VI. 1) built in the rock and embellished with scintillating steps, these again being hewn from the face of the cliff. And to the right an entire wall is covered with the most astounding façades of all. They are the Hellenistic tombs, the most renowned of all Petra's monuments, those with which we have become familiar owing to their frequent reproduction in cinema films. Beyond them, in the river valley, lies the crater in which the Petraean merchants elected to build their town, so that it should be surrounded on all sides by sheer rocks, in the face of which thousands of tomb-chambers were cut.

For the tourist Petra appears not only as a city of tombs but also as a city surrounded by rock-cut sanctuaries (VIII. 1). These are to be found everywhere, and they are generally in a good state of preservation. Steep paths run from the town of the living, past the encircling band of the city of the dead, to the mountain peaks, where, from time immemorial, local Bedouins would go to pay homage to their divinities, not in temples like their Hellenized descendants, but under the open sky. And Petra's main deities, Dushara, the god of the sun, and Allat, the moon goddess, stood there awaiting worship not in the image of men, but in the form of fetishes or obelisks (VIII. 2). Dushara's symbol was a phallic obelisk, or a black meteor fallen from the sky.

Such a meteor still stands in Mecca. Bloody sacrifices were performed in these mountain sanctuaries on rough altars hewn from the rock, the prototypes of the tomb-monuments. Yet it was not only the half-savage nomadic tribes, clans, or families of Arabs, who came to these platforms and altars to worship; the towns-folk also climbed up from the city along the steep and sacred paths (IX. 2). The city temples represented a tribute paid to fashion by the inhabitants; their real prayers were said on these mountain tops, where by day they felt themselves close to the Life-giver, the Eternal Sun, as they stood bathed in his rays; and by night they seemed bound in a stealthy union with the great magical goddess, the Silver Moon, whose light enveloped them.

A new vision appears. Through the clefts in the mountain there pours a torrent, a torrent of vivifying and life-giving water. And here, as would be expected, stands a sanctuary (IX. 1). It is a cave lying beneath an over-hanging rock, bathed in a strange and welcome twilight. Sacred paths lead to it, paths trodden by pilgrims who came in search of reviving water and were wont to eat a modest meal in this cave which they thus transformed into a dining-hall.

Tombs and rock-sanctuaries abound, but in addition there once flourished here a town of the living, a town such as Mecca was before the time of Mohammed, a town not unlike Jerash, Amman, and Palmyra, in other words a caravan city. It was a city of rich and wily merchants, but it was a fantastic and individual city as well, set as it was in its ring of red rocks. Little of it has survived, but its plan can still be traced. Quite recently, in fact, during the War, the German archaeologist Wiegand, director of the Berlin Museum of

1. A Spring and the Spring Sanctuary
2. Staircase up Jebel en Umer, leading to a rock sanctuary

IX. PETRA

Classical Antiquities, was able to draw up the plan of the town for the first time in its history. And to this some new additions have been made by the British Expedition to which I have already referred.

The general lines of the city's topography are clear. The three gorges which connect Petra with the external world form its main entrances; these are the Bab-es-Sik, of which I have already spoken, the Thughra in the south, and the Turkmaniye in the north. It seems probable that the area of the later town did not correspond with that of the more ancient. This was the fortress and cave-city with which the Bible and the early mentions of Petra have made us familiar. The fortified citadel probably stood on El Habis, an elevation overlooking the crater of Petra and her later buildings.

On the north, close to the fortress of El Habis, two romantic gorges—Es Siyagh and El Mu'eisra—have been explored by Mr. Horsfield and Miss Conway. They found there remains of several large and rich houses cut in the rock. Some of these houses were at a later date converted into tombs. Few unrifled tombs were found; these yielded pottery of a comparatively early date. This makes it probable that the rock-cut houses of the two gorges represent the dwellings of the inhabitants of Petra of the time when it first became a flourishing centre of caravan trade.

I may mention in this connexion that these rock-houses remind us of similar underground houses not uncommonly found in Africa. Few people are familiar with the wealthy subterranean city of Roman date known by the name of Bulla Regia in Tunisia, but Garian, a similar city near Tripoli, inhabited by

Arabs and Jews, has often been visited and those who have seen it will realize my meaning.

In late Hellenistic and early Roman times, Petra descended into the valley and changed its character from a subterranean to a surface-occupying town. It was probably at this period that it was enclosed by the walls whose line can still be traced, though it does not correspond exactly with that of the Byzantine walls which are very well preserved. The date of the earlier walls of Petra is uncertain, and it is idle to speculate about it so long as no excavations have been carried out along and under them. I may mention, however, that neither Diodorus whose description goes back to the late fourth or early third century B.C., nor Strabo who reflects the conditions of the late second century B.C., refers to any fortifications of Petra. It seems therefore that in early Nabataean times the citadel alone was fortified and that it was the later Nabataean kings who built the walls at a time when they were able to benefit by the anarchy of late Hellenistic days and to create their Syro-Arabian empire.

Inside the walls the plan of the city was dictated by caravan trade. The main thoroughfare is the road which follows the course of the main river—the Wady Musa—which has been partially canalized and partially covered over. A so-called triumphal arch, an ornamental gate, the ruins of which still survive, was thrown across the river-street (VI. 2). On one side of this main street, on the western plateau of the town, temples and public buildings were arranged in terraces overlooking the city. Two temples still stand as superb ruins, one of them—that of Kasr Firaun—even containing on the walls of its cella the remains of a sculptured stucco decoration. The general outlines of three large market-places are still recognizable. Here bargains were concluded, here bankers, merchants, middlemen, and their agents carried on their business, here gold and precious stones changed hands, here ginger peel and thyme smelt sweetly and the air was filled with the pleasant perfume of incense and that of other odorous leaves and roots brought from India and Arabia.

Part at least of the residential quarter of the town still consisted of houses cut in the rocks even in later times, whilst part was formed by houses on the opposite side of the main river-street. Here the walls of the big palace, the palace of the king of kings, may have stood, side by side with those of other large dwelling-places.

The ruins, as a whole, both those of the town and of the sanctuaries, of the houses and of the tomb-façades, are splendid and singularly romantic, but they reveal little of the city's history. Its buildings still lie obscured by the dust of ages, the façades of the tombs are still undated, the inscriptions are monotonous and poor in content. All theories as to the historical development of Petra and the evolution of its architecture are still 'in the air'. The guesses of those who consider that Petra ceased to be of importance at the time of Trajan are as unconvincing as those which suggest that the second century A.D. was the time of its greatest prosperity. The only definite information which exists at present is that obtained by the French Dominican Fathers Jaussen and Savignac, who industriously studied the inscriptions and architecture of similar tombs of Petraean merchants at their caravan city El Hegra. We now definitely know that in the first century A.D., that is to say in early imperial times, all the types of those Petraean tombs which have been so impressively arranged in order of evolution by modern scholars were in use. But one type of tomb is missing, that with fully Hellenized façades, a fact which proves that these are later than the reign of Augustus, and may belong to the days of Trajan. Yet they are so rich and splendid that they cannot possibly have been built during any period of the city's decline.

Consequently I suggest that Petra, the caravan city, experienced alternate periods of prosperity and of decline. Her career began at the time of the Persian monarchy; then followed the early Hellenistic period which was a difficult one for her both politically and economically. Her golden age dawned in late Hellenistic times, when her trade developed to an unforeseen extent. It is at this date that we begin to encounter Petraean merchants as far north as Sidon in Phoenicia and in Italy, for instance at Puteoli, where they formed a strong and wealthy community and even had their own temples. It is at this time too that the protection of all the more important caravan roads seems to be in their control and it is now that they create their own caravan empire. This period, perhaps with short interruptions, lasts for a little less than three centuries, and it is a significant fact that it is only during these three, that is to say from 164 B.C. to the time of Trajan, that we know the exact names of the Nabataean kings. The reign of Augustus seems to have been one of comparative decline, though we cannot be absolutely certain even of this fact.

After Trajan's reign Petra ceases to be the most important commercial centre in the new province of Arabia, although wealthy people still continue to live within her walls and to build rich tombs for themselves and their descendants. The centre of trade then gradually moves to Bosra, a city which also becomes the centre of political life. We do not know how long the period of final decline lasts in Petra, for the story of those years is as dark as that of her infancy.

This sketch of her rise and fall is based on an analysis of her architectural monuments, on a study of her coins, and on her inscriptions which are generally in the Nabataean tongue. Very rarely are they in Greek. The majority of them come not from the site of Petra itself, but from her dependencies in Arabia and from the region influenced by her commercial interests.

The coins and inscriptions, however, provide us only with a general conception of her development; they tell us the names of the Nabataean deities and kings, the names of some Petraean citizens, tribes, and clans. They hardly ever mention Petraean interests or occupations, political organization or economic structure. Occasionally one can learn from this source something about rulers and generals, about feudal dynasties of the military governors of separate provinces, but all of these belong to the Nabataean empire; we also encounter the names of the commanders of Petraean cavalry divisions and of Mearists occupied in protecting the caravan roads and the Syrian and Arab territories of the Nabataean kings. It is interesting to find that the titles of the military leaders and governors of these regions are not Aramaean but Greek; they are called strategi, eparchs, hipparchs, chiliarchs. It is obvious that the Nabataeans only felt the need for such titles when they had incorporated in their kingdom the Hellenized territories of the north and had to create a military and civil organization which should not seem entirely foreign to their new subjects. The Parthians had been likewise obliged to do this at the same period. It is on account of these new subjects that the Nabataeans called their officials by the names of strategus and eparch and their generals by those of chiliarch and hipparch, and it was also to please them that certain kings styled themselves 'Philhellenes', although to their old subjects they still remained 'the kings who brought back to life and saved' or 'the kings who loved their people'.

Behind these titles, behind these governors and divisions we feel, however, the power of those wily merchant princes who controlled enormous caravans travelling slowly from north to south and south to north, perhaps even without always calling at Petra. Nowhere else, not even in Palmyra nor in Jerash, is the pulsation of commercial caravan life so clearly to be felt as in the mixed city of Petra. Nowhere else does one scent so acutely the union between the fiery faith of the desert Bedouin, the caravan leader, with the feverish life of the merchant speculator; this wonderful union which was responsible for bringing Mohammed and his mighty religious empire into existence. I have never been to Mecca; but the atmosphere of Petra is very like that of Mecca and it was in Petra that I first realized how Mohammed's Arabs acquired those characteristics which enabled them to create a world-wide religion and a world-wide empire; which enabled them to fulfil dreams of the Sumerians and the Babylonians. Such dreams could never have affected the Jews, who were from the first too closely bound to one country, and of a national character insufficiently mobile or versatile. I can make but one suggestion to those who wish to understand the part that the Arabs have played in the history of religion, culture, and statecraft, and that is that they go to Petra, that they spend several nights in that fantastic crater, listen with open ears to the nocturnal chorus of jackals, and make a pilgrimage to the mountain sanctuaries. Thus they may feel something of the departed life of ancient Petra, the most wonderful of all the caravan cities in the region.

> Where through the sand of morning-land
> The camel bears the spice.

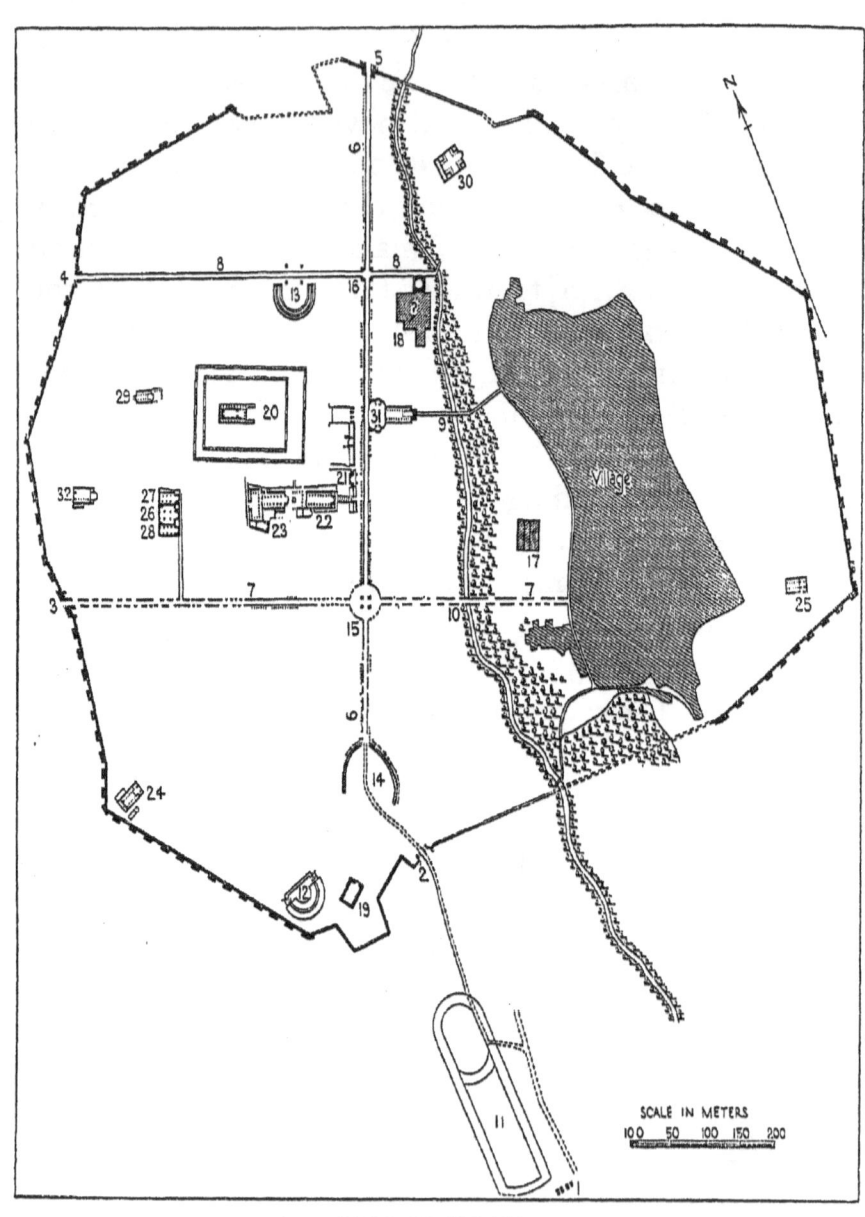

PLAN OF JERASH

GATES: 1. Arch, 2. Philadelphia, 3. Pella, 4. Gadara, 5. Damascus. STREETS, ETC.: 6. Antonine, 7. Pella, 8. Gadara, 14. Forum, 15. South Tetrapylon, 16. North Tetrapylon, 9. Artemis Bridge, 10. Pella Bridge. THEATRES: 11. Hippodrome, 12. South, 13. North. CIVIC BUILDINGS: 17. East Bath, 18. West Bath, 21. Nymphaeum. TEMPLES: 19. Zeus, 20. Artemis. CHURCHES: 22. Cathedral, 23. St. Theodore, 24. St. Peter and St. Paul, 25. Bishop Paul, 26. St. John the Baptist, 27. Damianos, 28. St. George, 29. Church over Synagogue, 30. Prophets, Apostles, and Martyrs, 31. Propylaea, 32. Genesius.

III

JERASH

THE creation of Petra was due to the important caravan routes running from India and Southern Arabia to Egypt and Syria. She was, in fact, one of the most prosperous cities of the Near East, not only during the Hellenistic period following upon the age of Alexander but also later under the aegis of Rome. In my first chapter I said a few words on the history of Transjordania and Petra, and I must here recall certain of these facts, and add to them several essential details to which I was unable to refer in the more general survey.

It seems obvious that Petraean trade developed at least as early as the prosperous days of the Persian empire. Definite intercourse had been established at that date between Petra and Egypt, Syria, and perhaps Babylonia, and also between Petra and the southern Arab kingdoms, though unfortunately we possess no clear information regarding either of these trades. The history during this period, both of Egypt and Syria, and of the southern Arab kingdoms, the Sabaean, the Minaean, and the Lihyianitic, is too little known.

As early as the fourth century B.C. the Nabataean kingdom was established, not as a society of robbers and pirates (as certain scholars suppose), but as an organized and commercial state, with a well-thought-out and carefully defined policy, designed to maintain an energetic stand for a liberty which was being threatened by powerful neighbours. We do not know what was the attitude of Alexander towards the

Nabataeans, but his more immediate successors were certainly not loath to lay their hands on this prosperous caravan city. The first attempt to do so was made by Antigonus the One-eyed and by his son Demetrius, probably the most energetic and able among the heirs of Alexander. Their aim was certainly to divert Petraean trade from Egypt, and to direct it towards the Phoenician ports; and they or their still more able predecessor Perdiccas may have been responsible for the foundation of the first Transjordanian military settlements, whose duty it was to safeguard caravans travelling northwards from Petra to the ports of Palestine and Phoenicia. But the efforts of Antigonus and Demetrius ended in failure and the Nabataeans retained their independence.

Relationships were not at once established between the Nabataeans and the Ptolemies, who ruled in Egypt as the successors of Alexander. We know little of the early intercourse of the two powers, but it is nevertheless evident that by the third century B.C. the Ptolemies, who controlled the greatest commercial port of the world, Alexandria, and were masters of the great commercial cities of Phoenicia, attempted to surround Petra with a sphere entirely under their own influence, in order to make her completely dependent on them and obedient to their orders. It is evident that the Ptolemies, in their endeavour to attract as much Indian and southern Arabian trade as possible to the harbours of their empire, and thus to compete in European markets with the Seleucids (who were in full control of the Euphrates route), could not tolerate the complete freedom of Petra, or the high customs-duties imposed by her on caravans *en route* for Alex-

Jerash 57

andria or Phoenicia. It is therefore in no way surprising to find that the Ptolemies took various measures for diverting the southern Arabian trade away from Petra in order to force that city into subjection. This policy explains the feverish endeavours made by Ptolemy II, the cleverest merchant who ever controlled Alexandria, to develop Egyptian intercourse with Arabia by the sea-route. It was for this purpose that he resumed and completed the work on the canal between the Nile and the Red Sea; that he founded a number of ports on the Egyptian coast of the Red Sea; that he probably helped to create a Greek port on the Arabian side, and that he established a firm Egyptian control over the Lihyianitic kingdom, which had succeeded to the Minaean in the control of the Arabian caravans.

The result of this policy was a close union between Egypt and El-Ela, formerly a Minaean and now a Lihyianitic caravan station. An interesting inscription on a sarcophagus which was probably found in the Fayum illustrates this state of things. It refers to a Minaean merchant, who was at one and the same time an Egyptian priest and a middleman between certain temples in Egypt and the merchants of southern Arabia. He provided the temples with incense and in return he sent fine linen (byssos) to Arabia in his own ships. This linen was a special product of the looms attached to the Egyptian temples.

The information that we have regarding Nabataean piracy in the Red Sea must also be connected with the policy of the Ptolemies, since the robbery of Ptolemaic ships by the Nabataeans was but a natural answer to Egyptian commercial policy on the Red Sea. The result was a punitive expedition of the Egyptian navy under Philadelphus or Euergetes I which for a while put an end to the endeavours of the Nabataeans to become a maritime power.

The activity of the Ptolemies in Phoenicia, Palestine, and Transjordania was inspired by the same policy. It was both for political and commercial reasons that they waged war after war against the Seleucids, in order first to establish and later to retain their control over these countries. Without being masters of Palestine and Transjordania the Ptolemies could never organize an efficient defence of their Sinaitic frontier, nor would they be in a position to reduce the Nabataeans to obedience. The control of the Phoenician cities was a natural addition to the control over Palestine and Transjordania. We must not forget that Tyre and Sidon were the oldest and the best harbours of the Palestinian, Phoenician, and Syrian coast, and that from time immemorial these cities were the *debouchés* of the Arabian and Asiatic trade of the Near East. In the hands of the Seleucids Tyre and Sidon were formidable naval bases against Egypt, and at the same time good starting-points for keeping down the endeavours of the Ptolemies to control the most important caravan routes of the Near East.

No wonder therefore that the Ptolemies, successful in their endeavours to transform Phoenicia and Palestine into Egyptian provinces and to establish a protectorate over the Ammonite sheikhs of Transjordania, made strong efforts to consolidate their power in these countries. One of the means for reaching this goal was to Hellenize these centres of Semitic life and civilization. We know very little about this side of their policy; but the little that we do know points to a policy of intense Hellenization carried out by the Ptolemies both in Palestine and Phoenicia and in Transjordania. City building, urbanization, was one of the means by which this policy could be achieved in the most efficient way, and we know that these kings pursued this policy both in Palestine and in Transjordania. The recent excavations of such cities as Bet-shur, Gazara, and Maresha in Palestine show how deep was Ptolemaic influence in these Semitic cities; and the creation of many cities in Transjordania bearing dynastic names such as Philadelphia, Berenice, Philotereia, and Arsinoe shows that still more has been done in this respect in that region. Here the Ptolemies were not the first urbanizers, for Macedonian colonies existed here before their time. But they did their best to make these Macedonian military colonies strong and prosperous in order to keep down the hereditary proclivities of the Ammonites towards highway robbery.

The results of this Ptolemaic policy in Transjordania are fairly well known, for the famous archives of Zenon have yielded scores of letters and other documents, most of them of the year 259 B.C., throwing clear light on Egyptian activity in the country of the Ammonites and especially on the brisk commerce established between Transjordania and Egypt at this time. Zenon spent a year in Palestine and Transjordania as an agent of Apollonius, the powerful finance-minister of Ptolemy Philadelphus. No wonder that letters written by him or addressed to him during his stay in Palestine reveal many features of the policy of the Ptolemies in both Palestine and Transjordania.

Since Zenon became secretary-general to Apollonius a couple of years after his return to Alexandria, other letters of the same character were kept by him as originals or copies in his files. Let us take a look at some of them which refer to the Transjordanian country.

A lively epistolary intercourse was going on between Tubias, Emir of the Ammonites, and both Apollonius and his master Philadelphus. From these letters and other documents of Zenon's correspondence we learn that Tubias had at his disposal some Ptolemaic soldiers, who were quartered in Rabbath Ammon, the capital of Tubias, which was renamed Philadelphia either by Ptolemy Philadelphus or else by Tubias in his honour. This shows that Tubias was practically a vassal of Philadelphus in much the same way as his modern successor rules as a vassal of the British Crown.

The relations of emir and king are most friendly. In excellent Greek the former writes to the latter about some presents which he is sending him through Zenon and Apollonius. These presents consisted of horses, of large and strong Arabian donkeys, of wild asses, of cross-breeds between wild asses and domesticated donkeys, and of dogs. It is evident that the emir knew how fond was Philadelphus of rare animals and how many efforts he made to improve the Egyptian breeds by imports from abroad. It is interesting to see that there are no camels on this list, although we know that at this time their importation to Egypt had just begun.

While animals were sent to Philadelphus other presents were dispatched to Apollonius: young slaves of noble origin, with pink cheeks and bright black eyes of almond shape, were among Tubias's gifts to the Chancellor of the Exchequer.

While this diplomatic intercourse was going on between the court of Philadelphia and that of Alexandria, brisk life reigned in Transjordania and Palestine. Groups of Egyptian citizens probably on behalf of some grandees of Alexandria were travelling from one place in Palestine and Transjordania to another. Starting from Gaza, the chief Ptolemaic harbour in Palestine, they visited all the important marketplaces of Palestine and Transjordania, came in touch with the Nabataeans of Petra in the South and with the Aramaeans of Damascus in the North. Everywhere they were buying goods for export; slaves and horses, results of raids of the Ammonites into the territory of the Seleucid rivals of the Ptolemies, loom large among them.

But the most important traffic was in Arabian goods, brought to Transjordania and Palestine by the Nabataean caravans: incense and myrrh are the staple commerce. It seems therefore that the measures taken by the Ptolemies to establish control over the Nabataeans were in the main successful and led to an *entente cordiale*, the result of which was a lively caravan trade both between Petra and Alexandria and between Petra and the Asiatic dependencies of Egypt. No wonder therefore if a contemporary of Zenon tells us that it was the traffic with the Nabataeans which made Ptolemaic Syria and Phoenicia 'rich in gold'.

In view of all these facts it is more than probable that the history of the Macedonian fortresses of Transjordania as caravan cities goes back to Ptolemaic times. Gerasa, however, was not one of them. At this time it was probably still a modest village of Arabs tending their flocks and occasionally cultivating some land.

Towards the end of the third century a change came to Transjordania. Palestine and Phoenicia were lost by the Ptolemies to the Seleucids, who were still the rulers of Mesopotamia and of a part of the Iranian plateau. Having got possession of Palestine and Transjordania the Seleucids naturally imitated the Ptolemaic attitude towards the caravan trade. Masters of Palestine, Transjordania, and Phoenicia, they tried to divert Arabian traffic from the road via Petra and Alexandria to their own maritime cities of Palestine, Phoenicia, and Syria. We do not know how far the Seleucids of the second century B.C. were able to achieve this end, but there is some evidence that Petra was at this time more closely connected with Seleucids than with Ptolemies; we hear, for instance, of the appearances of Nabataeans (that is to say of Petraean merchants) in Phoenician towns and in Delos, the main Seleucid port in Europe.

At all events it is certain that Antiochus III and his followers, especially the famous Antiochus IV Epiphanes, made renewed efforts to carry on the systematic Hellenization of Transjordania which had been begun by their predecessors. Some of the cities must be regarded as their own foundations, not as earlier urban centres developed by them. One glance at the map of Nearer Asia suffices to explain the aim of this town-building and town-developing policy of the Seleucids.

Transjordania itself is not a fertile country either for the agriculturist, the horse-breeder, or the stock-rearer. Only small agricultural and pastoral centres could hope to prosper there. In the neighbourhood of Jerash a certain amount of iron is to be obtained.

But it was not any desire to work indifferent iron-mines, nor any agricultural consideration, that drove the Seleucids and their predecessors to Hellenize and colonize Transjordania, by founding colonies, stretched as a chain connecting one fertile plain with another along the great caravan road which links Petra to Damascus, Phoenicia, and Syria on the one hand, and to Jerusalem and the ports of Palestine on the other. These Transjordanian towns, which were steadily Hellenized by the Seleucids throughout the second century B.C., were actually fortified caravan towns, and it may well be that it was only under Seleucid rule that Amman, or rather Philadelphia, first became a real Greek city. And we may be practically sure that it was Antiochus III, or even Antiochus IV, who first established at modern Jerash a Greek colony in the place of a local village. This village had served as a centre for the half-nomadic tribes of the Gerasenes; now it was to be called Antioch of the Gerasenes or Antioch on the Chrysorrous, the name of the stream running through the town. The ruins of this Antioch still stand.

The above statements on the early history of Transjordania are as yet hypothetical. The country has called forth little scientific study, except for that of certain roads of Roman date. The course of the caravan routes which traversed the land at that period is already certain, but we are reduced to mere guesses as regards the network of caravan roads of the Hellenistic era, and can do no more until detailed archaeological surveys, based on accurate air maps, shall be carried out by specialists. Nevertheless I am of the opinion that the growth of the Transjordanian towns is to be accounted for by trade alone. In the later times, it may be noted,

Jerash was connected by excellent roads both with Amman and Bosra. No certain proofs, however, exist for the connexion between Jerash and Damascus and Jerash and Palestine, even in Roman times.

We know how short-lived was the last effort made by the Macedonian kings of Nearer Asia to control the waves of national reaction against the foreign Greek element. Palestine under the Maccabees became a centre of this reactionary feeling. We know how Roman assistance—for even after their victory over Antiochus III the Romans still continued to regard the Seleucids as serious enemies—enabled the Jews to break free from the Hellenizing Seleucids, and how Rome permitted these barbarians to destroy everybody and everything Hellenistic with the greatest steadfastness and cruelty. The Transjordanian towns, and amongst them the newly founded Gerrasene Antioch, which was captured and destroyed by the Jews at the time of Alexander Jannaeus (102–76 B.C.), became the victims of this reaction. It seemed as though the end had come to this unfortunate city, this new centre of Hellenism on the Chrysorrous, almost before Seleucid culture had had time to take root. But fate directed otherwise.

Of events in Transjordania and Jerash in the first century B.C. little is known, but it was undoubtedly during this period that Nabataean trade entered upon the most prosperous period of its development. It is not without reason that Petra's finest monument, the El Khasne, which we have mentioned above, belongs to this period and not without reason that we find references to the rule of the Nabataean kings in Damascus.

Jerash

The rise of Petra to splendour was much assisted by the anarchy reigning on the Euphrates; this being caused by the steady advance of the Parthians and their conquest of the land of the two rivers. The lasting war between Seleucids and Parthian Arsacids was responsible for a temporary disorganization of the caravan route from Seleucia along the Euphrates, and for a time it became more advantageous for caravans to travel to Petra from Gerrha on the Persian Gulf, or from Charax, than to go from Gerrha to the mouth of the Euphrates and thence northward along the river. Not less important was the fact that a weakened Egypt was no longer able to impose its wishes upon the Nabataeans. As a result of all this, the Nabataeans acquired control both over the caravan road across the Sinaitic peninsula, and even over part of the Red Sea route to Egypt. Their kingdom was thus extended considerably to the south and west, and their port on the eastern shore of the gulf of Elan (Akaba) became the open harbour of Leuce Come (White Village). This absorbed the previously existing harbours and entered upon a lively intercourse with the Egyptian harbours of the Ptolemies.

We do not know how much this Nabataean success affected Transjordania, but it seems probable that the dawn of its prosperity, if not the very renewal of its life, is to be dated from this period. Bosra's history provides not infrequent proof of this, and so does the discovery at Jerash in 1930 of the first Nabataean inscription which seems to date from the first century B.C.

We have, however, no definite information about this: all that we do know for certain is that an important event in the history of Transjordania took place when Pompey put an end to the independence of Petraean Arabia, of Syria and Palestine, and gave 'freedom' to the cities of Transjordania. Henceforth the place of the Seleucids in the Near East was filled by the Romans, who came as new Hellenizers, treading in the steps of Seleucid tradition. In Syria from the first their policy was akin to that of the Seleucids, and the towns of Transjordania owe their late greatness and prosperity to this fact. It is therefore only natural that in Jerash Pompey appears as a new founder of the city, and this finds expression in the introduction of a new system of chronology which we may call the Pompeian era (starting in 64 B.C.). It looked, then, as if a new dynasty had come to power in that year, a dynasty not actually Hellenic, but certainly Philhellene.

Pompey's policy was in the main continued by his successors in Syria. For more than a century and a half local kings, whose names are known to us, ruled at Petra as vassals of Rome, and continued to control the Arabian caravan trade. Roman policy in this connexion is not entirely clear, but in the early period of the empire it seems to have been to strengthen Egypt by means of independent connexions of that country with India and southern Arabia, rather than the protection and development of the caravan trade through Petra. This is at any rate the impression given by the rather skimpy information which we possess on Augustus' Arabian campaigns and on the policy which his successors—more especially Nero—adopted on the Red Sea.

The towns beyond the Jordan could not, however, remain unaffected by the greater stability which life reached at this time both in Syria and all over the

Roman empire, especially during the early decades of the first century A.D. As a result of this stability a period of great prosperity began for Syria and Palestine. Witness the great building activity of Herod the Great and his dynasty, these splendid heirs of the Maccabees and obedient vassals of Rome, who ruled for a while a huge Syro-Palestinian kingdom. Signs of this prosperity have been revealed also at Jerash by the systematic excavations recently begun there. These prove that the early first century was a period of feverish building activity in the city, whose general lines were laid out in this period.

But the greatest period of prosperity began, both for Jerash and the Transjordan land in general, a little later. It was partially due to two series of events in the Near East: the rising of the Jews against Nero and Vespasian, and the policy of the Roman emperors towards Alexandria. The Palestinian war of A.D. 70 led to the attempt of the Flavian emperors to surround the Judaean centre of fanaticism by chains of Hellenistic cities, and thus to enclose Judaism in an iron ring of Hellenism. The towns of Transjordania formed the links of one of these chains, that along the Jordan. There Vespasian and Domitian settled strong groups of Roman veterans, either of Greek origin or thoroughly Hellenized. Powerful Roman garrisons appeared again in some of the cities of Transjordania in order to uphold these new supporters of Hellenism and of Roman influence. It is very probable that alongside this military policy the Flavians took some measures for promoting Petraean trade and for directing it towards the Transjordanian towns. This fact is suggested by some inscriptions recently unearthed at Jerash.

It cannot, one fears, be denied that this policy was also partly directed against Alexandria, and that the damage which might have resulted from it to this city was intentional. Alexandria in the first century of our era had become too wealthy and too prosperous, and its inhabitants had come to look upon the Romans both with envy and disdain. Opposition had raised its head more than once in Alexandria, and it was only due to the energetic measures taken by the Roman officials there that Jewish pogroms had not developed into veritable risings. It is consequently not surprising that the Flavians and their followers were anxious to divert a part of Alexandria's eastern trade to other provinces of the Roman empire, and that they chose for this purpose the towns of Transjordania and did their best to develop their trade.

Seen in this light the policy of Trajan and his followers seems reasonable enough, and the extraordinary, almost fabulous, growth of the Transjordanian towns in the second century A.D. is also explained. I have already described the way in which Trajan took a firm hold of Petra and made her a part of his new Arabian province, clearly explaining to the inhabitants that henceforth their trade was not only to be with Egypt by way of the Red Sea, but also with Damascus and the coasts of Phoenicia and Syria by way of the Transjordanian towns. It cannot be doubted that Trajan's schemes were due both to the situation in Alexandria and Palestine which we have just described, and also to his attitude towards Parthia and Mesopotamia, of which I shall speak more in my next chapter. His policy in Arabia and Transjordania was followed by his successors Hadrian, Antoninus Pius, Marcus

Aurelius, and Commodus, and later by the dynasty of Severus. It was during this period that Jerash was most prosperous and that her finest monuments were erected. The town now spread over a wide area on both sides of the river, becoming a typical caravan city: but more of this anon.

With the third century A.D. this prosperity was interrupted. The towns of Transjordania fell into ruin and decay. It is not impossible—though we have no direct information about it—that the new masters of the Iranian Orient, the Sasanian Persians, who many times in the middle of the third century swept all Mesopotamia and Syria down to the sea, included in one of their plundering and ravaging raids both Petra and the Transjordanian cities. This may have been one of the causes of their decay, though the main cause was certainly the anarchy and ruin which reigned all over the Roman empire during most of the third century and affected first and foremost the caravan trade. We must not forget that its brilliant development in the second century A.D. had been entirely due to the ever-increasing prosperity of the Roman empire at that time.

We cannot tell whether Petra ever recovered from her third-century downfall, but Jerash had a later period of revival, and gradually and slowly regained some importance as a Christian city. Modest churches were built from the fourth century onwards, by the side of her temples, and along with them synagogues appeared. The Sun and the Moon were replaced by the all-conquering Cross, but the commercial life of the city experienced little more than a slow and sickly recovery.

The real revival of Jerash took place in the time of

Justinian, and the reason for this will be elucidated at some future date by those who are prepared to devote serious study to the history of caravan trade of late Roman and Byzantine times. One thing, however, is certain, and that is that in Justinian's day there was a revival of caravan trade. It again followed the Transjordanian route, passing through Petra or through the towns which had superseded her in Arabia, and it had a marked effect on the life of Jerash. It was at that date that there appeared there, beside the ruins of the temple of Artemis, a huge church, the cathedral of Theodore Stratelates, with a holy tank and mighty Propylaea rivalling the similar heathen buildings standing near by. These, too, were everywhere turned into churches, and painting and mosaic-work blossomed in them. Yet thought was still given to that part of the population which had remained heathen or was still but half Christian, for it was on their account that at about this time the long-honoured holiday of the Semitic Maiumas was revived, in the very teeth of the Fathers of the Church who considered the celebration of the Maiumas an immoral and loose institution.

The rebirth of the city was, however, but shortlived. The Sasanian storm swept over her, to be followed by Arab rule both in Moslem and pre-Moslem days. These rulers of the East played a part in the ruin of Jerash, but it was not they who dealt her and the other towns of Transjordania their final death-blow. Whatever destruction may have been wrought in her Christian churches by Omar II, the iconoclast (717–20), it brought less damage to the city than the earthquake of the 18th of January 746, which ruined many of the greatest of her buildings. Yet neither Omar nor the earthquake was the real cause of her final ruin. The real cause was the change in the organization of caravan trade in the times of Arab domination. The trade took a new route and one which missed Jerash. Some faint life continued to linger there; remains of an Arabic city of the twelfth to the fourteenth century have been recently uncovered. The progress of excavation will show how great an importance this city of the twelfth to the fourteenth century enjoyed. So far as we can now tell its revival was both partial and short-lived. Very soon afterwards Jerash became what she is to-day, one of the most romantic of Syria's numerous ruins and one of the most promising sites for the work of modern archaeology.

What have the archaeologists accomplished there? Ten years ago a visit to this site was a difficult and complicated affair. Now nothing seems easier. If you step into a motor-car early in the morning in Jerusalem, you find yourself in Jerash by lunch time. No wonder then that in the nineteenth century visitors to the ruins were counted in units, whereas to-day they run into hundreds: and they will soon go there in thousands. It is likewise not surprising that in the past archaeologists were content to photograph the ruins of Jerash and to copy her inscriptions, whereas now the time for a scientific and systematic excavation of the site has arrived.

We, the archaeologists of the twentieth century, are working on the basis established for us by our predecessors of the eighteenth and the nineteenth, those travellers who were the first to collect the inscriptions of Jerash, to draw and photograph the ruins of the most important buildings, to measure them and to make a general plan of the city. After this work of preparation the first excavations at Jerash were undertaken by Professor Garstang, the Director of the British School of Archaeology at Jerusalem.

During his tenure of office, however, Transjordania came to be reorganized as an independent state with an interesting constitution: at the head is an emir who lives in a very new but small palace at Amman, the capital of his kingdom. He consults a Cabinet, composed of ministers elected by the local population, and to each of these native ministers an English adviser is attached. The emir is also provided with an army—the Transjordanian legion—whose officers are partly English. The government was probably much the same under the Ptolemies. One of the important departments of the Transjordanian Government is the Service of Antiquities; of this again a native and a British director are in charge. The British adviser, a well-known architect, Mr. L. L. Horsfield, took up his residence at Jerash, and, following in the steps of Professor Garstang, started a new era in the history of the town, both by systematic excavations and by a partial reconstruction of the city.

In this Mr. Horsfield was and is helped by many foreign institutions: first, the British School collaborated with him in uncovering the ruins. Soon Yale University, at the advice of the late Professor B. Bacon, took an active interest in the work and helped both Mr. Horsfield and the successor of Mr. Garstang (Mr. Crowfoot) to carry on their work. Since the withdrawal of the British School, the work is being done by Yale University in collaboration with the American School of

1. 'Triumphal' arch outside the city

2. The pear-shaped square. To the left on the hill are the ruins of the Zeus temple and to the right those of the theatre

X. JERASH

1. One of the side fronts of the Temple of Zeus

2. The seats of the theatre

XI. JERASH

Oriental Research at Jerusalem, and with the help and advice of Mr. Horsfield.

For the first two years of Yale's work our aim was to study the Christian antiquities of the site, while Horsfield was studying its heathen monuments. Now we are all engaged in studying the most important monuments, whether Christian or heathen.

It is not my intention to give a detailed account of the work that has been accomplished, since much of what has been done still remains to be published, and I do not wish to infringe on the rights of those who are entitled to write of it. I will give here only a general description of Jerash at the time of its greatest prosperity —the first and second centuries A.D. No sufficient light has yet been thrown on the difficult problem of what it was before, or what befell it after, that time. Even the most recent excavations have failed to reveal the Hellenistic town, and only very gradually are they displaying its Christian successor, the Jerash of the fourth and following centuries.

Here, as at Petra, the ruins give us a clear idea of the skeleton. The walls which enclose Jerash stress the peculiarity of the surrounding country. Their date is uncertain. It may be that we must assign the core of them to Hellenistic times. Perhaps some work on the fortifications was done in the early Roman period, especially before and during the great Jewish revolts against Nero and Vespasian. Repairs and reconstructions may have been made in the third and the following centuries.

The three outstanding features of Jerash's skeleton are its main colonnaded avenue, the city's 'spine'; its large temple, which is the heart; and the pear-shaped market-place, surrounded by columns, which may be considered as the belly. Quite isolated stand the majestic ruins of the theatre and the temple of Zeus overlooking the southern gate, as if to protect the city from this side.

If Jerash is entered from the Amman road the first building which one sees is typical of most towns in the Roman empire. It is a triumphal arch, a symbolic gateway erected to the glory of the empire and the emperor (x. 1). In Jerash, as in Dura, this arch stands outside the town. The dedicatory inscription has unfortunately perished, so that we do not know the date of its construction, though it closely resembles the southern gate. One is led to conclude that they are contemporary; but the date of the south gate also is still unknown.

The next ruin that the visitor passes lies on the left of the road from Amman, but still outside the town. It is a large stadium (more than 200 metres long and about 80 wide) of the usual form, with seats and the twin 'boxes of honour'. A curious misunderstanding is connected therewith, for most scholars call it a 'naumachia'. It remains for him who first gave this name to explain how a naumachia—a place in which mock sea-fights were enacted—could exist in a half-desert region, where water was worth its weight in gold. The building itself fails to reveal the slightest trace of appliances by which the track, which has the form of a rectangle with a rounded end, could be filled with water. The real purpose of the building is self-evident; it was a stadium for athletic contests. But it probably also served some more prosaic use of greater service to a caravan city, such as a horse-, a camel-, possibly also a cattle-market, and it may well have been here that caravaners bought new supplies and sold their surplus animals. The use of a stadium for this purpose was probably dictated by the wish to provide seller and purchaser with facilities for testing the animal before settling the transaction. At a later time, perhaps during the second Persian invasion, the northern part of the stadium was cut off and made into a smaller circus.

A few minutes beyond the stadium a caravan coming from Amman would reach the southern gate, a beautifully built and richly adorned arch with three passages.

It is characteristic that the walls here project in order to enclose within the fortifications the high hill on which stand two impressive buildings (X. 2). These are still in excellent preservation, and consist of a large and rich temple and a theatre. It is difficult to account for their position at the very gates of the city, and to explain why these buildings are differently orientated from the rest of the town. In the town the roads are straight and run from south to north and west to east, and there can be no doubt that this general layout dates from early Roman times. The temple and theatre, which do not fit in with this scheme, cannot therefore have been built by the Romans; they are an heritage from the older Jerash of Hellenistic days.

The temple, dedicated to Zeus the Olympian in the Roman period, has never been excavated and little is therefore known of its early history. The only known fact about it is that in the first century A.D. money had to be raised for its construction or reconstruction. This work was only completed in A.D. 163, when the temple assumed its Roman garb and was dedicated to Zeus (XI. 1).

The history of the theatre (XI. 2) is less vague. Its hall, which would hold four thousand five hundred spectators, was built in early Roman times; the stage underwent frequent reconstructions, the dates of which have not yet been scientifically determined. My impression is that in its earliest form it dates back to the Hellenistic period, and if this is really so, and if the monuments on the hill were really constructed at this date, it may not be too rash to make the following reconstruction.

In pre-Hellenistic times there probably stood there a temple consecrated to the local Semitic god, for later inscriptions tell us that at a later date Olympic Zeus resided on this hill accompanied by hierodules (sacred slaves), who may perhaps be regarded as an Eastern heritage left by the former temple. This, like other Syrian temples, may have been connected with a theatre-like building used for religious purposes. In Hellenistic times the local sanctuary was transformed into the temple of Zeus and a large Greek theatre was built as well. Perhaps the hill became an acropolis and citadel, which may even have been fortified. Finally in early Roman times, say, the first century A.D., both temple and theatre were reconstructed, enlarged, and re-decorated. It was probably then that the former was surrounded by a peribolos with a monumental staircase connecting its terraces with the pear-shaped area from which stretched the main civic artery—the avenue bordered by columns. When the city wall was built, the fortified citadel was certainly enclosed within the defences; it may even have continued to serve as the citadel.

Jerash

Caravans entered the Roman town directly after passing the city gates. There the first architectural group which confronted them consisted of a court, unusual both in size and shape, being of the form of a flattened pear with monumental gates at each end. It was excellently paved, and bordered by two disconnected porticoes of Ionic columns, enclosing only a part of it (x. 2). Trial excavations conducted this year have proved that, in its present condition, it dates from early Roman days, that is to say from the time of the city's reconstruction. At an earlier period there was no square at this place. The excavations showed that a deep ravine between two hills (the acropolis and the hill near the river) was filled up with debris to create the level floor of the Roman square. The same excavations, however, failed to reveal the real purpose of this peculiar square, but I am of the opinion that at Jerash, as at Petra, the first architectural feature which travellers must have encountered on entering the city would be one of several caravanserais. These took the shape of market-squares, surrounded by shops, store-rooms, and goods-yards, similar to those which are still to be seen to-day in caravan towns. Caravans must have halted on these squares; there the camels were unloaded, the goods were placed in the store-rooms, and the travellers washed and tidied themselves. It was only after assuming clean, elegant, and civilized attire that the visitor made his way into the clean and elegant city.

The wide avenue (XII) leading out of the pear-shaped court was the pride of Jerash, just as it was the pride of Petra and the pride of every Syrian town. It was flanked by columns numbering in all over five hundred, though to-day only some seventy are still preserved, and it was intersected at two places, at the beginning and the end of the central part, by two fourfold gates, the tetrapylons so typical of Syrian towns. Between these the more important edifices lined either side of the avenue. To east and west of the tetrapylons, crossing the avenue at right angles, stretched colonnaded roads, of which the one leading to the bridge across the river passed under the first tetrapylon.

The central part of the main avenue was flanked by unusually fine buildings. We are well acquainted with those standing on its north side, where, just beyond the first tetrapylon, there open out to the visitor approaching from the south the most splendid series of façades. First appears a fine nymphaeum, which was recently excavated and partially restored by Horsfield. It was a three-storied building with a rich decorative façade, in style somewhat reminiscent of the stone decoration of the theatre, and it served simultaneously as a temple, a water-conduit, and a cistern. It was adorned with niches, statues, and multi-coloured marble facings, and ever-flowing water added to the decoration (XIII. 1).

Next to this an elegant propylaeum, entrance gate to a remarkably decorative staircase, comes into view. This once led to a small temple, a modest neighbour of the temple of Artemis, and perhaps the abode of her divine consort. He probably withdrew in awe of his wife's greatness to this quiet retreat, as did Hadad from Atargatis in many places, and as did many another deity of Syria and Asia Minor; for here the Great Goddess, the incarnation of the 'Eternal Femi-

1. The main colonnaded street of Jerash. Behind on the hill stands the Temple of Artemis

2. Part of the colonnaded street

XII. JERASH

1. The Nymphaeum (monumental fountain on the main street)

2. Entrance to the Church of St. Theodore (formerly to a pagan temple, next to the Temple of Artemis)

XIII. JERASH

nine', dominated over the masculine in the sphere of religion, if not also in the sphere of everyday life. In Christian times when the temple was transformed into a Christian church, the main architectural features, such as the monumental staircase, were retained, but the building gradually developed into the splendid basilica of Theodore Stratelates, of which I shall speak in greater detail below (XIII. 2).

Beyond rose the fine entrance to the temple of Artemis, Jerash's divine protectress, who in Roman times added to her Greek name that of Fortuna, the city's 'Luck'. This entrance is planned with amazing daring and ability, and has all the subtlety characteristic of high technical development such as we see in the illusionary grouping of Graeco-Roman architecture in imperial times. The main entrance to the temple was from the principal colonnaded avenue standing at right angles to it. The approach from the other side of the river also led to the colonnaded avenue; the road first crossing the bridge and then passing through a narrow rectangular court bordered by Corinthian columns. Monumental gates connected this with another and wider court, shaped like an isosceles trapezium. Its longer side faced the colonnaded avenue and was adorned with a large threefold triumphal arch. This second courtyard is a veritable *trompe-l'œil*—a marvellous achievement of illusionary architecture, where everything tends to stress the imposing lines of the arches. The road passes under the triumphal arch and then runs to the propylaeum. In Christian times this entire group of buildings between the street and the river was converted into the church of St. Procopius, but the fundamental lines of the original structure can still be discerned.

The Propylaea have been admirably restored by Horsfield (XIV. 1). The simplicity and grace of their fundamental lines render them most distinctive, though the plan is simple and by no means original. They consist of a monumental triple gate, whence a large and straight staircase leads to the entrance of the peribolos. Here the plan is so admirably worked out that though the Propylaea are now ruined they cannot fail to impress the spectator, so long as he is able to divert his mind from purely decorative details. Yet in illusionary architecture even these details are essential, for they provide the building with the necessary effect of light and shade. To realize the full merit of the construction one must first and foremost appreciate the success of the architect in solving his most difficult problem, that of grouping together upon terraces a number of buildings of different periods and styles.

Hundreds of people passed through these Propylaea as they went to bow before Artemis, the queen of the city; Jerashites of every kind, rich and poor, men, women, and children, the travellers and merchants whom the caravans periodically deposited in the town; important caravan leaders, ordinary camel- and donkey-drivers, free men or slaves—one and all went to make obeisance to their mistress, to wash in the pure waters of her fountain, to absolve themselves from sin in her presence, and to lay before her their offerings and vows.

The space between the three façades of these buildings was occupied by large two-storied shops built of stones, a veritable Burlington Arcade. All were built up against the terraces of the temple and of the small

1. Monumental Propylaea (gate) leading to the great Temple of Artemis

2. Front of the Temple of Artemis

XIV. JERASH

theatre which will be described later; all were uniform, and it is obvious that this shopping centre must have been town property, and that the leases of the shops must have added an important and steady sum to the municipal revenue.

The temple of Artemis is undoubtedly a most imposing ruin, for to-day twelve of its columns still stand *in situ*, topped by splendid and admirably preserved Corinthian capitals (XIV. 2). It would be easy to re-erect the columns which have fallen from the porticoes surrounding the peribolos and from the colonnades, for they all lie strewn around just where they fell when earthquakes shook them down. Beneath the temple stretch mighty vaults, in which a museum has now been arranged, comprising architectural and epigraphical material from the ruins. Beautiful and well preserved as the ruins are, the temple is still a riddle to us and still stands mysterious in its splendour. When was it first built? Who built it, and how? Had its site been sacred even before the foundation of the caravan city? One day perhaps the excavations begun last year will provide answers to all these questions. The only thing we know now for certain is that the Propylaea of the temple in their actual form were built in A.D. 150.

Such are the main outlines of the city. Like Petra, Roman Jerash appears as a town whose splendid development was largely due to caravan trade, and whose ground-plan either consciously or unconsciously adapted itself to caravans. Everything else in the town was of secondary importance and it is not surprising to find that time has obliterated most of it. The group of buildings, however, which rises beyond the temple of Artemis, as though it were some annex belonging to it, seems to be of more than secondary importance, consisting as it does of a closed theatre with a curious square in front of it. This may have been something in the nature of a forum, where in Roman times the populace met and the elders congregated. Here may also have been a meeting ground for religious ceremonies and for the performance of sacred music and dances of a ritualistic character. The place closely resembles the temple of Artemis in Dura which I shall describe later, though here everything is on a much larger scale.

Such is the town which stands on the west bank of the Chrysorrous. The topography of the quarter on the east bank, which was connected with the western by two stone bridges, is not clear. The ruins there were never important and now almost all trace of them has been defaced by the village built above them by Caucasian emigrants, who migrated to Turkey in 1860 and were transported to Jerash in 1878; one or two of them can still speak Russian. It seems unlikely that this section of the town was ever occupied by buildings of the old Hellenistic city; it more probably represented an overflow from the main town on the opposite bank, with residential houses, suburbs, and utilitarian buildings. Even at present the ruins of a large and luxurious bath survive, but this bath is far less sumptuous than that which stood on the western bank.

In Jerash, as in all the cities of the ancient world, a second and no less imposing town rises immediately behind the town of the living: this is the town of the dead, full of remarkable monuments. There is no point in describing them here, for they are neither as strange nor as beautiful as those of Petra or Palmyra. Yet the town would seem incomplete without them, for they were the buildings first encountered by a traveller coming from Damascus or Palestine, Philadelphia or Bosra, or from the other cities of the Decapolis. The temples and chapels, the huge massive sarcophagi, the step-pyramids set upon heavy bases, the façades cut in the rocks—all appear in fantastic sequence, and it was probably they that prepared the visitor for the splendours of the town of the living.

One of the most curious monuments of Jerash stands among these tombs: it is a huge tank or pool in the northern necropolis, into which flow many springs, no doubt the main water-supply of the city. It is not a cistern like those in many other cities of the ancient world but an open reservoir, such as can be seen in America to-day (xv. 1). From this reservoir water came through a sluice into an aqueduct, entering the city west of the so-called Damascus gate. It then turned round the rear of the 'Artemis-complex' and ended in the beautiful nymphaeum of the main street described above. The tank is divided by a cross wall into two unequal parts. The whole mass of buildings near the south end of the pool has been recently excavated by Dr. C. Fisher, but there still remain some problems connected with it.

Along the south side of the tank runs a terrace bordered on the water-front by a colonnade. On the other side of the terrace stands a little theatre with seats for about 1,000 spectators (xv. 2). The southern entrance to the terrace was adorned by an arched gate, near which was found long ago a large block of stone with a long Greek inscription of which I am going to speak presently. We may note that from the seats of the theatre, if the theatre actually had a normal stage, the tank could not have been seen. Even if the stage building was very low 'those seated on the extreme sides of the semicircular auditorium would have found it difficult to watch what may have been going on below', says Dr. Fisher in his manuscript report on his excavation.

Had it not been for the inscription mentioned above, a late Greek text of the year A.D. 535, we could never have guessed at the nature of this group of buildings. This inscription, however, clearly proves that the feast of Maiumas was celebrated here. This was one of the most renowned religious ceremonies of heathen Syria and was especially abhorred by Christians because of its ritualistic submersion of naked women, in the presence of an audience seated in a theatre-like temple of a type peculiar to Syria.

All the elements essential to this ceremony seem to lie before us at the end of the reservoir, and it seems easy enough to reconstruct the action in our minds. We can, in fact, form a very vivid picture of the ceremony as it must have been performed on this site in adoration of the goddess of Jerash. But, unfortunately, the results of last year's excavations make it difficult to assume that the small theatre was built for the purpose of watching the ceremony which was taking place in the tank. For, as I said, it was probably impossible to see from the steps of the theatre what was taking place in the reservoir. One must therefore conclude that, if the ceremony of the Maiumas as it was enacted at Jerash was connected with the theatre, then it could not have been connected with the reservoir; or, vice versa, if it was performed in the reservoir then it could have had nothing to do with the theatre. Excavations give rise to, but they may also destroy, many of our hypotheses.

Such was the general aspect of Jerash in the early Roman empire. Of the life of the inhabitants we know but very little. Numerous inscriptions from the town enable us to reconstruct the past of certain of its buildings and the cult of its deities, but in general they only tell us, in connexion with its inhabitants, insignificant and uninteresting things just as likely to have been of common occurrence in any other town of the Roman Empire.

A very careful study of the inscriptions does, however, teach us something. We learn, for instance, that the city was not entirely Greek, that the Greeks were, in fact, submerged by the local Semites, the ever-increasing number of Arabs and Jews; so, though, to outward view, the town was Greek, its basis was Arab, and the same is true of its religion.

Neither at Jerash nor at Petra do inscriptions attribute civic prosperity to the caravan trade, for ancient inscriptions speak but rarely of such prosaic facts, though those of Palmyra are an exception. Nor would the general aspect of the city or the character of its monuments make us realize that the town was once peopled by caravan merchants. At Petra and at Palmyra this is not so; at both the whole ground-plan is that of a typical caravan city.

In spite of this I am firmly convinced that Jerash was a caravan city. A few days of careful study prove it. Thus when we look at the unproductive territories, the poor vegetation and the indifferent mines, it is clear that only transit-trade could enable her to acquire the wealth necessary for the construction of the buildings which I have just described. The money for these buildings came from the pockets of the inhabitants, and they can hardly have received exterior financial aid, for it is unlikely that any of the emperors would have contributed to its adornment. If an emperor lent help to any particular city he always had special reasons for it. Philip, for instance, was interested in the fortunes of the neighbouring Canatha; we must not forget, however, that he was an Arab by birth; Septimius Severus had made Leptis in Africa the city of his dreams, but he was a native thereof and dearly loved it. No such connexions can be established for Jerash. It was the caravan trade alone which could have provided the enormous sums of money needed for building the beautiful monuments of the city. This fact is significant and must be taken into account by those who devote themselves to the study of the economic history of antiquity. It gives us a clear idea how large were the expenses connected with the caravan trade and the profits derived from it.

The fundamental lines of the Jerash of the early Roman empire were not altered when the town became Christian and when mighty Artemis was transformed into a wicked demon. The superficial aspect no doubt underwent a change. One by one the finest buildings were transformed into Christian churches, even during the period of neglect and devastation in the third and fourth centuries. These early churches are small and simple and cannot compare with the heathen ruins, but when the period of complete revival dawned in the fifth and sixth centuries, especially in the reign of Justinian, the Christians set themselves the task of creating a new Jerash at least as brilliant as the old. They erected it above the ruins of the buildings of the heathen age.

Thus the cathedral of Theodore Stratelates, the warrior saint, rose beside the temple of Artemis, on the very ruins of the temple of her warrior-god husband. The cathedral with its Propylaea, its monumental staircase, its admirable paintings, and its fine mosaic and sculpture, is actually little more than a Christian imitation of the earlier pagan temple, but one detail of its construction, which has been recently revealed, is peculiar. This is the interesting character of the courtyard, and 'ganglion' of the complicated buildings which gradually came into being here.

This courtyard lies between the church of the fifth and sixth centuries and the one facing the road, an earlier building, probably to be assigned to the fourth. An impressive fountain stands in the centre, and a fine staircase leads from the court up to the later church. In front of the fountain, immediately behind the apse of the later church, stands a bishop's throne. It seems obvious that the Christian nymphaeum was erected here in the place of an earlier heathen fountain. But we can trace this farther, for Epiphanius, Bishop of Cyprus, writing some time about 475, refers in a passage of his *Panarion* to the miracles of the Christian world, and names certain places where water in the springs, that is to say in the fountains, turns to wine on the anniversary of the feast of Cana in Galilee, a day which coincides with that of the Transfiguration. Amongst the names on this list we find that of Jerash, where the miracle is said to have occurred in the

'Martyrium'. There can be no doubt that the Christian miracle took place on the spot formerly sacred to the heathen mysteries, and it seems obvious that a similar miracle occurred in or near the temple of Artemis in heathen times.[1]

The church of St. Theodore was not the only Christian building in Jerash. Even before our excavations had begun, three other churches were known, and all of these we studied carefully. We found that they all dated from the sixth century, that is to say from the time of Justinian. Our excavations revealed six more churches and one synagogue (in this last we discovered a floor mosaic which depicts the Flood). Indeed, wherever there were ruins marked by a large mass of stone, the very first turn of the spade served to reveal a Christian church. All these churches were of the same date, and it was under Justinian that Jerash became thoroughly Christianized. At that time she appears to have been far from being poor, and though it is, of course, true that all her churches were built of the stones taken from heathen edifices, all their interior decorations were nevertheless new and individual. All the paintings and the wall and ceiling mosaics which once embellished the interiors have now disappeared, but we have fragments of those which covered the floors. Two of these are especially impor-

[1] We must remember that in these parts of northern Arabia Artemis' masculine equivalent was Dusares, the god of fertility, identified by the Greeks with Dionysus. This deity, this 'Arab god' as the inhabitants of Jerash called him, was accorded almost as great a worship at Jerash as that offered to Olympic Zeus and to Artemis herself. Three dedications to him have already been unearthed there. We may well suppose that the Arabian Dushara or Dusares might have appeared in his statues and bas-reliefs not only in the garb of the Greek Dionysus but also as a god of war. This would account for the cult of the warrior saint which was established in Christian times in his sacred precinct.

1. The great water tank outside the City

2. The theatre built on the slope of the hill above the great water tank where the inscription of Maiumas was found

XV. JERASH

tant to the historian and archaeologist, for their borders are composed of schematic views of ancient towns with their names written beside them. The majority of these views have disappeared, and Fate has so willed it that two of the surviving ones depict the same scene, namely a view of mighty Alexandria and her famous lighthouse, the Pharos. Side by side with Alexandria is represented the town of Memphis.

I will not discuss the importance which these mosaics have for the history of Byzantine art and for the study of the topography of Alexandria and Memphis in Byzantine times; the subject has been dealt with by Mr. Crowfoot, whose luck it was to discover these mosaics. It is, however, to be noted that chance has preserved here the views of the two towns, Memphis and Alexandria, which represent respectively the dawn and the end of Egyptian culture. In Justinian's day both appear as of equal importance, not because of their role as transmitters of an historical tradition many centuries old, but because they are the bearers of a new culture, the culture of the Christian empire. What we see represented in them, as a symbol and standard of the time, is not the great buildings of the past, but the mighty temples of the Christian cult. These are not only the heirs of the bygone culture, but also an embodiment of an entirely new civilization. The place filled by St. Sophia at Constantinople, by the Vatican, the Lateran, and Santa Maria Maggiore in Rome, or by the fine cathedrals at Alexandria and Memphis, was filled in Jerash by the martyrium of Theodore Stratelates, as well as by many other churches in the city.

The East is amazingly strong, amazingly full of

vitality, Greek heathen civilization had flourished in Jerash for centuries; Greek Christian culture superseded it. Yet as soon as the successive waves of the Persian Ormuzd and of Mohammed broke over her, this ancient Grecian edifice, seemingly so stable, crumbled as though it had faded into a mirage. The crescent appeared on the horizon and soon came to dominate the ruins both of heathen and Christian towns, whose columns and porticoes slowly fell into the decay in which we now see them.

IV

PALMYRA AND DURA

THE caravan roads of the Persian empire leading from India and Iran to Palestine, Syria, or Asia Minor created their own towns just as the Indo-Arabian route had done. Amongst the most ancient cities so created were those of Damascus, Hama, Homs, and Aleppo, all of them notable for the fact that not only were they prosperous in early times but remain important centres of commerce to-day. Much later, in the Hellenistic period, the city of Seleucia grew up on the banks of the Tigris, and still later Palmyra rose to importance in the heart of the desert, midway between the valley of the Euphrates and the rich fields, woods, and ports of Syria and Phoenicia. Contemporaneously with Seleucia Dura appeared on the Middle Euphrates and, though it was never destined to rival the above-mentioned cities in importance and wealth, its historical significance is quite as great as theirs.

The history of the oldest caravan cities of Syria is somewhat obscure. To begin with none of them have ever been excavated and few of them ever will be, since most of them remain prosperous commercial towns to-day. Literary records or references which throw light on their existence in Babylonian or Assyrian times are scarce, and have never been the subject of comparative study. References dating from Persian and Hellenistic times are even rarer, and the few that exist are of slight historical importance. The case of Seleucia, of Dura, and of Palmyra, three caravan cities characterized by their Hellenistic and Roman culture, is very different, for their topography and monuments are now being gradually elucidated. Seleucia grew up as the blend of a caravan city and of a large river port; Dura is a combined caravan station and frontier fort, whilst Palmyra remains distinct as the largest caravan centre of Roman times in the Syrian desert. Seleucia is at present undergoing scientific excavation, but it is still too early to discuss the results of the work. As regards Dura and Palmyra, much material is already available, for at the former systematic excavation has now been going on for seven years whilst the latter, whose extraordinary columns have always made a romantic appeal to all travellers who have seen them, has recently become the subject of more or less systematic examination, begun by a private Danish expedition, and now conducted by the Syrian government. As a result the history and topography of Dura and Palmyra are gradually becoming clearer, and already it is possible to point to several basic facts which, when formulated, will facilitate the work of future discoverers.

I have already laid stress on the probability that in early times caravans coming from the lowlands of the Euphrates and Tigris, or from the highlands of Persia, travelled northward and westward, either across the Syrian desert or round it and up along the Euphrates. It is probable that even at this date these caravans used the rich sulphur springs lying half-way between the Euphrates and Damascus, as well as the oasis which surrounds them, as a stopping-place on their westward road. Near one of these springs a temple must have been built at a very early date and soon afterwards a village must have grown up around it.

Palmyra and Dura

This village, which the Bible calls Tadmor, but which was later named Palmyra, served as a centre for the tribe which owned the oasis. Yet a tribal centre, springs, and an oasis do not alone transform a village into a caravan city; for this purpose facilities for the exchange of goods and comfortable rest-houses are necessary. Tadmor was not a caravan city and it lacked the requirements essential to such. In addition the older caravan cities of Damascus, Hama, and Homs, standing on the fringe of the desert, were already trading centres and were not prepared to tolerate a rival to their commercial importance. As a result some time was yet to pass before Tadmor-Palmyra could develop into a caravan city.

Fortresses for the protection of the Euphrates caravan route must have stood on the banks of that river from the earliest times, and Dura was probably one of these; for the name, common to several Assyrian fortress towns, is derived from the Assyrian word *dûru*, meaning a fort or burgh.

We know little of Tadmor-Palmyra in pre-Hellenistic times and nothing whatever of Dura. Our first reference to the latter dates back to the year 280 B.C., when a certain Nicanor, a general of Seleucus, Alexander's successor in Syria, founded a fort and a colony of Macedonian soldiers on the site and called it by the Macedonian name of Europos. If we consider the reason which prompted this act, it becomes obvious that Dura-Europos could not have stood alone on the banks of the Euphrates: she must have been one of a long chain of Macedonian fortress-colonies, created in order to protect both the Euphrates route and also the points at which the river could be most easily crossed. This route was an extremely important one for the Seleucids, masters as they were of Iran on the one side and of Asia Minor on the other, for it connected Seleucia, their Babylonian capital on the Tigris, with Antioch, their capital on the Orontes. Without this route intercourse between Greek Syria and Asia Minor—the centres of the Seleucid kingdom—and her rich Persian satrapies in the East would become impossible. Hence the Seleucids naturally endeavoured not only to render this road absolutely secure and free from nomad incursions, but also to Hellenize it and to stud it with Greek forts and colonies.

It is thus that Dura was founded, and it was for this reason that its founder populated it with soldiers, who were at the same time prosperous landowners. Documents tell us that the lands of Dura, partly planted with vines, were divided amongst these colonists, but so far excavations there have failed to reveal exactly where these lands and vineyards lay. The land referred to may perhaps have lain on the left bank of the Euphrates which is still irrigated and fertile to-day, or it may have been that on the right bank, the side on which Dura itself stands. To-day the land near the city of Dura is partly desert (the plateau behind the city walls), partly covered with wild tamarisk groves (the alluvial strip bordering the river). In all probability it was not so in ancient times. The existence outside the city walls of a special enclosure apparently for the cattle of the citizens and for the pack-animals of the caravans suggests that with more abundant rainfall the now desert plateau behind the town might have been in the past good seasonal pasture land. On the other hand, the bareness of the alluvial strip along the river might be accounted for primarily by the inertia of the inhabitants and the neglect of the irrigation-system which probably had a very early existence here. Some traces of canals still exist on some parts of the alluvial land near Dura both up and down the river and in fact large tracts of similar land up the river are still cultivated by the natives.

Whatever the reason for its creation, it can definitely be stated that Dura was no large commercial centre in its early days. At that time the main Euphrates caravan routes did not run as they do to-day by way of the Syrian desert to the towns standing on its edge and thence to Syria and Phoenicia; they followed a rather more northerly direction. One of them starting from Antioch passed through Apamea-Zeugma, where it crossed the Euphrates, then turned south-east on the left bank of the river and crossed it a second time at Nicephorium; the other ran through Aleppo, probably following much the same course as the road to-day, without crossing the Euphrates and joined the first road at Nicephorium. Both roads then followed the right bank of the Euphrates southward to Seleucia-on-Tigris. The many roads which connected Asia Minor and Mesopotamia reached Syria either at Antioch or at Edessa.

At this date no mention is made of Palmyra; all that is known is that the period was not one of great prosperity for Damascus, and the same is probably true of Hama and Homs. This fact is curious when we remember that the roads leading across the Syrian desert to the sea were shorter and therefore cheaper than those to the north, yet the reason why the Seleucids abandoned them is obvious. They led to

Phoenicia by way of Damascus, and at that time Phoenicia was in the hands of the Ptolemies, who also had control of Damascus. The Ptolemies were the chief rivals and enemies of the Seleucids and it is therefore not surprising that we hear nothing of Palmyra at this date and that Dura, which is geographically so closely connected to Palmyra, was no more than a fort and an agricultural colony, passed by caravans which made only the shortest halts within the city walls.

This was the situation in the third and at the beginning of the second centuries B.C., when the Seleucids were strong and whilst they continued to control Mesopotamia and Iran. The capture from the Ptolemies of Phoenicia and Palestine by Antiochus III must have brought about certain changes, and it is possible that trade via the Syrian desert was then resumed, thus bringing to Damascus a new period of prosperity. But we know little of all this, and we can presume that in general the situation remained unchanged.

More important events were brought about by the changing situation in the East, in Mesopotamia, and Iran; namely, the resurrection of Iran and the formation and rapid development of the Parthian monarchy. Here again our knowledge is incomplete and one-sided, for all our information is derived first from Greek and later from Roman (that is to say from hostile) sources. The Greeks and the Romans regarded the Parthians as barbarians, lightly veneered with Hellenic culture. The Parthians from their point of view tell us nothing of themselves. Their coins merely provide us with a chronology; few of their inscriptions have survived and

Parthian historical traditions were only on one occasion made use of by a classical writer, Pompeius Trogus, who refers to them in connexion with the aims and personality of Mithridates the Great. Archaeology likewise has so far failed to throw much light on the Parthians, in spite of the many ruins of their palaces and forts which still exist. All these ruins, with the one exception of Hatra, lie on the sites of older cities; and excavators, in their attempts to penetrate to the earlier levels as quickly as possible, have tended to regard the Parthian remains only as tiresome obstacles to be dealt with as summarily as possible.

Of late, however, more interest has come to be taken in the Parthians and their successors, the Sasanians, as a result of which attention is being given to the Parthian levels and archaeological information is increasing in proportion. Thus we find Andrae working at Ashur, carefully excavating and planning a fortified Parthian palace. The same scholar has made and published a scientific study of Hatra, that curious city of the Mesopotamian desert not far from the middle Tigris, which used to be the capital of a strong Arabian kingdom, vassal of the Parthian kings. An expedition of the University of Michigan is digging in the ruins of Seleucia and carefully recording its finds of the Parthian period. In the Iranian lands occasional discoveries by Sir Aurel Stein, Sarre, and Herzfeld are throwing from time to time some dim light on the Parthian period of Iran. But this is only a beginning, and Parthia is still an enigma.

Facts must nevertheless be taken into account, for it is impossible to eliminate Parthia from the history of the ancient world. A reading of Hellenic and Roman historians, more especially of Tacitus and Cassius Dio, provides one with the same picture of a Parthia weak and worn by internal strife, populated by barbarians, enemies of Hellenic culture, and ruled by uncivilized kings, who are cruel, weak, and cowardly.

And yet, already in the third century B.C., we find that Parthia was able to unite a section of Iran and partially to reconstruct the Persian empire, whose traditions stimulated her and acted as her guiding star. We find that none of the able kings, descendants of Seleucus, ever succeeded in breaking Parthia or in regaining possession of Iran. Instead, Parthia steadily expanded; a part of India became Parthian; all Iranian lands inclined towards her; she stretched her arm steadily westwards, and in the second half of the second century B.C. all Mesopotamia was in her possession. One may argue that the Seleucids were weak and otherwise occupied; but even so one must remember that the Romans led by Pompey, Crassus, or Anthony were never able to conquer Parthia, in spite of the great prowess of these generals. And it seems likely that even Caesar's legions would not have conquered, or at least not have retained, Parthia, since all those who preceded and came after him were singularily unsuccessful. Only one explanation of the fact is possible: to offer such a resistance Parthia must have been a strong and cultured power, with a firm though flexible structure, of which we know only very little and with a peculiar creative civilization of her own of which we do not even know the outlines. Hence a thorough and systematic study of the few ruins which can give us a picture of Parthia is of outstanding importance; and Dura and Palmyra, of which we shall have more to say below, are to be numbered among these ruins.

Attention has already been drawn to the fact that at the end of the third century and the beginning of the second, Parthia was expanding ever farther westward. After the fierce attempts to frustrate this western expansion made by Antiochus III and Antiochus IV—the two greatest Seleucids—the one by means of a campaign against Parthia, the other by means of a more thorough Hellenization of the more important Euphrates towns, we find that Mesopotamia was falling to the Parthians piece by piece. By about 140–130 B.C. lower Mesopotamia was already Parthian, and Parthia remained in its possession for many centuries to come.

Sometime during the late second or early first century B.C. Dura became part of the Parthian kingdom and the seat of a strong Parthian garrison. One wonders whether the city simultaneously became a centre of caravan trade, and whether Palmyra's development as a caravan city dates from the same time—a possibility which seems all the more likely when one considers the disorders and disturbances which broke out on the Upper Euphrates at this period.

Let me remind the reader of some facts. It was at this date that Osrhoene became an independent state with Edessa as its capital, to be ruled over by a native dynasty whose kings all bore Arabic names, the most popular being that of Abgar. Edessa was later to become famous in the history of Christianity. Commagene, the neighbour of Osrhoene, followed the same example, becoming an independent state with a semi-Iranian culture and a semi-Iranian ruling family. The sanctuary of Nimrud-dagh with its sculptures and inscriptions gives us a good idea of the character and history of this petty semi-Hellenistic kingdom. Not very much later the age-old city of Emesa (the modern Homs) became an independent kingdom with an Ituraean dynasty of kings, most of whom bore the name of Sampsigeramos. Likewise we hear that Chalcis 'under the Lebanon' was 'founded' at about the same time by an Arab called Monikos. It is probable that to this Arabian kingdom belonged the city of Heliopolis (modern Baalbek), later a rich and flourishing Roman colony. The ruins of its beautiful temples built in Roman times and dedicated to the north Syrian gods, Atargatis and Hadad, who were equally worshipped at Edessa, still stand in their proud glory and attract hundreds of tourists. A little later at the time of Pompey, Chalcis became one of the capitals of the short-lived Ituraean kingdom founded by a Greek—Ptolemy, son of Mennaeus.

A number of minor Arab principalities were well-nigh as effective as these greater states, not only in size and population but also in their role of bandits and robbers. In addition, at some time during the first century B.C., the Nabataean caravan kingdom extended its rule over Damascus. It was probably as a result of this that Palmyra came to be connected with the main caravan routes of the Nabataeans. These events must have rendered it more profitable for the late Seleucids and the Parthians to communicate by way of the desert, through Dura and Palmyra.

In spite of this, the later years of the second century and the early ones of the first were not a prosperous period for Dura and Palmyra. The trend of events was still uncertain, and wars with Syria were almost

Palmyra and Dura

continuous; Parthia was feverishly intent on conquering Syria, and Hellenism was presenting a stubborn resistance to her onslaughts. Such conditions did not tend to establish the prosperity of the Euphrates caravan route and, as we have already shown, its temporary decline led to the rise of Petra. Hellenism could certainly not have withstood the Iranian attacks had not Rome, the heir of Seleucid tradition and the mighty upholder of Hellenic culture in Syria, come to her aid. Rome's first step was to destroy the Black Sea kingdom of Mithridates and then to put a stop to Iranian expansion in Asia Minor.

In annexing Syria it was Pompey's aim to erect a dam against the wave of Iran which was attempting to swamp that country. Long and fierce wars resulted, with which we all connect the names of Crassus and Carrhae and of Anthony, who both failed in their attempts to conquer Parthia. It is in Anthony's time (41 B.C.) that we first hear of Palmyra, which had already become a sufficiently wealthy centre of caravan trade to excite the general's desire, but not so well established that its inhabitants could not collect their possessions and fly in search of safety towards the Euphrates, possibly to Dura. This development of Palmyra is not contradicted by what I have just said, for even anarchy cannot kill caravan trade, and the safest route in this disordered region for the few caravans which still travelled from Parthia to Syria was that leading across the desert by way of Palmyra. It was this route that the caravans followed and the city continued to develop, but much change was still essential before it could become really prosperous. In any case, as recent discoveries have shown, Palmyra was able to lay the foundations of her great temple as early as 32 B.C.

The defeat and subsequent death of Crassus, and Anthony's lack of success, clearly proved to those who would admit it that nothing was to be accomplished by force in the Euphrates region, and the Romans came to realize that the conquest of Parthia was too expensive and complicated an undertaking for even the empire to contemplate. Yet the Parthians had to recognize that Rome would never cede Syria to them. Neither state, in fact, could hope to gain permanent control over the whole of Syria and Mesopotamia, and both acknowledged the need for peace on the Euphrates, where there were centred commercial interests of vital importance to both. It therefore became essential to compromise and to reach some sort of understanding, a fact which Augustus realized clearly enough. Hence his diplomats were able to accomplish what the republic's generals had failed to do. They encouraged the resumption of caravan trade across the Euphrates, and they reverted to the centuries-old intercourse which had always subsisted between Syria and Iran. An issue of coins by Augustus, in honour of a return by the Parthians of the standards and prisoners captured from Crassus, is an important feature of this policy, for in reality it celebrates the temporary introduction of the Pax Romana on the Euphrates and with it the renewal of the Euphrates caravan trade.

It is possible that at some future date documents will be found in the ruins of Palmyra equal in importance to the wills of Ptolemy VII (Euergetes II), of which the text was recently found at Cyrene, and of Attalus III of Pergamum, which we know from an inscription of Pergamum, all of which attest the triumphs of Roman diplomacy. I mean by this, documents which established Palmyra as a neutral between the two rival empires and laid the foundations of her brilliant development as caravan city. It is hardly probable that such documents would take the form of a definite treaty between Parthia and Rome. One would rather expect to see on the one hand letters from Augustus to his Syrian legate and on the other from the Parthian king to his Mesopotamian satrap, and these might state the terms of some understanding between Rome and Palmyra and between Parthia and Palmyra. Whatever the form of such a correspondence, its effect can hardly be doubted, since it must have enabled Palmyra to become a neutral, semi-independent town, wherein the goods of those two officially hostile powers, Parthia and Rome, might be exchanged. For trade to have flourished as it did, both the powers must have definitely guaranteed Palmyra her liberty and safety, and it seems probable that they both undertook to safeguard her boundaries, and to protect the city, agreeing at the same time to recognize the form of government which they had themselves set up in Palmyra.

It was this understanding which led to the amazingly rapid development of Palmyra into one of the wealthiest, most luxurious, and most elegant towns in Syria. One would almost imagine that she had sprung from the desert sands at the wave of a magic wand, so rapidly was the old and apparently small and unpretentious temple of the village of Tadmor transformed. Already at the time of Augustus and Tiberius it was one of the most important sanctuaries of Syria, which could vie in magnificence with any of the then existing temple groups in that province.

The caravan road which traversed Tadmor became in Palmyra one of the grandest avenues to be found in any town in Roman Syria. Hundreds of columns lined it, tetrapylons subdivided it, avenues intersected it, and balconies opened out upon it. Land lying close to the springs at which the caravans halted was wrested from the desert, built over with fine houses, and transformed into the busy centre round which the commercial and the political life of the town was developed. At the same time the first monuments of the dead began to appear, the oldest tomb inscription in Palmyra dating from the year 9 B.C. It was then that the merchants of Palmyra, having used up all the scanty sulphur springs of the neighbourhood, brought to the rapidly growing town all the water which lay below ground in the desert for an area of many miles around.

What became of Dura at this time? We know that until the Romans captured the city in A.D. 164, Dura had remained a Parthian fort, occupied by a strong garrison and ruled by a Parthian governor-general who controlled the life of the city. Consequently, in spite of the fact that her population had been Macedonian and continued to speak Greek, it nevertheless became more and more Iranian—as Iranian, in fact, as was the population of Panticapeum (Kertch) in southern Russia at this time. Simultaneously the inhabitants of Dura also became Semiticized, for the majority of its women folk were of Semitic origin. Yet the culture of the city remained Greek, with a slight Iranian admixture, and not Graeco-Semitic.

The period of Parthian rule was that of Dura's

greatest prosperity. I have already said that originally Dura was probably little more than a Seleucid, and later a Parthian, frontier fort, a fact which must account for her military features, her great walls, and her citadel. With Palmyra's foundation Dura grew from a mere fort into the point of departure of the main caravan route from the Euphrates to Palmyra. A glance at the map will show that Dura is the nearest crossing-place of the Euphrates and if, in addition to this, it was also, as we have every reason to suppose, the most northerly fort on the Euphrates owned by Parthia, it was naturally by way of Dura that the Parthians dispatched the majority of the caravans from Palmyra destined for Mesopotamia and Iran, and there that they received those returning to Palmyra. The garrison of Dura was responsible for the safety of the roads leading to the west, south, and east across the Euphrates, and this fact alone was sufficient to lead the caravan merchants to pass through Dura and even to halt there for a longer or shorter period of time.

As a result of this Dura's wealth increased. Her Macedonian landowners developed into Levantine merchants, furnished the caravans with wine, oil, bread, vegetables, beasts of burden, and all other necessities, and levied in return various taxes from all caravans which stopped at, or made use of, Dura. These taxes were distinct from the main customs-dues which were probably levied by the Parthians. A study of the ruins shows that in the first century A.D. Dura must have been a large and rich town. All her best and richest religious buildings date from this time.

Thus the two temples of Artemis Nanaia and of Atargatis and Hadad with the accompanying 'theatres' and with their wealth of sculptures and paintings; the great temple dedicated to the Palmyrene divine triad in the north-western corner of the fortifications, with its wonderful frescoes, painted at the expense of wealthy citizens; the corresponding temple in the southern corner of the fortifications with a chapel dedicated to the warlike Sun-god Aphlad of the neighbouring village of Anath (the modern Anah) on the Euphrates; and finally the recently discovered temple of a local Atargatis, the Artemis Azzanathkona, again with a fine 'theatre'; all these received the shape they now bear in the last years of the first century B.C. and in the early years of the first century A.D.

It is a well-known fact that the wise policy of peace and quiet in the Near East which was adopted by Augustus and his successors underwent a change early in the second century A.D. We cannot here speak of Trajan, yet it is important to lay stress on the fact that it was he who consciously reversed Augustus' policy of compromise and acquiescence in the East and turned from diplomacy to strategy and to wars of conquest in place of negotiation and treaties. In this Trajan followed in the steps of Caesar and of Anthony for, like them, he was probably convinced of the possibility of a conquest of Parthia so that the entire civilized world could again become a single kingdom as it had been under Alexander the Great. Only the outlines of Trajan's Parthian campaign are vaguely known to us, but it is a fact that he was able temporarily to wrest Mesopotamia from Parthia and to transform her into a Roman province.

We know also that, on their southward march down the Tigris and the Euphrates, the two armies of Trajan found little Parthian resistance. While one army was descending the Euphrates both on foot and in ships built higher up on the river, it certainly occupied Dura-Europos, for one of its legions erected a triumphal arch on the caravan road near Dura. The ruins of this arch, previously regarded as a monumental tomb, were excavated and studied by the Yale expedition. The fragments of a short Latin inscription tell us that this arch was built in honour of Trajan. Nothing can express more clearly than this the military importance of Dura.

Trajan's conquests could scarcely have pleased the people of Palmyra and Dura. A permanent occupation of Mesopotamia by Rome portended no good to Palmyra, since her office of middleman between Parthia and Rome would soon be at an end, and therewith her period of wealth and independence. She was faced with the prospect of becoming no more than a Roman provincial town, impoverished perhaps by a hopeless struggle with the older caravan cities of the region. It was thus that Trajan's policy, although it left Petra almost unaffected, threatened to deal a veritable death-blow to Palmyra.

But Mesopotamia did not long remain a Roman province, since continual risings broke out both there and in the empire which prevented Trajan from carrying out a real conquest of Parthia. Soon after the first set-back in his Parthian campaign the emperor died, and his successor Hadrian reverted to Augustus' policy in the Near East. As a result, first Mesopotamia and then Dura were restored to Parthia and Palmyra's anxiety was set at rest. Hadrian was in this way Palmyra's new founder; and the citizens, quick to appreciate his act, came to call themselves with just reason 'Hadrian's Palmyrenes'. We do not exactly know what was Hadrian's policy towards them, but we do know that in his day the city was no ordinary provincial Roman town, but retained a large amount of autonomy. This is proved by a fact recorded in the Palmyrene tariff, namely, that the customs-dues were neither determined nor collected by a Roman procurator, but by the council of the city itself, which may possibly have been directed by a Roman advisory board. Whether such a board existed or not, the impression remains that notwithstanding the liberal treatment of Hadrian, Palmyra came into closer contact with the West. She became more Greek than she had been before, her constitution was strongly Hellenized, and for the first time in her history many of her citizens came to adopt Roman citizenship and to add to their Semitic names Roman family-names (like Ulpius, Aelius, &c.). It was perhaps under Hadrian's rule, or a little later, under Marcus Aurelius, that Palmyra was first occupied by a Roman garrison, a fact which is proved by some inscriptions (as yet unpublished) found on the site of the largest Palmyrene temple. These inscriptions help to explain certain similar texts which were discovered in the city many years ago.

Palmyra enjoyed a period of considerable prosperity during the reigns of Hadrian and of his immediate successors, until the outbreak of the civil wars of the third century A.D. Most of the more important buildings in the city were erected at this time, and the larger number of the tomb-towers were raised during the second century A.D., although many of the more important of these are a little earlier in date. Most of the large columns which line the impressive avenues were set up at this period, and it was probably also then that Palmyra's territories became really extensive. It was from these territories that she was able to provide the Roman army with divisions of its best cavalry of mounted archers, divisions which we afterwards find scattered all over the Roman empire. Even more significant is the great development of Palmyrene trade at this time; her merchants were no longer content to serve simply as middlemen between Parthia and the commercial towns of Syria. For they now sent caravan upon caravan to all the more important trading cities of Parthia, and had agents or, to be more precise, trading colonies, in Babylon, in Vologesia, in Spasinu Charax. In the west the Palmyrenes now went beyond Damascus and the Phoenician towns, establishing their commercial agencies far beyond the limits of the east. We hear of them on the banks of the Danube, in distant Dacia, in Gaul, and in Spain, as well as in Egypt and in Rome. There, in the world's capital, they had their own temples, dedicated to their own deities, and adorned with altars and statues.

It is this development of the trade of Palmyra, these far-reaching commercial connexions, and the concentration of large financial interests in the city, that explain what may at first glance seem strange, namely, her close intercourse with Petra. For not only did some of the caravans of Parthia, *en route* for Petra and Egypt, pass through Palmyra (instead of crossing the desert from south Mesopotamia straight to Bosra), but also the caravans of Petra, carrying south Arabian goods destined for the Phoenician ports, made their regular route via Palmyra instead of via Damascus; which proves that Palmyra was not only a caravan city but also an important centre of caravan banking and finance.

The spasmodic efforts of Hadrian's successors to revert to Trajan's policy and to take advantage of the difficulties with which the Parthian kingdom was beset were but incidents in the later history of Palmyra. The Parthian kingdom was now on the eve of its decline, its power was soon to pass into the hands of another dynasty, the Sasanian, and its mantle was to fall to another Iranian tribe, the Persian. The first Roman campaign against Parthia since Trajan's death was directed by Lucius Verus, brother of Marcus Aurelius, and owed its complete success to the ability of Avidius Cassius, who at a later date was an unsuccessful claimant of the throne of the empire. The war led to the subjection of northern Mesopotamia, and with northern Mesopotamia Dura also fell. In A.D. 165 this outpost ceased to be a Parthian fort and was occupied by a strong Roman garrison.

This change in nationality did not really affect Dura, for she still remained a caravan city. But it is probable that from this date frequent wars on the Euphrates drew a considerable number of caravans towards other routes, for instance, from the Parthian caravan cities straight through the desert and not up the Euphrates to Palmyra.

From the time of Septimius Severus a policy of conquest on the Euphrates becomes traditional. Severus, himself half a Semite, was the founder of a Semitic dynasty. In the politics of his successors Caracalla, Heliogabalus, and Alexander Severus a number of able women played leading parts. Foremost among these were Julia Domna, the wife of Severus, and her followers Julia Maesa, Julia Mammaea, and Julia Soaemisas, all of them Hellenized Semites, who had been educated in Seleucid traditions. They dreamt of a Roman empire with an eastern capital, to be a revival of the Greek empire of Alexander the Great. Their aim became the conquest of Parthia, but although Parthia was in her death-throes, neither Severus nor his dynasty could finally conquer her. Affairs had reached just as much of a deadlock as they had under Marcus Aurelius, Rome retaining only northern Mesopotamia. In spite of every possible effort the Severi were unable to add southern Mesopotamia to their list of conquests, and after the death of Septimius Severus his policy met with a series of disasters. His heir, Caracalla, was killed by his own soldiers during a campaign against the Parthians, and Alexander Severus scarcely escaped with his life from the hands of Ardashir, the first Sasanian king.

In Palmyra the period of Severan rule was one of great change and innovation. This half-Semitic dynasty appears to have liked and trusted the Palmyrenes, for several of them were admitted at this time into the ranks of the Roman aristocracy and an even greater number—almost all the aristocracy of Palmyra in fact —acquired Roman citizenship. The name of Septimius and that of his son Caracalla-Aurelius became component parts of the names borne by Palmyrene Roman citizens. To these two names was often added that of Julius, the name of Septimius' wife and Caracalla's mother. Palmyra, together with Dura and other Syrian towns, was granted the title of a Roman colony, but this did not reduce her to the level of a provincial town and she retained throughout a good deal of her freedom and autonomy.

Notwithstanding their Roman names the citizens of Palmyra remained unchanged. They still retained their peculiar form of government of which I shall speak in greater detail below, and it seems that the only change which the policy of Septimius Severus brought about was to draw them nearer to Rome and to bring them into closer contact with the ruling dynasty.

We see the same phenomenon appearing in military life. In early imperial times we know little of the military organization of Palmyra. It is, however, very improbable that in the first century A.D. she was occupied by a Roman garrison. Such a garrison does not appear before the time of Trajan; and even at that time Palmyra certainly had her own police force inside the city, which provided for the safety of her caravans and for the upkeep of her caravanserais (catalymata) and of the wells (hydreumata) on the caravan roads radiating from her territory.

We know nothing of this police force, but we may suggest that the normal safety of the caravans was entrusted to their leaders, the synodiarchs, prominent and rich citizens of Palmyra. Each one of them certainly had at his disposal an armed force probably consisting of archers mounted on camels and horses. The patrons of the synodiarchs, and of the military escorts of the caravans, were the two gods Arsu and Azizu, of whom I will say more later. Unfortunately we do not know whether the caravan escorts were parts of a Palmyrene corps of militia, recruited or hired or both by the city of Palmyra, or mercenaries hired

Palmyra and Dura

for each occasion by the leader and the members of a caravan.

A permanent force was required for the safety of roads, wells, and caravan stations. Everybody knows what a well means to the life both of caravans and of the Bedouins of the desert. It is certain that the Nabataeans had organized such a protection on the caravan roads which depended on them, and that when these roads were taken over by the Romans from the Nabataeans the Roman caravan roads were guarded by a set of fortified camps of larger or smaller size. There is, therefore, no doubt that there was the same protection for the Palmyrene caravan roads, and it is more than likely that within the Palmyrene territory the roads were guarded by a Palmyrene militia, whose chief commander was the highest magistrate of Palmyra—the strategus.

In war-time—and since the times of Trajan wars had become very common in eastern Syria and Mesopotamia—when the safety of both the city and of the caravan roads was affected by the unruly attitude of the nomads of the desert, the city, with the consent or on the initiative of the Roman government, would appoint a special magistrate, a kind of commander-in-chief of the armed forces of Palmyra, and would let him act as a military dictator. We know, from some recently discovered inscriptions, one such chief-magistrate in the reign of Antoninus Pius and two for the period of Septimius Severus—one in charge of the city (in A.D. 198) for maintaining 'peace', another in the next year acting as strategus against the nomads.

It is curious to find that under Caracalla or Alexander Severus a twentieth Palmyrene cohort was stationed at Dura. From this Cumont has concluded that Palmyra was at this time allowed by the Roman government to have a special regular army of her own of about twenty cohorts, that is to say of at least ten thousand men, Palmyrene soldiers led by Roman officers. But the theory that Palmyra possessed an independent army, however attractive it may be, is not convincing. It seems more likely that, after the time of Septimius Severus or Caracalla, Palmyra, which received from one of these emperors the title and the rights of a Roman colony, no longer provided the Roman army with irregular cavalry divisions (*numeri*), as she had formerly done, but that she furnished mixed regiments or cohorts as other sections of the Roman empire did. It was one of these cohorts that the Romans sent to Dura to serve as her garrison or as a part of her garrison.

In this period of ever-renewed wars Dura constantly gained importance as a Roman military centre, losing at the same time her importance as a caravan city. Recent discoveries have shown that Dura, which had received a strong garrison immediately after her conquest (in A.D. 165), became an important rallying point for Roman armies on expeditions against the Parthian empire. For she was, without doubt, the strongest fortress on the southern frontier of Roman Mesopotamia, and lay on the ordinary route of Roman armies down the Euphrates towards Ctesiphon, the Parthian (later the Persian) capital of lower Mesopotamia; it was the same route which had been followed by Trajan. This military importance of Dura accounts for the fact that part of the city was transformed, in the time of Septimius Severus and Caracalla, into a regular Roman military camp with a fine 'praetorium' as its centre, with a 'champ-de-Mars' for training the troops, with baths and temples. We shall know more of the role played by Dura in the military expeditions of Septimius Severus, Caracalla, Macrinus, Alexander Severus, Gordian III, Philip the Arab, and Valerian, when the excavation of this camp is completed and all the inscriptions, parchments, and papyri found in its ruins have been published and illustrated.

Palmyra's autonomous organization and her independent militia force account for the role which she played in the second part of the third century A.D. Here I will not go into the history of this troubled period in the life of the Roman empire, for the anarchy, the frequent wars, the rapid succession of emperors are familiar to everybody. In the East this unrest threatened Rome with the loss not only of Mesopotamia but of Syria also. The new Sasanian power in Persia was stronger and more vital than the Parthian monarchy of the Arsacids, and attacks on the Roman empire became increasingly frequent and energetic, at the very time when the structure of the state was being undermined at home by bloody civil wars. The emperors after Alexander Severus were so engrossed in their gallant effort to put a stop to this disintegration that they were obliged to ignore the way in which the autonomous city-state of Palmyra was gaining in power. They disregarded not only the development of Palmyra's army but also the way in which one of her leading families—the Julii Aurelii Septimii (whose members frequently bore the names of Hairan, Odenath, and Vaballath)—was gradually growing into the ruling family and becoming a dynasty of petty princes. Such a course of development was not unusual in Syria.

Great excitement reigned in Dura when the sweeping Persian invasions led by Ardashir, the first king of Sasanian Persia, and his successor Shapur began. In a private house in the centre of the city, of which more will be said in the last chapter of this book, among the business documents written by its owner on the walls of his office, we read a hastily scratched text which says: 'in the year 560 [A.D. 238] the Persians descended upon us'. This was the terrible and famous invasion of the Roman empire by Ardashir. Feverish activity reigned at this time at Dura. Never before had she been faced with capture by such enemies. Her role had been to serve as the starting-point for expeditions of an aggressive character. This is the reason why the old fortifications of Dura, inherited from the Parthians and shattered by the earthquake of A.D. 160, though kept in order and repaired to a certain extent, were never rebuilt or modernized. Even the buildings of the city which leaned with their backs on the city wall were not disturbed. The Persian danger aroused the Roman garrison of Dura from its apathy. Great efforts were spent by them in rebuilding the fortifications as quickly and as efficiently as possible. It would take too much space to describe the work done by the Romans in the decade from 238 to 250. Suffice to say that the most important part of it consisted of doubling the defences on the desert side by a thick mud-brick wall in order to make it safe from the siege machines of the Persians. In vain!

A little more than half-way through the third century another great Persian attack, led by King Shapur,

Palmyra and Dura

took place. Shapur seized all Syria and advanced as far as Antioch. During this invasion Dura was taken and for a while occupied by the Persians. Among thousands of coins found in the ruins of Dura none are later than A.D. 256. Valerian organized a campaign to save the Near East and when this ended disastrously with his capture in 260 at Edessa, Odenath, the uncrowned king of Palmyra, began, as an ally of the Roman empire, a war against the Persians and other enemies of Gallienus, the successor of Valerian; a war which lasted for eight years and was crowned with success upon success. It was, then, in no way surprising that such victories should have tempted Odenath to look upon himself as the successor of the Arsacids. So he adopted first the fitting title of King of Kings, and then another which is interpreted in several ways, either as 'Restitutor totius Orientis' (a purely honorific title borne before him by the Roman emperors only), or 'Corrector totius Orientis', which might represent an office we do not know. It appears later in documents of the time of Vaballath; to Odenath it is given by the same Vaballath in a posthumous inscription.

Odenath, King of Kings of the Iranian type, and the recognized *alter ego*, if not possible rival, of the Roman Emperor in the Orient, spent most of his rule outside Palmyra fighting the Persians. At Palmyra he was represented during his absence (from A.D. 262 to 268) by a member of the Palmyrene aristocracy—a half-Iranian, half-Roman gentleman—Julius Aurelius Septimius Vorodes. The title which this man bore at Palmyra is highly interesting. He was *procurator* (governor) and *iuridicus* (judge) according to the

Roman terminology, and *argapetes* (military governor) according to the Iranian. Nowhere is such stress laid on the two-sided character of Palmyra, on the double face which she always showed—Iranian on one side, Roman on the other—as in the above-mentioned titles of Odenath himself and of his representative at Palmyra.

I will say no more of the dark years which mark the close of Palmyrene prosperity, of the rule of Vaballath, Odenath's son, of the regency of his mother Bat Zadbai, more famous under her name of Zenobia, or of the breach with the Roman empire. How Vaballath created an empire of his own, comprising Syria, Egypt, and Asia Minor, and how Zenobia achieved world-wide renown are events with which the historian is familiar. It was caravan trade which had first been responsible for the development of Palmyra; it was the same trade that created a caravan state and a caravan empress; and it was not by a freak of chance that Egypt became a part of this trade-complex, since Egypt had already been in the sphere of the commercial influence of Palmyra for some considerable time.

Zenobia's caravan kingdom was but short-lived. We know how the Roman empire recovered, how unity was restored, and how Aurelian succeeded in capturing and destroying Palmyra and in forcing Zenobia, the caravan queen, to figure in his triumph.

The fortunes of Dura in the period of the short splendour of Palmyra are dark. We do not know how long the Persians were in possession of the city which they thoroughly pillaged and partly destroyed. Nor do we know whether Odenath during his victorious campaign down the Euphrates occupied the city and restored some of her monuments. The temple of the Palmyrene gods, and some monuments of the main gate, were certainly restored after the time of Alexander Severus, but the exact date of these restorations is unknown. On the other hand, no coins (except two of Shapur), and no inscription dated later than A.D. 256, have been discovered at Dura. This restoration and reoccupation evidently did not last very long. After the victory of Aurelian over Zenobia and the suppression by the same emperor of the subsequent revolt of Palmyra, Dura was never again occupied by Roman soldiers. She remained a no-man's land between the Roman and the Persian empires and became a piece of desert. When Julian passed by Dura, on his abortive campaign against Persia in the vain hope of reviving Roman rule on the Euphrates, Dura was already a ruin, and the desert had begun to encroach on the once prosperous settlement. Palmyra was to survive Dura for some considerable time, though after a slow decay she too gradually crumbled, and when the caravan trade again revived in Arab hands she was left to one side. To the varying fortunes of this trade she had owed, first her splendour, and then her ruin.

V

THE RUINS OF PALMYRA

THE ruins of Palmyra and Petra are undoubtedly among the most romantic relics of the ancient world; nowhere are there ruins which can compare with them; there is an exotic savour about them which we find nowhere else. Those wonderful tomb-façades which stand out against a background of coloured rocks in the fantastic Petraean valleys cannot fail to stamp their memory for ever on the mind of every visitor who sees them, and Palmyra evokes sensations no less vivid and no less romantic. I had read many descriptions of this city before my first visit and had looked upon them as purple patches of romantic writings. Yet I must admit that I felt the spell of that same romantic enchantment which all previous travellers have experienced when, after a long day's journey across the desert, the outlines of her tomb-tower-mausoleums first became visible against the horizon, then slowly detached themselves from the smoke-like film of wind-blown sand, until at last the columns and arches stood clear-cut before me against the grey-gold background of the desert. This was all the more remarkable since travellers can now reach Palmyra in a swift Ford or Chevrolet and put up at a comfortable hotel, whereas, twenty years ago, the journey was made on camel-back and in the company of an armed guide, for the sheikhs of Palmyra have always been noted for cruelty and rapacity.

These most romantic remains of antiquity were first seriously 'discovered' during the most romantic period

1. The ruins of Palmyra drawn by the architect Cornelius Loos in 1711

2. General view of Palmyra. In the foreground is the modern cemetery; behind it the colonnaded street; and in the background the hills surrounding the city, and on the top of one of them the Turkish Citadel

XVI. PALMYRA

1. Tower tombs outside the city; behind on the top of a hill the Turkish Citadel

2. One of the Temple tombs

XVII. PALMYRA

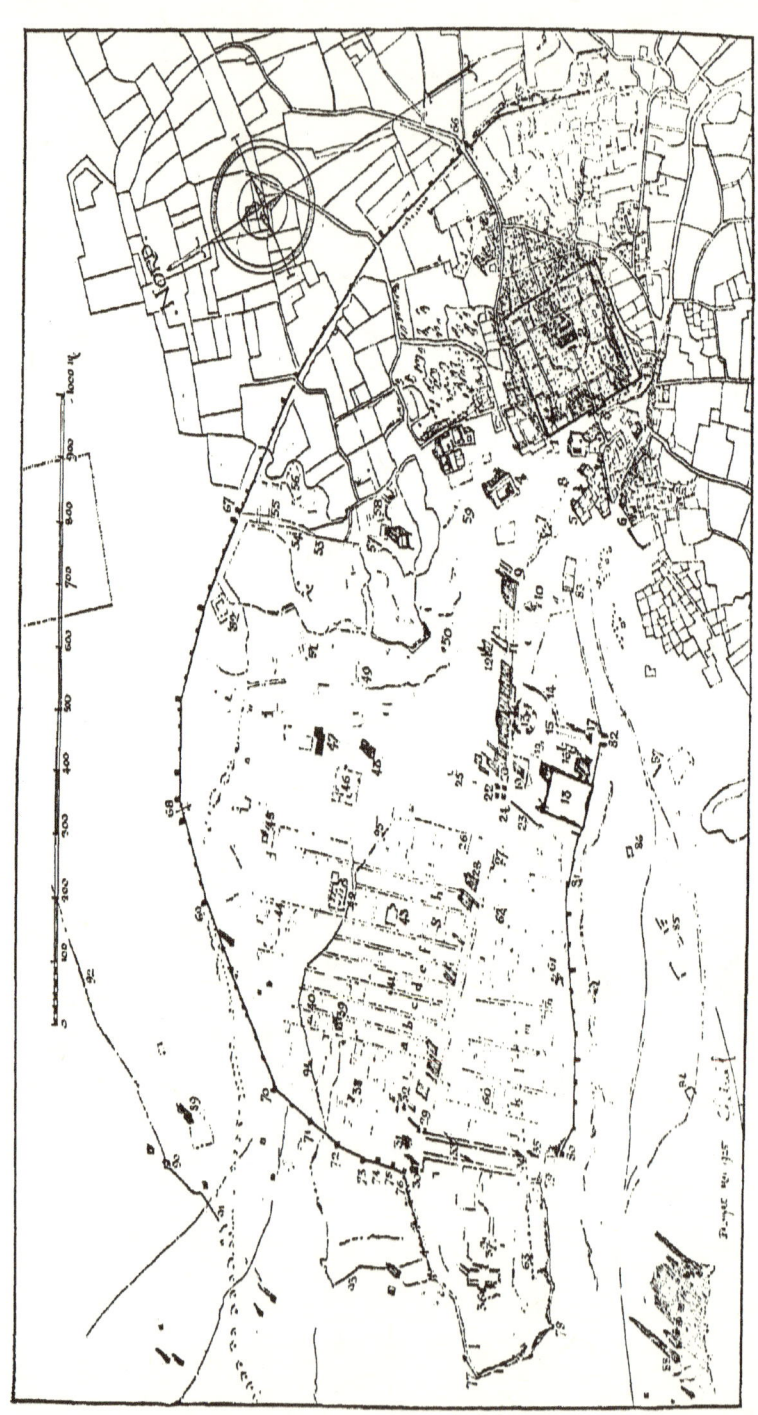

PLAN OF PALMYRA
1–3. Main gate. 9. Triumphal arch on main street. 13. Theatre. 18. Caravanserai.
From *Syria*, 1926, pl. xii, by permission of *P. Geuthner*.

of European history, the eighteenth century; classicism was then still powerful, but the romantic reaction against it was just setting in. Palmyra, as a matter of fact, had already been visited by English merchants from Aleppo in 1678 and again, and with greater success, in 1691. As early as 1695-7 William Halifax, who was a member of the second expedition, published drawings and a diary of his journey in *The Philosophical Transactions*, and in 1693 Hofsted, another member of the same expedition, made a detailed oil-painting of the city, which now hangs in the hall of Amsterdam University. These pioneer works only attracted the attention of specialists and archaeologists. The next visitor to Palmyra was a certain Cornelius Loos, attached to the staff of Charles XII of Sweden during his Poltava campaign, and later the architect of the Stralsund government offices. When his king was imprisoned by the Turks at Bender, Loos, who was with him, beguiled the king's time by designing new uniforms for his troops. Then, in March 1710, Charles sent him to Syria, Palestine, and Egypt to draw pictures of ancient monuments, and on his travels Loos saw Palmyra and stayed there for some time, making drawings of her more important ruins. In 1711 he handed in his sketches and a report to the king, but a part of them was lost in the battles between Turks and Swedes which were fought at Bender. The remainder were preserved and are now in the Library of Upsala University, though unfortunately neither the drawings nor the report have ever been adequately published. I know of them through the kindness of Professor Anderson of Lund, who printed some of them in a newspaper article (XVI. 1).

Palmyra was first really introduced to the modern world in 1753 by the English artist Wood. Little is known either of his work or of his life, excepting that he visited the city in 1751 in company with the wealthy traveller Dawkins and that his description met with an enormous success throughout the civilized world. It was in fact due to this book that the French friends of Catherine the Great of Russia christened her capital 'the northern Palmyra', presumably comparing her thereby to Zenobia, in much the same way as they had formerly compared her to (the no less romantic though far less probable) Semiramis. Although this was no flattering comparison either for Catherine or for the Russians, the name of Northern Palmyra stuck to St. Petersburg. Wood's book has remained a classic to this day. Since then no one has written any 'general work' on the subject although her antiquities, her statues and busts, and the remains of her stone prosopography are to be found in all museums.

To the Russian traveller, Prince Abamelek Lazareff, the author of an interesting volume on Palmyra, we owe the longest known text, the Palmyrene tariff, written in the Palmyrene dialect of the Aramaean tongue. The Prince was personally responsible for its publication with the aid of the late V. V. Latysheff, the Marquis de Vogüé, and Professor H. Dessau. The stone itself on which this tariff is inscribed was, by the efforts of the former Russian Archaeological Institute at Constantinople, moved to the Hermitage Museum a short time before the War. No less important was the expedition led by the late Th. I. Uspensky, a member of the Russian Academy, and by B. V. Farmakovsky, which made all the arrangements for transporting the tariff to St. Petersburg. This expedition was also the first to copy and to publish the frescoes which were discovered by chance at about that time in the painted tomb which the Palmyrene guides of to-day point out to tourists as the tomb of Zenobia. In reality it was, as shown by its inscriptions, one of the many tombs carved in the rock by some private citizen. He and his descendants, besides burying members of their own family in it, carried out a profitable business by selling portions of it to strangers. In the realm of scholarship the recent expedition undertaken by the two famous Dominicans of Jerusalem, Pères Jaussen and Savignac, is the only one that can compare in importance with this Russian expedition.

Quite recently the unchecked robbery of the ruins of Palmyra, carried out by tourists and merchants alike, has come to an end, and now the era of archaeological expeditions and explorations, aiming at a more or less thorough record of the antiquities existing above ground, is equally reaching a close. Thanks to the French Academy of Inscriptions, to the Syrian government, and to the administrators of the French Syrian mandate, the hour has at last struck for subterranean excavations to be made and, more important still, for the thorough protection and restoration of the ruins. This has happened only just in time, for since the introduction of motor-cars the despoiling of Palmyra had made giant strides. In a few decades scarcely a column or an arch would have been left standing on the site; they would have fallen, as have hundreds of those which Loos and Wood saw still standing in their places, laid low as much by the hand of time as by any other agency.

It is not the aim of this short chapter to give a detailed description of the ruins, for such a description would necessitate months and months of careful work on the original site, and of excavation beneath the more important buildings or groups of buildings. Yet a few words must be said about the remains in general.

However slight may be our topographical knowledge of the town, the main outlines stand out clearly—more clearly in fact on the sand-covered skeleton than they would in an entirely excavated site, where details tend to obscure features of major importance. The large and magnificent 'city of the dead' rises in front of the 'city of the living', which it almost rivals in brilliance. For the traveller of to-day first catches sight of this necropolis consisting of stone tower-mausoleums, elegant in proportion yet severe in outline (XVII. 1). The ancient traveller, on the other hand, saw as he approached something more than these tomb-towers: he was confronted by the porticoed façade of the tomb-temples richly painted within and decorated with a series of sculptures and reliefs (XVII. 2). He also viewed still more modest constructions above the ground—plain mounds, below which lay rich underground halls carved in the rock, their walls adorned with paintings, their niches occupied by sarcophagi. The tombs are precious documents for the historian, partly on account of their peculiar architecture which is in no way Greek, hardly even Semitic, in style, and partly because of their admirably preserved interior decoration, executed in painting or in sculpture and representing stylized yet realistic portraits of scenes of religious import. Their main value, however, lies in the fact that their positions indicate the lines of approach to the city—the caravan roads—whilst the portraits and numerous inscriptions give us much historical information regarding the wealthiest members of the Palmyrene merchant aristocracy. It is distressing to think how easy it would have been to compile a complete historical prosopography of Palmyra, had not the majority of these tombs been despoiled by Arabs and Europeans alike, had not the busts and inscriptions they contained been scattered among hundreds of public and private collections both in Europe and in America, without any exact description of their place of origin.

Behind the city of the dead rises that of the living (XVI. 2). We do not know for how long this city remained an open one, unprotected by walls or, in other words, how long its temple alone was fortified. Only a thorough examination of the walls can give us the answer to this question, and no one has yet attempted this task. All that we do know is that the surviving walls are of late date, and belong partly to the time of Zenobia, partly to an even later period.

As at Petra and at Jerash, so again here the walls fail to determine the main outline of the city, for caravan trade was responsible for its contour. Palmyra is the most typical caravan city of antiquity; far more so than Petra, where the roads and buildings are slightly obscured by the town's peculiar topography. At Jerash the early period in the life of the city is still a problem, and we are therefore still uncertain how much influence it exercised on the building of the later caravan city. In Palmyra, on the other hand, the outlines of the caravan city stand out quite unmistakably.

All the caravan roads leading westwards converge in the town into a single street, the main caravan artery, to be espied by the traveller in the distance as he descends from the desert hills bordering the city on this side. It is this road which is responsible for the fame of Palmyra in modern times, and its imposing grace, its column-lined avenue, and the arches marking the points of departure of its cross-roads well deserve their fame. Equally interesting and majestic are the tetrapylons and the pedestals fastened to the columns upon which stood the statues of the men responsible for their erection along the main street. The pride which the Palmyrenes took in this colonnaded avenue proves in fact that it was not only a main street, but that it was also a main artery, a very spine, without which the city could not live (XVIII. 1).

The colonnaded avenue was bordered on each side by at least three hundred and seventy-five columns, and of these some hundred and fifty still remain *in situ*. It runs almost directly from east to west, though at one point there is a sharp and sudden bend, at the same time concealed and marked by a fine threefold arch— a veritable marvel of 'illusionary' architecture. The reason for this change of direction is clear: architecturally it would have been simple enough for the road to run straight across the city into the desert, but in actual fact its course was determined by the 'haram' or main temple. It is clear enough that where the mighty columns of its peribolos rise a temple must have stood from time immemorial, and when the caravan city first came into being there could, of course, be no question of moving such a temple, the site of which had been preordained by religion and not chosen on account of the lie of the land or because of the direction which caravans were to follow. The caravan road conse-

The Ruins of Palmyra

quently obeyed the dictates of the deity. The main street probably assumed an especially impressive character between the arch and the temple and it may even have become a kind of sacred dromos, like those which led to Babylonian and to Egyptian temples. As yet, however, it is only the chance discovery in this part of the street of a fine exedra (semicircular seat) which in any way supports this theory.

Only two years have elapsed since this main temple of Palmyra was freed from the hundreds of poor Arab huts built over and around it. The work was due to the efforts of the controlling archaeological body of Syria and mainly to its director, H. Seyrig. As a result of it, the outline of the temple now stands out clearly. I will not describe the building in detail, for it is both the right and the duty of those who excavated it to do so; a few words only will suffice for my purpose.

Many inscriptions found in the temple tell us that the great 'haram' of Palmyra was built in approximately the same form as it stands now, in the last years of the first century B.C. and the early first century A.D., and that it was dedicated to the great Babylonian god Bel. The cella retained its original shape to the end of its existence, while the court was rebuilt, on a larger and more ambitious scale, probably in the second century A.D. There is no doubt, however, that a court and a peribolos existed when the cella was first built. The plan of the temple as built at the time of Augustus is surprising in its originality, its strangeness and asymmetric conception. The oblong, rather narrow cella, divided into three unequal parts, is surrounded by a Corinthian colonnade which once had gilt bronze capitals. The capitals have disappeared and the portico of the cella now stands denuded of them. The main entrance into the cella opens in one of its long fronts; not, however, at the centre of that front but on one side. A superbly massive portal badly attached to the cella, with pediment-sculptures which remind us of the famous frescoes of Dura, forms the frame of the entrance-door. A colonnaded court probably surrounded the cella. The now existing peribolos, with its fine columns and monumental entrance, is in all probability an extension of the earlier colonnaded court (XIX).

At the very first sight it is apparent that the temple, as built in the early first century A.D., is not a Greek building. I feel certain that the shape of the cella was dictated by the fact that it replaced, probably on a larger scale, an earlier cella of the same orientation and the same plan, a cella of a Sumero-Babylonian temple which previously existed on the spot. This cella was moved by Greek architects from the narrowness and darkness of the courtyard of the Babylonian temple into the brilliant sunlight of the Greek temple-architecture, and was surrounded, to its great surprise, by Greek columns. Instead of the usual Babylonian court, with an altar in the centre and two-storied rooms around three of its sides, a colonnaded portico surrounded the isolated cella. The whole became a strange mixture of Babylonian and Greek elements. This explanation would account for the curious plan of the temple, and for the lack of architectural harmony between the cella and its encircling colonnades.

The temple and the caravan road, religion and lucre: such are a caravan city's main interests, and in these early Palmyrene days religion probably assumed the

1. Part of the colonnaded street

2. General view of the interior of the caravanserai

XVIII. PALMYRA

1. Front view of the Temple of Bel

2. Side view of the Temple of Bel

XIX. PALMYRA

role of an active protector, for the temple must originally have served at the same time as a fort, in which the population could seek shelter from the incursions of the nomad Bedouin, doubtless of frequent occurrence.

A third and no less important feature at Palmyra, just as at Petra and at Jerash, was the caravanserai, the open place where the caravans halted and the men settled their business and performed their ablutions before entering the temple. We know where the caravanserai at Palmyra was situated since its position is indicated by the most monumental tetrapylon in the main street. The area between this and the ravine has never been properly excavated, although the large buildings which surround it are peculiar. Their plan indeed is so confused as they stand to-day that excavations should be undertaken there as soon as possible. One building especially deserves to be studied, for its mighty walls surround a rectangle containing interesting interior porticoes and a fine and monumental entrance. In my opinion this building is a typical caravanserai of a typical caravan city, a fact which is indicated not only by the general plan, but also because numerous inscriptions have been found there, some of which sing the praise of worthy caravan leaders and lay stress on their able, disinterested, and devoted service to the merchants and the city (XVIII. 2).

There are other buildings of interest in the city's main square and one of them, recently excavated, is especially so. It is a theatre-like construction standing near the tetrapylon, and though M. Gabriel, who excavated it, is convinced that it is a regular Greek theatre, I am not of the same opinion. There are indeed similar theatre-like structures in several Syrian towns, but Syrian theatres in general have not the same character as Greek. To find regular Greek theatres in Jerash and Amman seems natural enough, for these towns were inhabited by Greeks. But in Palmyra, with her curious constitution, her tribes and tribal organization, and her all-pervading religious enthusiasm, a theatre in which the tragedies of Euripides and the comedies of Menander would be played seems to be even less suitable than one destined for the sort of drama which was improvised at the court of the Parthian king. We may remember how Vorodes the conqueror of Crassus allowed the head of the Roman general to be used as a butt in a performance of the Bacchae of Euripides. At Palmyra the real purpose of the theatre-like building in the main square was probably quite different, even if Greek plays were occasionally performed there. It was rather the centre of political and religious life, where the 'fathers' of the town foregathered. Here the oldest tribal sheikhs, most of them rich merchants and some synodiarchs—faithful caravan leaders—must have come together; here the common members of the tribes must have assembled to vote the honours due to tried and trusted caravaners, and here also the citizens must have met to witness religious ceremonies, dances, hymns, or sacrificial offerings. It was chiefly for purposes of this nature that auditoriums were erected in the non-Greek regions of Syria.

Such then was the main artery, the very centre of Palmyrene life. On either side of this the city spread out in a multitude of transversal roads, some of which were bordered by columns and led to temples, markets, and public buildings. At a later date, in Christian times, churches also appeared. Ruins of one of them may still be seen. One of the most important temples in this part of the town still survives in almost perfect condition, elegant despite its massive build and its rich decoration. It was dedicated to the mighty Baal Samin and recent discoveries have shown that it was but a part of a great group of buildings dedicated to the same deity. Sculptured fragments and inscriptions found by chance tell us of the existence of other temples consecrated to other gods. It is, for instance, certain that somewhere there stood a rich temple in the name of the twin Anatolian and Syrian deities, Hadad and Atargatis. We also know almost exactly the site of the temple of the Syro-Babylonian Ishtar-Astarte, whilst inscriptions and reliefs testify to the existence of others dedicated to the caravan gods Arsu and Azizu. It remains for future explorers to reveal more of these sacred edifices.

The houses of the gods were rich, but the public buildings, the tombs, and the private houses belonging to the wealthy citizens were quite as magnificent. Two of the latter have been recently excavated and were found to be even finer and more elaborately ornamented than those belonging to the rich merchants of Delos. The splendid colonnades of their central courtyards are those of palaces rather than of houses; even more palatial are the rooms opening on to the courtyards which are worthy of any Italian palazzo. Except for those which belong to the streets or to the temples, or those erected in honour of city notables, most of the columns which are to be seen either *in situ* or fallen come from the peristyles or colonnaded atria of private houses. Time alone will show whether the more modest houses of the middle-class inhabitants, the shops and houses of Pompeian type, or the districts inhabited by craftsmen and workers, stood side by side with these palaces or whether they were situated in other quarters of the town. But, however this may be, it is characteristic of Palmyra that the first houses to be discovered belonged to members of an aristocracy which was responsible for the architectural outlines of the city, for its wealth and beauty, for its peculiar social and economic organization.

In speaking of these houses I have used the words peristyle and atrium, thus inviting a question which I cannot undertake to answer, namely whether these colonnaded Palmyrene courtyards are of Greek origin. In the most distant past the column was known to Mesopotamian builders, and the colonnaded courtyard was familiar in Babylonia. Alongside with the Babylonian courtyards we also find similar constructions in the Hittite 'hilani', the Persian 'apadana', and the Parthian palaces, so that it may well be asked where the Palmyrene house originated. Until more Parthian palaces have been studied, and more Palmyrene houses excavated, it will be wise to refrain from laying stress on any one of these possibilities.

We ask ourselves what sort of life the Palmyrenes lived in this fairy-tale city created by caravans and intended for caravan trade. Though we have a slightly better idea of it than we have of the life of Petra or Jerash, our knowledge is still very limited. Hundreds of Palmyrene inscriptions are interesting and informative; thousands of statues, busts, or bas-reliefs and numerous painted portraits or wall-paintings bring us into contact with the external aspect of the inhabitants: much is also to be learnt from such unimpressive relics as tesserae of clay bearing figures and inscriptions, which once served as entrance tickets to banquets, or religious or private receptions organized in connexion with the cult of the gods and the dead. But unfortunately neither the inscriptions, the sculptures, the paintings, the tesserae, nor the domestic utensils, have as yet been collected, nor has any full description of them been published.

Yet we do possess sufficient material to enable us to draw a rough sketch of the life of Palmyra. The first thing that comes to notice is the mixed racial character of the inhabitants. Semites, no doubt, were in a majority, and most of the inscriptions are in their language, an Aramaean dialect written in an alphabet peculiar to Palmyra. But there are also numerous Greek and Palmyrene bilingual inscriptions and some others in Greek alone or in Latin. The same is true of the names, for here again the Semitic predominate, though alongside them occur a certain number of Greek, Latin, or Iranian origin. Greek residents seem to have been few, for most of the Greek names are borne by emancipated slaves. Occasionally, but rarely, members of Semitic families took Greek names. It is obvious that the Palmyrenes disliked their hereditary Greek enemies, and tried to debar them from settling in the city; and the Romans do not seem to have insisted that a policy of 'open doors' should be adopted. The Palmyrenes appear to have enjoyed complete freedom in this respect. Apart from the freedmen, Greek and Roman names were borne by civil and military agents of the Roman government and by the soldiers of the Roman army, though there were but few of these in Palmyra. There were also Iranians, classed as members of the ruling Palmyrene aristocracy, and, in opposition to the Greeks, not regarded as foreigners.

A careful analysis of the Semitic names would probably show that not all were of one stock. It seems, nevertheless, improbable that all the ruling families were descended from the original inhabitants of the oasis, the Aramaeans or Chananaeans, whoever they may have been. I feel certain that at the dawn of her greatness, trade connexions and funds came to Palmyra from without, from Babylonia, from Damascus, from Safaitic Arabia, and from Petra, perhaps also from Palestine (after the destruction of Jerusalem?). This is indeed clearly proved by the number of religious cults of foreign origin which existed in the city. It may have been this which was implied when, in the year A.D. 85, two notables of Palmyra, Lisams and Zebida, sons of Maliku, son of Ildîbêl, son of Nesa, of the clan of Migdath, erected a dedication to the Arab Šamš 'the god of their forefathers'.

The social structure was very peculiar, for although clan-division is usual amongst Semites, we find here, among dozens of clans, four only which tower above the others. One wonders if the members of these clans alone possessed exclusive political rights and if they alone provided the counsellors, magistrates, and caravan leaders. Whether this was so or not, we often find these four clans working hand in hand, and Palmyrene notables considered it a great privilege to be honoured by them. Unfortunately the life of these various clans and their interrelationship is little known to us. The powerful clans were naturally not always at peace with one another, for in Palmyra, just as in Syria and Mesopotamia to-day, long and hereditary feuds were usual among Arabs. Interesting light is thrown on these ancient quarrels by an inscription of very early date, of the year A.D. 21. It was carved under a statute of Hašaš, at the expense and by order of two clans, those of the Bene Komara and the Bene Mattabol. Both of them are names which figure frequently in Palmyrene history and there is no doubt that they were the two most powerful and influential bodies in the city. The text of the inscription reads as follows.. 'Since he, Hašaš, has come to their head [that of the two clans] and arranged peace between them, he now attends to their close co-operation in all things great and small.' It is characteristic that in the abridged Greek version of this text the two clans are referred to as 'the people of the Palmyrenes'.

The priests who attended upon the gods worshipped at Palmyra formed a strong and powerful group, a varied and complicated hierarchy, which has never yet been the subject of a careful study. Some of them officiated in temples; others were associated with interesting religious bodies grouped round the temples or possibly round the tribal sanctuaries. Numerous busts have been found representing the male members of prominent and renowned Palmyrene families, clothed in priest's attire. On their heads are poised tiaras of the typical (cylindrical) shape, adorned with the crowns and busts of the gods whom they served. In my opinion this proves that the priesthood here was not always hereditary as it was in the Egyptian, Babylonian, Semitic, and even in the Iranian world, but rather a purely honorary name and office, as in Greece and Rome.

We also find along with an occasional (possibly Iranian) priestly title, that of 'symposiarch' or chairman of religious banquets. He is accompanied by a large staff of followers or assistants. Much wine was consumed during these feasts by gods and mortals alike, and in an important inscription a priest-symposiarch boasts that old (probably local, not imported) wine was served at one of these repasts. This proves that in antiquity Palmyra possessed a flourishing agriculture. Beside wine, barley, vegetables, dates, and, as we learn from the tesserae and from the tariff of Palmyra, olive oil, were native products. Undoubtedly those who participated in these holy feasts received a clay 'jeton' like so many of those found in the ruins, which seem to give us such a clear picture of the city's social and religious life. Many of them bear inscriptions which refer to the priests, of Bel or of some other god. Sacred feasts were held not only in honour of the gods. It was the belief of the Palmyrenes, possibly one borrowed from the Greeks, that the dead became members of the divine family, heroes or semi-gods. In accordance with this belief the dead were represented as sanctified heroes stretched on rich couches and wearing fine garments. In their honour funeral banquets were served in which they were supposed to take part. Some of these clay tokens were certainly tickets distributed to those who attended those post-mortal banquets—surviving members of the family of the deceased, members of his clan, or of the religious association (*thiasos*) to which he belonged.

One wonders whence this idea of holy banquets

1 and 2. The great triad, Bel, Yarhibol, Aglibol
3. Arsu, the caravan god

XX. THE GODS OF PALMYRA
(for description see p. 150)

1. Atargatis

2. Atargatis and Hadad

3. Allat the warrior-goddess

4. Tyche of Palmyra

5. Tyche of Palmyra or Bel

XXI. THE GODS OF PALMYRA
(for description see p. 151)

came to Palmyra. The question is difficult and complicated. I cannot discuss it here. I may, however, point out that in Parthian Mesopotamia both deities and sanctified dead were represented lying on couches; this may be due to Greek influence on the religious ideas of the population of Mesopotamia.

The structure of the great family of Palmyra's gods and goddesses is just as complicated as that of its population and priests. Bel was supreme in the main temple. To him and to Baal Samin (both of them gods of the upper world and both of them termed in Greek 'Zeus'), were added the gods of the Sun and the Moon called Yarhibol and Aglibol (xx). As a triad, Bel, Yarhibol, and Aglibol were probably worshipped in the great temple. Sometimes a fourth, or even a fifth, member was added to the triad. We find such groups of three or four often depicted in Palmyrene reliefs and tesserae. It is probable that, of the three or four gods of the triad, two were not Babylonians but the local gods, Yarhibol and Aglibol. The great Baal Samin became in the Roman period a rival of Bel, being called, or rather described in hundreds of dedications, as 'the blest in eternity, the good, and the merciful', and we may suppose that he was a Syrian addition to the Palmyrene pantheon. A curious figure is Malakbel, the 'messenger of Bel', the acolyte and minor *alter ego* of Bel, no doubt a Babylonian like Bel himself.

In the same way as Bel, Shamash and Ishtar were also of Babylonian origin, but the latter soon merged into the Phoenician Astarte. The semi-Elamite Nanaia too, who was also worshipped at Dura and of whose cult we shall say more later, and Nergal, the god of the underworld, likewise came from Babylonia. Yet Babylonia was not the only country whose gods were represented at Palmyra. From north Syria, and ultimately probably from Asia Minor, came the mighty couple Hadad and Atargatis (XXI), while Eshmun was derived from Phoenicia in addition to Astarte. He was depicted as Asclepius on Greek tesserae. A fair number of gods came from Arabia: these were Šamš (in Arabia the Sun-god was feminine but in Palmyra she became identified with the Babylonian Shamash) and Allat (the Arab Athena) (XXI. 3) and that interesting god Chaî al Qaum, a kind and benevolent deity and an abstainer from wine-drinking. He is probably the rival of another Arab deity, Dushara or Dusares, the Arabian Dionysus. Arsu and Azizu each had a temple in Palmyra, and were very important deities. On tesserae, coins, and reliefs, Arsu is depicted as a young soldier riding a camel, or else is shown standing by the side of a camel which he leads. Sometimes even he is actually depicted as a camel, the beast which is his holy emblem. Azizu, who is young and handsome, is represented on horseback. While Arsu is certainly of Arab origin, for his cult was practised at Petra, and the Safaitic Arabs worshipped him under the name of Roudha or Radhou (originally a female deity), Azizu is possibly not an Arab, for he was worshipped at Edessa where the god Monimos was his equivalent. Both are acolytes of the Sun; one, the Morning Star, precedes the Sun in religious processions, the other, the Evening Star, follows behind. Azizu is probably one of those numerous mounted deities who were worshipped by the Syrians and whose cult was carried far beyond the confines of that land by Syrian soldiers and merchants. Even in

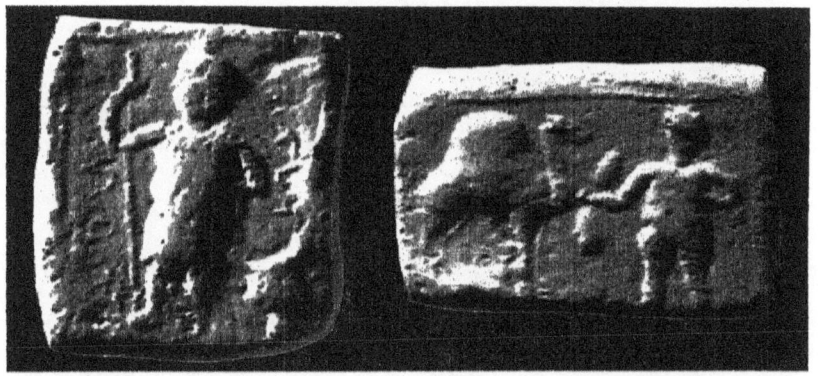

1. Arsu and Azizu. 2 and 3. Arsu

XXII. THE GODS OF PALMYRA

distant Dacia we find a number of dedications in which he is addressed as 'Deus bonus, puer phosphorus Apollo Pythius' (xx. 3 and xxii).

In Palmyra, Arsu and Azizu, the Arab and the Syrian, were originally what they remained, the gods and patrons of caravaners, their mighty protectors, their strong defenders, the holy synodiarchs. On tesserae they sometimes appear with Shamash the Sun-god or Yarhibol-Malakbel. With all these gods was associated the Moon-god—Aglibol. To these kind and merciful deities, the guiding lights of night and day, all those who spent long nights and days in the desert offered their fervent prayers. We have already met these guiding stars of caravans for, side by side with Petra's Fortuna (Tyche), they gaze down on us in the form of the Greek Dioscuri from the façade of the wonderful El-Khasne at Petra. These were the first deities to be greeted by the caravans entering the Petraean valley, and it was to them that travellers fervently commended themselves in the thousands of inscriptions cut upon rocks and on the walls of temples and gates which the caravans passed during their long journeys.

It is surprising not to find, in the long list of names of foreign gods and goddesses of Palmyra quoted above, any name of an Iranian deity. There are, naturally, no really Greek and Roman gods at Palmyra either, but at least the Greek and Roman Pantheon was represented here by some Greek names given in Greek inscriptions to Oriental gods, and by Hellenized figures of the same gods in statues and bas-reliefs. No similar Iranian religious influence can be traced at Palmyra. The only divinity of the Palmyrene Pantheon who may claim Iranian origin is a god with the name Satrapes, known to us by a bas-relief and a tessera. On this last he appears in the company of Arsu and Azizu. Yet we know that he came to Palmyra not from Iranian lands but from Phoenicia and Asia Minor, where he was worshipped long before Palmyra was founded, i.e. at the time when both Phoenicia and Asia Minor were satrapies of the first Persian empire.[1]

I regard this absence of Iranian elements in the Palmyrene religion as based on a fallacy. I cannot enter here into details. Suffice to say that the Babylonian gods who came to Palmyra reached her at a time when Babylon was a Parthian city and Babylonia was looking towards one of the Parthian capitals—Ctesiphon. In Babylonia the Parthians took over the Babylonian gods and created a kind of syncretistic religion which well reflected the composite character of the Parthian empire in general. This religious syncretism I regard as one of the leading features of Parthian religious development. I may quote a parallel phenomenon in the Kushan kingdom of northern India, where purely Iranian, pre-Zoroastrian gods appear on the coins under the forms, and with the attributes, of Greek gods. Somewhat similar was the evolution of religion in Mesopotamia. The Parthians themselves were in all probability Zoroastrians, although the Parthian kings regarded it as imperative to give official recognition to the gods of the constituent parts of their multinational empire. Thus it was that Bel, the great lord of Babylonia, whose cult was widely spread all over Mesopotamia and Syria, became one

---

[1] The name of Ormuzd which appears in a recently discovered tomb of Palmyra is almost certainly the name of a man, not that of a god.

of the gods of the Parthian empire. Nothing now prevented a good Zoroastrian from paying his reverence to Bel, from coming occasionally to his temple, and from addressing prayers to him as if he were another Ahuramazda. In view of this fact the Babylonian clergy had to make some concessions to the ritual habits of the Parthians, i.e. to Iranize somewhat the cult of their own master and lord, the merciful Bel.

As a god of the Parthian empire Bel came to Palmyra in his somewhat Iranized aspect, and with various Iranian elements in his cult. Some facts support my hypothesis as stated above. In one inscription of Palmyra there is a list of the priesthoods of Bel. One of the names of these priesthoods finds no explanation in the light of Semitic languages and seems to be of Iranian origin. Moreover, the most important gods of the Palmyrene Pantheon, especially the warrior-gods Bel, Yarhibol, and Aglibol, as represented in sculpture and painting, sometimes appear in Parthian dress and wearing Parthian arms and weapons. The same is true of Arsu and Azizu.

I have already said something of Palmyra's political constitution, our knowledge of which is still deplorably slight. Its origins are hidden in obscurity, and though the terms used in the time after Hadrian are Greek, it does not mean that it was at all essentially Greek. A strategus probably represented the republic and commanded the militia. Two archons acted as representatives of the civil government. Immediately under them was a treasurer and an overseer of the markets and caravanserais, and then came the officials who levied the dues and taxes. The powerful senate had a special president. The tax-contractors were likewise important, as we learn from the Palmyrene tariff, a document which consists of a carefully edited, corrected, and enlarged edition of the tax and especially customs laws, formulated in A.D. 137 by the senate, under the presidency of a proedzos, and in the presence of a secretary and archontes.

It is a pity that we know so little of the relations between the magistrates and the senate or of the age-old organization of the powerful clans in which the population was divided and which had their own corporate and religious life. Still more deplorable is it that we know so little of the relations between the city of Palmyra, her magistrates and senate, and the central government of Rome. Who, beside the commander of the garrison, represented Rome? What income was derived by Rome and in what way? Why is it that so few Roman emperors and governors of Syria were honoured by statues and other monuments in the city of Palmyra, while such honours are so prominent in much smaller and poorer cities of Syria? Time will probably bring to light some written monuments which will explain these riddles.

Both the standard of life of Palmyra and the trend of politics were obviously set by the merchants who financed the caravans. They had established offices in the East and West, they owned ships both in Parthian and in Roman ports, and they lent and borrowed money for commercial enterprises. A series of inscriptions in honour of presidents of Palmyrene 'fondouqs' in foreign countries, of synodiarchs—caravan leaders—and of archemporoi—presidents of commercial companies—make us familiar with them and their activities. It is a curious fact that though Palmyra's representatives were scattered all over the world, and Palmyrene caravans travelled in all directions, the above-mentioned inscriptions speak exclusively of 'fondouq'-presidents who resided at, and of caravans which travelled to and from, Babylon, Vologesia, Forath, Spasinu Charax, and other minor centres of the Parthian empire, all of them cities lying at the mouths, or not far from the mouths, of the Tigris and the Euphrates. No mention is found of 'fondouqs' or commercial agencies at Damascus, Emesa, or Hamath, or in any other city of the Roman empire, or of caravans travelling northward or westward. This seems to imply that Palmyra derived her main income from her commercial connexions with Parthia. On the other hand, it means that these commercial relations with Parthia, the caravan journeys to and from Parthia, were a risky enterprise and full of dangers, while the relations with the Roman empire were safe enough not to be worthy of mention in inscriptions which praised outstanding services of prominent citizens.

Most important is the information which the aforesaid inscriptions yield as regards the 'fondouqs', commercial settlements of the Palmyrenes in various cities of the Parthian empire. The 'fondouqs' appear as important centres of Palmyrene life, as almost independent political bodies inside the foreign cities, reminding us of similar European 'fondouqs' of the Middle Ages and the Renaissance in the Orient and of the European settlement at Shanghai in China of our own days, now so well known to all the readers of European newspapers. Palmyrene temples which towered above Palmyrene caravanserais, offices, and store-houses in these settlements are mentioned, for example, in some Palmyrene inscriptions in honour of the presidents of the settlements. One of these inscriptions seems to speak, strange to say, of the erection at Vologesia, by the president of the Vologesian 'fondouq', of a temple in honour of the Roman emperor Hadrian. A temple dedicated to the cult of a Roman emperor in the heart of the Parthian kingdom sounds almost nonsensical. And yet we must not forget that Hadrian must have been both very popular and very influential in Parthia. He had just restored, after the glorious expedition of Trajan, Mesopotamia to the Parthian king and revived the regular commercial relations between the two empires.

Another interesting feature revealed by one of the inscriptions of the 'fondouq' presidents is the fact that the Palmyrene settlements in Parthia drew a sharp line between the Palmyrene and the Greek merchants. The two groups appear in this inscription as two separate bodies. It seems that the Palmyrenes did not regard themselves as members of the Greek world, and were proud of being 'just Palmyrenes'.

The 'fondouq' presidents were important persons both in Palmyra and in Parthia. It is probable that they were endowed in their 'fondouqs' with an almost royal power, though the communities of the resident merchants were in possession of a certain amount of autonomy and self-government. They certainly regarded themselves as offsprings of the Palmyrene 'demos'.

In conclusion, in order to give an idea of the texts which illuminate the life of the Palmyrene 'fondouqs'

1. Young priest

2. Veiled woman

3. Schoolboy

XXIII. THE PEOPLE OF PALMYRA

(*for description see p.* 152)

The Ruins of Palmyra

and the personalities of the great merchants of Palmyra let me give some lines of one of these texts. The inscription which I am going to quote was recently found beside a filled-in well in the desert south of Palmyra by Father Poidebard during one of his geographical-archaeological air-expeditions. It is cut on a large column which probably once stood beside the water bearing the statue of Soados, a Palmyrene notable, and served as a guide to caravans travelling to or from Palmyra or moving from well to well.

I will translate several lines of it: 'The Senate and the people have honoured Soados, Boliades's son, the son of Soados, the son of Taimisamsos, the pious man who loves his native land, who on many and important occasions protected in a noble and generous way the interests of traders and caravans and of his co-citizens established at Vologesia, as testified in the letters of the god Hadrian and the divine emperor Antoninus, his son, and also in an edict and a letter of Publius Marcellus as well as in those of the governors of the province his successors. He was also honoured for all this both by means of decrees and statues by the Senate and by the people [of Palmyra], by the caravans and by individual citizens.' It is in memory of all these services that his country erected four statues to him in Palmyra, and the senate and the people three statues outside the town: one in Spasinu Charax, one in Vologesia, and one in the caravan station of Gennaes.

Another inscription gives a good idea of a synodiarch's duties. Near the caravanserai of Palmyra lies an enormous architrave with an inscription which was first copied by Professor Ingholt. It is a decree in honour of Ogelos, a distinguished Palmyrene, published by the four tribes of Palmyra in A.D. 199 to celebrate 'his courage and valour' and in honour of the activity displayed by him during several of his military campaigns against the nomads, as well as for assistance rendered to merchants and caravans throughout his (obviously numerous) synodiarchies.

Palmyrene culture is also quite peculiar. It presents a complicated picture difficult to define. A number of facts which throw some light on it are known to us, but the subject has never been adequately studied. If a section of the population consisted originally of nomad Bedouins they must have soon forgotten their Bedouin customs in the new town, where they came into contact with merchants and bankers who had migrated from the older commercial cities like Babylon, Damascus, Petra, or other towns of Syria and Babylonia to this young and prosperous centre of caravan trade. For years many Palmyrenes had lived in the cities of Parthia and quite a number of Parthians had probably migrated to Palmyra. Many Palmyrene citizens were no strangers to the West. As merchants and soldiers they resided for years at Alexandria and in other cities of Egypt, in Rome and Italy, and even in the western provinces of the Roman empire. From time to time one Palmyrene or another would become a member of the ruling aristocracy of the Roman empire. Some Roman emperors (e.g. Hadrian and Alexander Severus) accompanied by their armies, their officers, courtiers, and quite a number of Roman officials, had visited Palmyra at irregular intervals and had mixed with the Palmyrene aristocracy. And all this intercourse must certainly have affected the life of the town and have marked it with a distinctive stamp.

The Ruins of Palmyra

It is thus not surprising to find that the rich merchants of Palmyra, residing in their fine houses of Babylonian type, lived a peculiar life, unique in its complexity. All the members of the aristocracy naturally read and wrote in two languages, Aramaean and Greek. An attractive tomb statue, now in the collection of the Vicomtesse d'Andurain in Palmyra, represents a boy of a noble Palmyrene family holding in his hands a notebook composed of wooden tablets. On the open tablet of the book are written the last letters of the Greek alphabet (XXIII. 3).

If the intellectual life of the citizens savours of the Greek, their dress and furniture are neither Semitic nor Greek, but almost entirely Parthian in type. Look at the wide-patterned shalvari (anaksyrides—trousers) and embroidered robes worn by the men, at the beautiful rugs and carpets which cover their couches, note their embossed mitres, their drinking-cups and fibulae studded with precious stones, glance at the clothing of their wives and at the heavy jewellery covering them from head to foot—parallels to these features can only be found in Persia (XXIII. 1, 2).

More complicated still is the problem of Palmyrene art. The first impression is that it is entirely Greek, but I think that this first impression is incorrect. The sculpture of Palmyra represented by hundreds of statues, busts, and bas-reliefs, showing figures of gods and men and ritual scenes, presents in the treatment of the heads and bodies such softness and lack of vigour, such helplessness in modelling the limbs of a human body, such inclination towards the pictorial element and the minute rendering of details of dress and furniture (peculiarities which are entirely foreign to Greek sculpture and are typical of the Eastern plastic art in general), that we can hardly call this sculpture Greek or Graeco-Roman. If we look for affinities we shall see that the nearest parallels to Palmyrene sculptures will be found not so much in Babylonia, in Assyria, or in Persia, as in the north Semitic countries and in Anatolia, in the art which has been quite recently revealed by archaeological investigation of north Syria and Anatolia and which we call by the general name of Hittite. Such sites as Sendjirli, Carchemish, and Tell Halaf with their hundreds of statues and bas-reliefs show, in spite of the long stretch of time which separates them from the earlier Palmyrene sculptures, unmistakable affinities with Palmyrene plastic art. We may say, without being in great danger of misleading the reader, that the sculpture of Palmyra is the Hellenized offspring of Aramaean and Anatolian plastic art. The earlier stage in the development is represented by the famous late-Hellenistic sculptures of Nemrud-dagh in Commagene, where, as in Palmyra, the Syro-Anatolian Hellenized style is coupled with Iranian influence both in style and in the field of dress, arms, and weapons. This Graeco-Syrian style together with the Graeco-Babylonian which is represented by hundreds of alabaster and clay statuettes found in Babylonia constitute the two styles of sculpture which prevailed in the western part of the Parthian empire. The development in the eastern part which deeply influenced both the Indian and the Chinese art is different and does not concern us here. It is, however, not impossible that the two Mesopotamian schools of sculpture of the Hellenistic and Roman times had a certain influence on the development of

The Ruins of Palmyra 149

the so-called Gandhara art in India, and, vice versa, that late Iranian art influenced both Mesopotamia and Syria.

Not less conspicuous than sculpture was painting. While sculptural monuments survive in hundreds, those of painting are rare at Palmyra. The paintings which certainly existed in the private houses and in temples have all perished. Yet important finds at Dura show that they existed in large quantities, and that the houses and temples of Palmyra were as gay in their coloured dress as are the houses and temples of Dura. What remained of painting at Palmyra is found in the graves, especially in those subterranean funeral chambers cut in the rock which are typical in some parts of the 'city of the dead' at Palmyra. Like the sculptures, the wall-paintings of these chambers show portraits of the deceased who were buried in these chambers, both full figures and medallions supported by winged Victories, some mythological scenes, and some ornamental patterns. Here again we are first struck by the Greek character of the pictures, and it requires some closer study to discern elements which are not Greek. Since, however, Dura is much richer in paintings than Palmyra and Durene painting is to a certain extent very similar to that of Palmyra, I reserve the discussion of painting both at Dura and at Palmyra for the next chapter.

To sum up. The external aspect of Palmyrene culture strikes the eye with its complexity and peculiarity. It is an odd mixture of various elements: Iranian dress, arms, weapons, and furniture with a profusion of ornaments in gold and silver, of embroidered stuffs, of rich rugs and carpets; Babylonian, strongly Hellenized, temples and smaller houses; Syro-Anatolian Hellenized sculpture: and probably Graeco-Iranian painting—these are some of the most conspicuous constituent elements of this mixture. It is evident therefore that we shall never be able to understand Palmyra so long as we know the Western constituent elements only. Greek is but a thin veneer: what underlies this veneer comes from the various parts of the Eastern world—from Iran, Babylonia, Anatolia, and the north Syrian lands.

DESCRIPTION OF PLATES XX–XXIII
XX. THE GODS OF PALMYRA

1. The great triad of Palmyra—Bel, Yarhibol, Aglibol. Clay tessera of Palmyra showing on the obverse side the bust of Bel, crowned by a Victory standing on a globe; to the left the god Mars moving towards the bust. Beneath, impressions of two seals (female head looking to the left; figure of the god Mercury). On the reverse side to the left, figure of Yarhibol in military costume, wearing a radiate crown, and leaning on a spear or sceptre; to the right the figure of Aglibol with the crescent behind his shoulders, in the same dress and attitude. Right and left inscriptions giving the names of the two gods.

2. The great triad of Palmyra. Clay tessera of Palmyra showing the same three gods full face, standing in their temple. On the reverse side is shown the figure of a man (a priest?) reclining on a couch. To the left a large wine crater, to the right the moon and a star. Above, impression of a seal giving a portrait of a clean-shaven man turned to the right. Beneath, an inscription giving the name of the man (priest of Bel who issued the tessera): Malikho son of Wahballâth.

3. Arsu the caravan god. Tessera of Palmyra. On the obverse side bust of a youthful god; to the left a crescent (?); beneath, a bull running to the right. Beneath, the Venus star. On the reverse an armed god shown full face. To the left an inscription giving the name of the god Arsu.

XXI. THE GODS OF PALMYRA

1. Atargatis. Lump of clay from Palmyra showing the figure of the great goddess Atargatis, seated on a throne between two lions. She is leaning on a sceptre and holds in her left hand some flowers (?). To the right front, view of radiate bust (sun-god) and beneath bust of the Venus star and crescent. To the left veiled female (?) bust.

2. Atargatis and Hadad. Clay tessera of Palmyra. On the obverse Atargatis as above, on the reverse her divine husband Hadad, in Parthian military dress leaning on a sceptre or a spear. The inscription gives a personal name.

3. Allat the warrior-goddess. Clay tessera of Palmyra. On the obverse, front view of the goddess as Athena between two high vessels from which plants (reeds) are protruding. On the reverse buffalo reclining to the left; above him the crescent, to the right a cypress tree, beneath two altars.

4. Tyche of Palmyra. Clay tessera of Palmyra. On the obverse, bust of a goddess holding in her right hand a globe and in her left a palm branch, in a little shrine. On the reverse a priest seated in a chair getting wine out of a large crater.

5. Tyche of Palmyra or Bel. Bronze tessera of Palmyra. Bust of a youthful god or goddess, full face, holding an olive branch and wearing a calathos. On either side a star. The inscription says 'Fortune [who protects] the olive trees'. On the reverse, the sign of Bel (three Palmyrene letters) and a whetstone between two sacrificial knives.

XXII. THE GODS OF PALMYRA

1. Arsu and Azizu. Bas-relief showing a man sacrificing to two gods, one on camel-back wearing military dress and holding a spear in his right hand, the other on horseback in civil dress, holding in his right hand a spear. The inscription gives the names of the gods, Arsu and Azizu, and the name of the priest of Arsu who dedicated the bas-relief.

2. Arsu. Clay tessera of Palmyra. On the obverse front view of the god wearing military dress and leaning on a spear. Beneath to the right, a bull's head. To the right and left inscriptions giving proper names. On the reverse a laden camel, standing turned to the right, with his driver who holds a bag and a branch.

3. Arsu. On the obverse a laden camel standing to the right. Between his legs and above him two stars. Facing him a priest performing a sacrifice (burning incense). On the reverse front view of a priest holding two standards between two rows of three stars.

XXIII. THE PEOPLE OF PALMYRA

1. Young man reclining on a couch covered with embroidered carpets, wearing a richly embroidered Persian dress—a shirt with a belt, an over-cloak fastened with a circular brooch, wide trousers adorned with precious stones, richly adorned soft shoes, on his head a conical cap, near him on the top of a pillar his priest's mitre. His servant is shown wearing a similar dress.

2. Bust of a veiled woman wearing a costly diadem, ear-rings, a rich pectoral, and heavy armlets. Her mantle is fastened to the left shoulder by a brooch, from which hangs down the house key. Her tunica is richly embroidered. In her right hand she holds weaving and spinning implements. To the right her name.

3. Bust of a boy wearing a collar, dressed in a shirt and tunica fastened to his right shoulder by a circular brooch. In his right hand he holds a stylus and in his left his schoolboy's tablets on which the last letters of the Greek alphabet are written—ϕ, χ, ψ, ω.

VI

THE RUINS OF DURA

THE rather prosaic history of Dura is quite different from that of romantic Palmyra. Before 1920 the site was visited almost as rarely by archaeologists as by tourists; in fact I have never heard of a single tourist's visit. It is not that the city is inaccessible, for it stands now, as it stood hundreds of years ago, on the important caravan road along the Euphrates, about half-way between Deir es Zor, a large trading and military town on the middle Euphrates, and Abu Kemal, a small village on the borders of Iraq and the territory under French mandate. Only two or three of the more enterprising archaeologists had passed that way and even these seem to have taken little interest in her mighty towers, her walls, and her citadel. So it is only quite recently that Dura has come to be mentioned in archaeological and historical works, and what I have said regarding her history is entirely based on the data provided by excavations carried out in the last few years.

Though the story of the discovery of the site is known to archaeologists, it is sufficiently significant and romantic to warrant re-telling. It was in 1920, at the very end of the War, that Captain Murphy, the commander of an English detachment of Sepoys, discovered, purely by chance, in the north-western corner of the ancient city, near the fortifications, ruins of a temple decorated with interesting frescoes, while he was engaged in digging trenches and building blockhouses all over the ruins of Dura. Soon it was established that

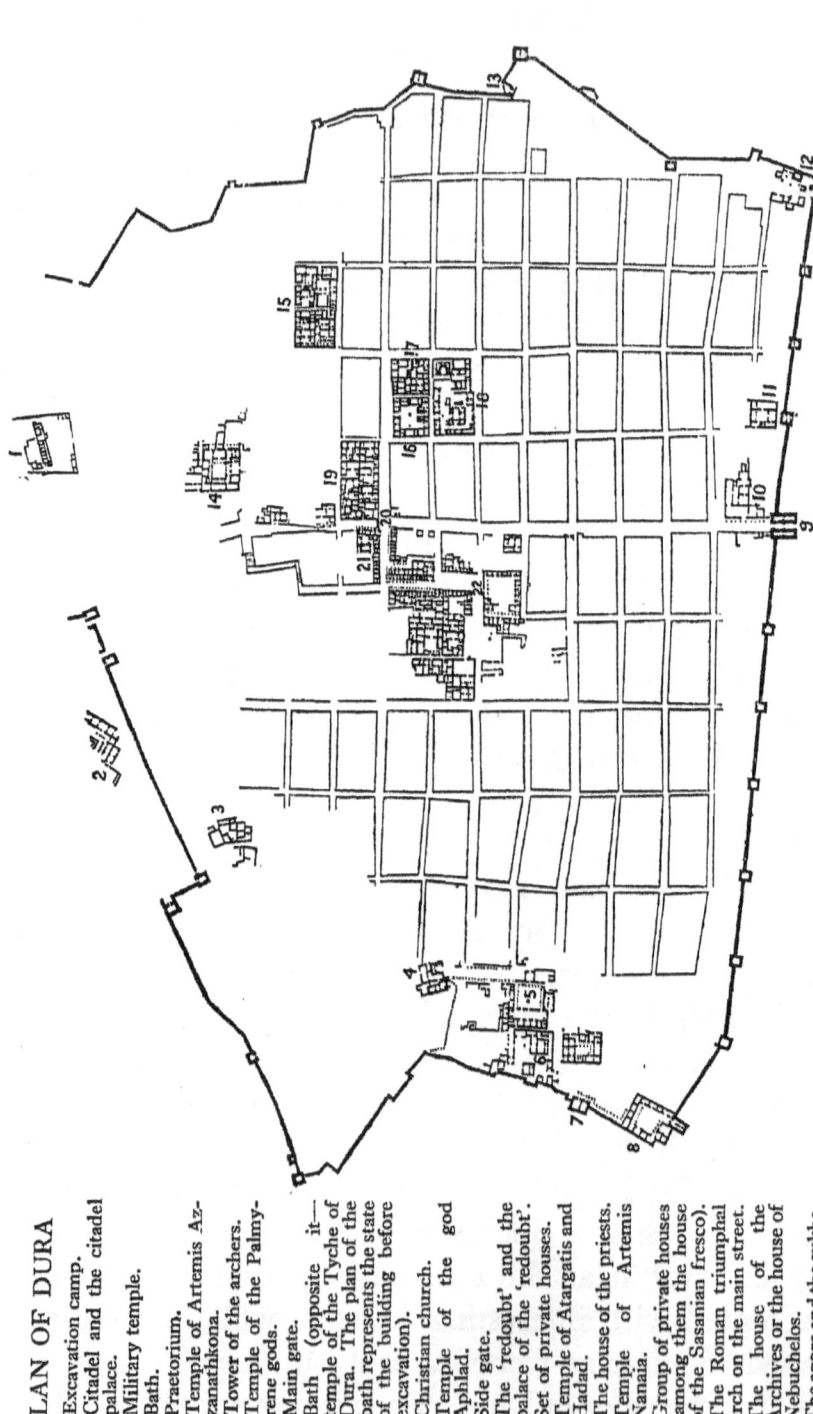

PLAN OF DURA
1. Excavation camp.
2. Citadel and the citadel palace.
3. Military temple.
4. Bath.
5. Praetorium.
6. Temple of Artemis Azzanathkona.
7. Tower of the archers.
8. Temple of the Palmyrene gods.
9. Main gate.
10. Bath (opposite it—temple of the Tyche of Dura. The plan of the bath represents the state of the building before excavation).
11. Christian church.
12. Temple of the god Aphlad.
13. Side gate.
14. The 'redoubt' and the palace of the 'redoubt'.
15. Set of private houses.
16. Temple of Atargatis and Hadad.
17. The house of the priests.
18. Temple of Artemis Nanaia.
19. Group of private houses (among them the house of the Sasanian fresco).
20. The Roman triumphal arch on the main street.
21. The house of the Archives or the house of Nebuchelos.
22. The agora and the sukhs.

these frescoes adorned the walls of a sanctuary which, during its last period of use, was dedicated to the worship of the three Palmyrene military deities: Bel, Aglibol, and Yarhibol. Captain Murphy reported his discovery to the late Miss Gertrude Bell, director of antiquities in Iraq, at the very moment when the famous American Egyptologist, James Breasted, happened to be in that country, and Miss Bell requested him to go to Dura and examine the frescoes. When Breasted reached Dura he found the British detachment about to leave the town and he only had one day in which to carry out his examination. In that day he was able to sketch and photograph the frescoes, to make a plan of the sanctuary in so far as this was possible without digging, and to jot down a rough outline of the town and its fortifications.

After the end of the War Breasted lectured on the discovery to the French Academy of Inscriptions and this body instantly decided to undertake excavation on the site, which by this time was already within the French mandate. The Belgian archaeologist Franz Cumont, an associate member of the society, was nominated director and it was made possible for him to work at Dura for two years on end. His workmen were soldiers of the French Foreign Legion, amongst whom were several Russians. Many interesting objects were brought to light, and the results of the dig have been admirably published by Cumont in two large volumes, which appeared in Paris in 1926 under the title of *Fouilles de Doura-Europos*. Unfortunately neither the French Academy of Inscriptions nor the Syrian government had sufficient funds for the continuation of the work, although it was obvious that Cumont had as yet been unable to find the answers to all the important historical problems which Dura presented. In fact it can be said that Cumont's excavations raised these problems for the first time.

Although, as we have already seen, Dura cannot compare with Palmyra in wealth or historic importance, it is nevertheless precisely in such a town that we may most reasonably expect to find abundant material which will enable us to solve problems of the very greatest interest. The town was occupied for about six centuries (from about 280 B.C. to about A.D. 256) successively by Macedonians, Parthians, and Romans. It was destroyed and abandoned in the middle of the third century A.D. and never reoccupied. We should thus be able to trace in Dura the history of those Graeco-Macedonian islets set in the midst of a Semitic and Iranian sea by Alexander the Great and his followers, all along the main roads of the Semitic and Iranian worlds. We know the names of several of these islets, but very little of their life, activities, or culture. We also know, more or less, the result of the experiment, for it can safely be stated that the Iranian and Semitic waves engulfed these islets, although it is still impossible to say exactly how this happened, or to describe the islets at the date of this engulfing.

I have already stated how important it is for the historian to gain information about the civilization, history, and constitution of Parthia. The conditions of Parthian life are still unknown, though we can, no doubt, state that they were infinitely varied, being of one type in India, of another in Persia, and again of another in Mesopotamia. Dura, which was a city of the Parthian empire for about three centuries, naturally cannot present us with a key to all these problems, but she has already enabled us to formulate them, and at some future date she will undoubtedly help us to solve at least some of them.

One would expect that the majority of Dura's monuments should date from Roman times, the last period of her life. For while the Macedonian and Parthian periods in Mesopotamia still remain hidden in darkness, the Roman, if not in Mesopotamia at least in Syria, is a far more tangible element. Yet even here we find that our knowledge is incomplete and we may well ask whether enough has been done to increase it by a careful study of existing material. The influence of Rome is evident in Syria, but was she also powerful on the Euphrates? It is in this realm that some of the most absorbing problems of Roman history present themselves. Rome's Palmyrene policy must have been, for instance, one of the most interesting experiments in her flexible constitution, and it is even more intriguing to inquire into the effects wrought by Rome in a setting such as Dura, which was Macedonian-Iranian in character, though Semitic in origin, and therefore completely foreign to Rome. One wonders how Rome and Hellenism met there and how the Romans dealt with the problem of the territories lying along the banks of the Euphrates?

Such are in the main the most important questions to which we may expect to find at least partial answers at Dura. Cumont's diggings have allowed us to formulate these problems, and his excavations also give good hope that with the aid of luck—excavations are always to a certain extent a matter of luck—and with the assistance of close systematic and scientific study, Dura will provide much that is of value in the study of the said problems.

No doubt Cumont's dig showed, as we should expect, that Dura is not likely to yield first-class works of art in architecture, sculpture, or painting, or to produce any large amount of gold and silver in the form of jewels or gold and silver plate, or even state documents bearing on great political questions. It was never a large or wealthy town or an important centre of political life; it was a small provincial city lost on the boundaries of two civilizations, the Greek and the Parthian.

Yet we may reasonably expect to find an abundance of objects which should throw light on several sides of the life of the city during the six hundred years of its existence, and such as we cannot expect to find in the ruins of other cities of the ancient world.

For the sand of the desert has not only preserved what the earth generally preserves in other ancient sites, stone, pottery, and metal, but also wood, textiles, leather, and paper, and, among other things, texts on parchment and papyrus. We have learnt from Egypt how valuable such relics are, especially the texts on papyrus, since it is by these that we have come to know more about the past of that land than we do of that of any other part of the ancient world.

When it became known that no more funds would be forthcoming from French and Syrian sources for the continuation of excavations at Dura, I endeavoured, with Cumont's consent, to raise the required sum in America. Through the warm support of Professor James R. Angell, President of my university, Yale, I was able to collect the necessary funds, and the excavation of Dura is now being conducted by members of that University in collaboration with the French Academy of Inscriptions. For five years we have now been at work there. Three preliminary reports on the excavations have already been published, and it only remains for us to hope that the end of our research will prove as successful as the beginning. Formerly M. Pillet, architect and archaeologist, directed the work, but now Professor Clark Hopkins of Yale is in charge. F. Cumont and myself are responsible for the scientific-historical side of the work, and Yale, assisted by the Rockefeller Foundation, provides the funds for the entire expedition. I will try to give the reader some idea of what has been already accomplished there. Of the work of Cumont I will speak but briefly; of that of the Yale expedition in greater detail. But first I will say a few words about the journey to Dura, where I spent the springs of 1928 and 1930, and of the life which we led on the spot.

It is not very easy to reach the site either from Beyrouth or Aleppo; a long, tiring, and difficult journey must be accomplished, which takes at the very least three days, although the distance is not much more than 700 kilometres. It is best to devote four days and three nights to the journey, setting out from Beyrouth if one comes to Syria by sea, or from Aleppo if one approaches by train from Constantinople. There is a railway connecting Beyrouth with Damascus, Homs, and Aleppo, but few people travel by train in Syria, for motor-cars have supplanted all passenger traffic on the railway—any Syrian prefers to pay one pound (20 francs) and be shaken in an overcrowded Ford to travelling for double the price in an equally overcrowded, dirty, and stuffy third-class railway carriage.

From the main starting-points for Dura, Damascus, Homs, or Aleppo, a Ford or Chevrolet is the only means of conveyance, for in these regions the camel has once and for ever reverted to the world of legend at least for the European traveller. From Damascus or Homs the desert has to be crossed to Palmyra and thence to Deir es Zor; from Aleppo one must first reach the Euphrates and then follow the river bank to Deir es Zor. It must be remembered that the river is not easily navigable on account of its swift currents and frequent whirlpools and that only the heavy local barges can safely venture upon it; even they only do so down-stream, the empty barge being towed up-stream by a rope. From Deir es Zor to Dura along the river is a distance of ninety kilometres.

The journey, as I have already said, is long and tiring. Where roads are found their surface is appalling, but in most cases no roads whatever exist. The desert must then serve as one enormous road. It is wise to avoid the most sandy places, for here cars are liable to stick, and it is best to choose a path where the stones are small, as large ones not only shake the traveller to pieces, but are also apt to break the motor's springs. Where the surface is composed of gravel, mercifully strewn by the hand of God, is to be found the best motor-road in all the world. As it is impossible always to escape between the sandy Scylla and the stony Charybdis, one is often obliged to cross sand dunes at high speed or else be shot into the air by some large stone. Nor is the journey entirely a safe one, for, though the Bedouins still remember the severe lesson which the French gave them after the Damascus rising, they are sometimes carried away by their innate lawlessness. Thus they recently captured, in the English territory of Irak (so the French maintain), an English girl, whom they only consented to free after this virginal miss had informed the sheikh who wished to place her in his harem that she was already the mother of three children. More dangerous even than the Bedouin is the desert, the 'bled'. If there is a breakdown of the engine, if the tyre punctures, or if an axle gives way, one may have to sit there for hours without either food or drink, in the hope that help will soon arrive. It is thus safer for cars to travel in groups of two or three, well stocked with provisions in case of emergency.

Of the roads to Dura those followed by caravans in Seleucid times are the most interesting. They all lead from Antioch on the Orontes to Seleucia on the Tigris. Two of them—that through Aleppo to, and down, the Euphrates, and that following the Orontes to Apamea and running thence to Hamath and across the desert to the Euphrates—I know by personal experience. All Seleucid Syria spreads itself out before us as we travel along these roads, and as we gaze at the land it seems as if its life has hardly altered since the days of the great Antiochi, or even since Babylon, Hittite, or Assyrian times. It is interesting to observe the change in the type of habitation from one district to another. In the Orontes valley, where reeds grow in profusion but where there is no wood, the houses are made of reeds and clay, and dried dung is used as fuel. In shape the houses recall the Bedouin tent. As soon as we leave the valley behind *en route* from Apamea to Aleppo and the climb into the hills begins, the type of domestic architecture changes at once; reeds and clay are replaced by stone. Houses are few, but where there are any, they are tall, strong, and even graceful in shape. Instead of the 'tells' of the Orontes valley, under which lie the ruins of ancient reed huts, we are confronted with the most complete and best preserved ruins in the world, ruins for which northern Syria is renowned, whole villages, farms, monasteries, churches, and even small towns being preserved. There are hundreds of these in the hills of Syria, all of them of late Roman or Byzantine date, for after that period the mountainous region was deserted, perhaps owing to decrease of rainfall. One of the most interesting of these ruins, not far from Aleppo, is that of the ancient monastery of St. Simeon. Its churches stand on the hill, whilst in the valley below are the monastic buildings, a series of halls, chambers, shops, eating-houses, &c., intended for the use of pilgrims to the holy Stylite. The whole construction is absurdly reminiscent of the Troitzka-Sergeevskaia Lavra in Russia.

The traveller descends into the Aleppo valley, a woodless, poorly watered plain with heavy clayish soil, which serves as a kind of ante-room to the desert, and here again the landscape changes. Groups of cone-shaped clay huts emerge from the plain. Not a trace of stone, wood, or reeds is seen in these huts; everything is made of clay. These clay villages reminded me of the Russian apiaries, groups of hundreds of cone-shaped primitive beehives typical of the outskirts of the Russian villages. These curious beehives for men of the Aleppo plain are said to be very clean and comfortable within.

As one approaches the Euphrates there is yet another change of scenery and this is especially important to us in our study of Dura. Here the houses are of the usual four-cornered type, built partly in stone but chiefly in unbaked brick. Their ceilings are of thin tamarisk trunks gathered from the shores of the Euphrates or of palm trees brought from Mesopotamia, and the roofs are made of mud.

To-day, as in the distant past, the visitor to Dura can travel either by this route or across the desert to Palmyra and thence direct to the Euphrates. He may perhaps have to spend, as we did, a night at Deir es Zor, in a hotel where five or six beds devoid of bed linen but occupied by numerous not very pleasant but permanent inhabitants stand in a single room. If the traveller should happen to survive this ordeal, he will reach Dura as we did and it was in Dura that our life as excavators was to begin.

When any of my friends tell me that an archaeologist's life must be full of adventure, romance, and fascination I can answer that he should himself try that life for two or three months. Our craft or art is, no doubt, interesting enough in general, and it is especially so when we are discovering important objects. But in the main the job is dirty and dusty; it is either excessively hot or excessively cold, according to the time of the year, and, at the best of times, it is tiring and hungry work.

What did we find at Dura? At first glance it seemed a paradise; before us was the steep bank of the Euphrates on which we stood and beneath us lay a wonderful landscape; the river, wide, muddy, and swift, in the foreground and on its right bank groves of tamarisk where the wild boar still roams. Beyond the river stretched the interminable fields and deserts of Iraq. On the edge of this steep river bank stands the citadel of Dura, an oblong rectangle surrounded by high walls (XXIV. 1). Access to the interior is gained by two monumental gates, each protected by two towers, set in the longer side of the rectangle looking towards the city. On the Euphrates side the corresponding wall has long since crumbled and fallen into the river.

In this citadel we decided to make our camp until we had built a more permanent house at its foot. We turned the arches of the half-buried gates into a dining-room and study, we stored our instruments and finds in one of the roofless towers, and in the other we installed our kitchen. All this sounds poetic and comfortable enough and it really wasn't too bad. It was best at night, when the stars shone out brightly over the desert, when a cool wind blew up from the Euphrates, when the sound of the distant water-wheels drifted dim and regular across the river, when bats and night hawks flew above us, and when from time to time the stillness was broken by the cry of a fox or a jackal. It was beautiful, too, early in the morning, when the sun rose clothed in a mantle of pink.

But day follows dawn and with it comes prosaic reality. People have to eat and drink, and in the hot, parched air of the desert the latter is an ever-present essential. At first sight it would seem as though the problem of providing water would be a simple one, with the Euphrates in easy reach to bathe in or to draw water from. But we could hardly jump into the Euphrates from the towering cliff, and a four-mile walk was necessary to reach the water. Even when once there we found proof of the adage that 'there is many a slip twixt the cup and the lip', for close to the river the bank is steep and insecure and it may crumble at the first step. This may mean the end of one's life, for the Euphrates is swift and full of whirlpools and no one can hope to swim in it with safety. If you want to wash, you have to get a canvas pail, tie a rope to it, drop it in the river and pull it out, so that you can only wash by your own labour. And however thirsty you may be, beware of drinking Euphrates water, not because of its colour which is that of weak coffee, but because it is full of enteritis germs which bring on the severest dysentery. Thus you have not only to fetch and carry your water, but also to filter and to boil it before you can drink it. The same difficulties beset you when you attempt to satisfy your hunger. Both the desert and the Euphrates groves are full of game: two or three varieties of partridge strut there as sedately as though they were hens; pigeons, gazelles, rabbits, and wild plovers abound. Yet though there is game in abundance it is unprocurable, for all the firearms of the Bedouin have been confiscated by the French, and we ourselves had no time to go shooting. The Arabs own sheep and goats and meat is obtainable from them, but it is practically uneatable; milk is not to be found and the bread tastes like the chewing-gum so popular in my new country. So we ate tinned food.

But these ills were but half of our misfortunes. The greatest difficulty of all was that of obtaining workmen. The Bedouin is unused to work; he is weak, underfed, and lazy. Money does not tempt him; he works but to pay his tax and as soon as he has saved enough for this he disappears. He is, moreover, suspicious and insists on being paid in heavy Turkish mejidii; the slightest thing annoys him and when annoyed off he goes and there's an end of him. Added to this, he is a thorough barbarian: he smashes most of the finds and will try to steal as many of the others as he can. There is in fact no one who can be depended upon in this district, for even the Europeans in Syria are untrustworthy and of the worst type—they are mostly thieves and drunkards. On our first journey we were obliged to dismiss our European cook and chauffeur and to have recourse to armed force to get rid of them, so great were the difficulties they caused. All this is now forgotten, however. Both we and the local population are better used to each other and seeming order reigns, though below the surface the former conditions continue to subsist and will probably subsist for ever. The desert also becomes a natural enemy to archaeologists: it is dry and barren and as soon as you touch it, up rises a cloud of dust which will not fall, so that the excavator spends his day standing in dust, eating dust, breathing dust. It penetrates the pores of his skin and he returns home a veritable nigger. But there is no comforting bath awaiting him when he gets back. Sand storms come to make things even more difficult, and when these start in the morning they usually last for three entire days.

And yet the work at Dura is interesting and exciting. During these five seasons we have accomplished valuable work and have found many interesting things. These will be described presently: first I will say a few words on the character of the work, and I will quote one example to show that it can be thrilling enough. During the first season we were digging around the main gates of the city. They are threefold and under their vaults are doors giving access to the towers protecting the gate. The walls to right and left of these entrances are covered with hundreds of inscriptions, written there by soldiers belonging to the garrison, by merchants, customs-officers, and porters, all of whom have thus succeeded in immortalizing their names. The inscriptions are most numerous close to one of the doors, where stands a row of altars coated with plaster. On one of these an inscription is scratched, not cut, and, as I was examining it one day, I suddenly noticed a piece of stone protruding from below the thick coating of plaster. It was obvious that the plaster concealed something, so I took my knife, made the sign of the cross, and began to peal it away. To my delight there stood concealed beneath the plaster a lovely little stone altar bearing an Aramaean inscription. It was a most valuable find, and, emboldened by it, I began to remove the plaster covering the lower part of the altars and the space between them. When I had finished there stood before me another miniature altar with drawings and inscriptions engraved upon it—yet another most important discovery throwing much light on the later period of Dura's military history.

The reader may ask what exactly is the picture revealed by the discoveries of Cumont and of the Yale expedition. There can be no doubt that it is still too soon to define it, since the excavations are still in progress. But certain facts have definitely been established which are unlikely to be affected by future results, and it is of these that we shall speak.

So far it has unfortunately been impossible to trace the city's exact ground-plan. Cumont's plan was made with the aid of air photography and it has been rectified and brought up to date by my pupil Hopkins, who spent the whole of the second season of work at Dura (see plan 5, p. 154), and is now in charge of the excavations. Though its main lines are correct it still remains inexact with regard to detail and needs certain improvements. It is, however, the main lines that most concern us here. They show us the Dura of the third century A.D., and we find that at this period the city represented a most curious combination of a fort and a caravan town.

We are still unable to discover whether this had always been so, for our knowledge of the historical topography is still very vague. It may be that Macedonian Dura was on a smaller and more modest scale than the city whose ruins we are studying. It may have occupied only the limited space on each side of the Euphrates caravan road and may have been protected by one or two forts occupying the place where now the citadel and the palace of the so-called redoubt stand. We are as yet unable to prove this possibility, though if our funds last out, we shall be able to elucidate this question by means of systematic excavation of that part of the town lying between the citadel and the redoubt. Thus far, except for the supporting wall of the redoubt, we have no remains of buildings of the Seleucid period. All the buildings which we have excavated belong either to Parthian or to Roman times.

The outlines of Dura as it existed in the Roman and Parthian periods are clearly defined before us. The city lay on a piece of desert land enclosed on the north-west and the south-east by two ravines and descending towards the Euphrates. On three sides this strip of land is bounded by a wall and fortified by a row of towers (XXIV. 2), most of them square in plan and double

1. SE. part of the Citadel with the two towers and the gate. On the top of the rock are the ruins of the fortress

2. NW. gate and tower

XXIV. DURA. THE CITADEL

1. Hellenistic sustaining wall which surrounds the redoubt and gives it the appearance of a bastion

2. Entrance to the palace which stood on the top of the redoubt. The two columns in the foreground belong to a Propylon. Right and left of the main entrance are benches for those who guarded the door or waited for admittance

XXV. DURA. THE REDOUBT

The Ruins of Dura

storied. The wall dividing the city from the desert plateau in the south-west runs as straight as an arrow, while that overlooking the ravines makes its way along the edge of the cliffs right up the two ravines. The fourth, north-eastern, defence of Dura is the cliff overhanging the river and is separated from the city plateau by a third ravine running inside the city from south-east to north-west, where the modern Euphrates road from Deir es Zor to Abu Kemal runs. The Euphrates cliff is crowned by the oblong citadel described above which was certainly connected with, and included in, the city walls. This part of the wall, however, crumbled down into the Euphrates together with the north wall of the citadel. Since the ravine below the citadel (we shall call it the citadel-ravine) has not yet been excavated we do not know how this lower part of the city, between the citadel and the city-plateau (which may have been the oldest part of the town), was connected with the upper plateau, the main area of the later city. Another deep ravine now runs from the end of the main street of the upper city down to the citadel, from south to north, connecting the upper plateau with the bottom of the citadel-ravine. This ravine probably existed from time immemorial. It has never been a regular street open to men, beasts of burden, or vehicles. From the end of the main street a flight of steps may have descended to the citadel in ancient times. The two ravines inside the city give to the south-eastern part of the city-plateau the form of a bastion overhanging the two ravines. This natural bastion was called a 'redoubt' by Cumont. The steep slopes of this 'redoubt' are supported by walls of the Hellenistic period, and an important building of which

I am going to speak below rose on the top of it. I have already stated that the walls of the 'redoubt' are the oldest surviving monument in the city (xxv. 1).

Our recent excavations have enabled us to trace the history of the citadel with fair accuracy. The ruins standing on the citadel hill, which we were the first to discover, are of two periods, both earlier than the Roman. Probably the great earthquake of A.D. 160, of which we read in a dedicatory inscription found in the temple of the Palmyrene gods, threw a section of the citadel and its fortifications on the north side into the Euphrates, and since that date, or at least since the occupation of Dura by the Romans, the citadel has remained in a semi-ruined condition.

Both groups of ruins on the top of the citadel are, as I have said, of pre-Roman date. The older, of which some foundations alone survive, may belong to the Hellenistic age. The later, represented by the ruins of two large buildings of enormous square blocks of local stone quarried in the ravine near the citadel, cannot be much later than late Seleucid or early Parthian, as is indicated by the objects, more especially by the coins, discovered there. It is interesting to find that the early buildings are oriented more or less in accordance with the surviving citadel walls, while the later ones run south and north and have their monumental entrance set to face the transversal ravine and the buildings of the 'redoubt'.

One of these later buildings appears to be a large fortified palace—in fact a fortress-palace. It was entered from the south by way of an impressive hall bisected by a five-columned portico supporting the roof. Beyond this stretched a wide passage divided

The Ruins of Dura

into four sections by three columns, and this led to a large courtyard surrounded by a Doric colonnade with, I think, a cistern in the centre of it (XXVII. 2). Most of this building has now fallen into the Euphrates, but the rooms which flank the entrance, and five rooms on the west side whose walls were once painted, still survive.

Most of the walls of the neighbouring building have also fallen into the river, but the part which remains closely recalls the Parthian ruins of Hatra. If the first building was a fortress-palace, then the second was probably a great tower, the abode of the palace garrison, or perhaps a fire-temple. A round donjon built into the walls of the later citadel, possibly with the intention of protecting a great cistern or well, also belongs to this group of ruins.

The excavation and study of the citadel is not yet completed, but at present I think that in early Hellenistic times the top was an area of habitation, and that the surrounding cliff was not fortified. In early Parthian times a fortress-palace was probably built on the edge of the cliff above the ruins of the Hellenistic structure. It was differently oriented and was fortified with towers and a donjon erected above a cistern. Contemporaneously with the palace, or at a still later date, the fortifications constituting the present citadel were built.

There is, however, another equally possible solution of the problem. If, as Cumont and Renard think, the walls of both the town and the citadel were built in Hellenistic times, and if they are contemporary with the founding of the Macedonian colony, then the citadel walls, part of which form the donjon over the cistern, must be contemporary with the early Hellenistic building standing on top of the hill. Later, in Parthian times, the fortress-palace and tower were erected in place of this building in order to strengthen the citadel.

The redoubt has also had a complicated history. I have already said that the well-preserved portions of its walls standing on the three steep banks of the plateau are probably early Hellenistic. We do not know what the square space within these walls originally contained, but at the time when the fortress-palace was built on the citadel rock, a large palace of the Babylonian-Parthian type was erected within the Hellenistic walls of the redoubt (xxv. 2). This palace had a large open courtyard before the entrance, a monumental gateway, and a big inner courtyard with a bench running round it. Onto this inner court opened two extensive liwans or halls; in front of each stood two columns. A large rectangular hall with a pronaos opening out onto the ravine and facing the citadel was added to the north wall of the square Hellenistic building. All these buildings have suffered from frequent alterations, but even in Roman times this group must have been the residence of an important person, a high municipal or imperial officer. This, however, is still a purely hypothetical suggestion, for our work on the building failed to reveal either inscriptions, sculpture, or even informative graffiti. Nevertheless its plan so closely conforms to the little that we know of the life at the 'courts' and in the palaces of the kings and governors of Parthian and Sasanian Persia (for these, no doubt, followed the example of the Persian, Assyrian, and Babylonian kings) that we cannot be far wrong in our assumption. From time immemorial in the East only the 'courtyard' of the palace was open to the people, and this court always took the shape of a large open space in front of the palace.

Here, seated before a monumental entrance, the king or his representative would pass judgement and enforce law and order. It was so in the past and it remained so until recent days, when the term 'Sublime Porte' recalled the practice. Only favoured ones, who had waited for many hours amongst the labyrinth of passages, were admitted to the inner courtyard and into the liwan, the reception room, of the master. Beyond this place none but servants or relations penetrated. It is curious that the only important graffito found in this palace of the redoubt is an inscription which a cook scratched on his kitchen walls in Greek letters, but in the Latin tongue. In it he has immortalized the number of hams which he was going to serve to the Roman resident in the palace. In this connexion it is interesting to note that in 1930–1 we uncovered a large house of the same type as the palace in the redoubt. This house, which is certainly of Parthian date, and served either as the residence of a Dura notable or as a public building, stands not far from the temples of Artemis and Atargatis.

The masonry of the citadel is almost identical with that of the city walls and the two are certainly contemporary in date. The defensive walls which are strengthened by at least twenty-two towers are exceedingly impressive: mighty and severe is the line which they trace across the desert from either side of the monumental gates, through which admission to the town was gained. They then follow the twisting outline of the cliff rising above them. This year we discovered an interesting little gate set in the south-western wall, through which ran a path leading to the bottom of the ravine.

This is not the place in which to speak of the fortifications. But whatever their date we may note that in Parthian times they were solid, strong, and impressive. They were probably badly damaged by the earthquake of 160 B.C., which may have facilitated the Roman seizure of the town. During that period, or perhaps even in Parthian times, the walls of the towers were strengthened on the inside by constructions of brick, and later, perhaps at the time of the Persian attack, the walls facing the desert were reinforced on the inside by the addition of a huge glacis of unbaked brick. The inner 'contre-escarpe' on the south-western side is probably of an earlier date.

These mountains of brick were nevertheless unable to save the town from falling to the enemy, and even to-day, not far from the south-western corner of the fortifications, a ramp of earth rises gently against the city wall, its sides supported to right and left by walls of unbaked brick. It was probably along this ramp that there passed in close file Shapur's Persian soldiers, bringing ruin and destruction to the town.

A few more words must be said about the city walls and towers which were to us and to Cumont veritable archaeological Eldorados. Soldiers in charge of the defence would naturally deposit some of their belongings, especially their arms and clothing, in the towers. When, after the last attack which resulted in the capture of the city by the besiegers, the soldiers of the Dura garrison left the city or were killed in the battle, some of their belongings were left behind by them in the towers or dropped in their hasty flight in the vicinity of the walls. The conquerors probably did not pay very much attention to these pieces of equipment. They expected to find more and better loot in the temples and public buildings of the city. Thus it was that these pieces or armament and clothing remained where they had been left or dropped. When the city was abandoned, wind-blown sand accumulated in large masses in the towers and on both sides of the walls. In a short time it became so thick that rain could not penetrate to the objects. Consequently almost everything which lay here was found by us in comparatively good condition, somewhat eaten by worms but otherwise in an excellent state of preservation.

The most exciting finds near the towers were documents written on parchment and papyrus. Cumont found nine parchments near the double tower of the archers in the north-western wall. In our second campaign we added to these three parchments and one papyrus, found in the vicinity of the main gate (XXVI). We know now how these documents happened to be in these places. In our last campaign, that of 1931-2, we found in the ruins of a temple standing in the vicinity of the double tower of the archers, a room which probably served as a Public Record Office, of which more will be said below. This room was full of parchments and papyri. Most of them had completely decayed. Some —those which lay buried deep under the sand—were in a better state of preservation and they may yield important information about the life of Dura. From this place came the documents found along the walls of the south-western part of the city. Some of them may have been carried along by the retreating soldiers and dropped on their flight, some may have been left in the Record Office and blown away by the strong desert wind. In any case the desert sand preserved these venerable relics, which have already provided us with such abundant and important information on the life of Dura in the six centuries of its existence.

Along with these parchments and papyri the finds in the towers consisted mostly of pieces of clothing and of arms and weapons. Remains of textiles are rare in ancient ruins except in Egypt. Each new Syrian piece is therefore welcome to those who study the history of textiles. It must be admitted, however, that the Dura fabrics are not of the finest sort: most are fragments of camel-bags and plain shirts and cloaks. Still more disappointing were the arms and weapons. Most of them are very poor examples, which obviously did not belong to Roman legionaries. They must be assigned either to Palmyrenes (who never possessed either iron, steel, or even good wood in large quantities), or to other Eastern auxiliaries of Rome, or even to the last occupants of Dura—the Persians. In fact very few metal helmets, swords, spears, shields, or complete sets of armour were found. The most interesting find is without doubt a large chain armour, perhaps that of a horse, which in all probability belonged to a Persian *clibanarius* (see below, p. 195). Most of the soldiers, however, whose arms we found in the towers, were equipped with shields of leather or of wood stitched with leather, with nomad arrows, and with darts with wooden points. Yet one of the leather shields is exceptionally interesting, for its owner—a soldier of an auxiliary corps—had drawn on it in colour the itinerary of his return journey from the West to the East, that is to say

1

2

XXVI. DURA. THE MAIN GATE
(*for description see p.* 216)

1. The main street

2. Central court of the Fort

XXVII. DURA
(*for description see p.* 216)

from the Balkan peninsula to Dura. It thus provides us with a rare example of a very ancient map.

Such is the general aspect of the fortifications of Dura. Within the walls the topography depended in part on strategic considerations, but chiefly on the dictates of those two caravan routes to safeguard which the fortress was built. One is the road running along the Euphrates. In Dura it probably formed the main artery of the lower town. However, we are not sure whether this road actually went through the town or only past it, along the Euphrates bank, under cover of the protection formed by the citadel. Both the position of the redoubt and the existence of two gates of the town which are situated near the citadel seem to indicate the former alternative as the more likely. The exact line of this road is unknown and it must remain for ever unknown, for recent improvements to the modern Euphrates road have ruined this section of Dura from the archaeological point of view. The second large caravan road, forming the junction of the route from Palmyra and the western desert with that running along the Euphrates, defines the topography of the upper town (XXVII. 1). It passes through the straight desert wall of the town by way of the mighty threefold gate (XXVI), of which I must say more anon. Once in the town it became the main street, leading from south-west to north-east across the upper plateau, straight from the gate in the direction of the citadel and dividing the upper town into two unequal parts. Many transverse roads intersect it and the whole of the upper town resembles the draught-board pattern typical of towns of Hellenistic and Roman date. Unfortunately we have no idea of the lay-out of the lower town.

We do not yet know how all Dura's more important public buildings were grouped along her two main arteries, although we know the sites of five of her major temples. Two of these stand in the south-western part of the upper city. One was dedicated to Artemis Nanaia, the great Elamite and Babylonian goddess, who was also worshipped at Palmyra (xxx. 1). This temple assumed its later (Roman) form in the Parthian period, to be precise, in the first decade of the first century A.D. Neither Cumont, who first excavated it, nor we ourselves have been able to determine with certainty whether another, possibly Hellenistic, temple had previously stood on this site, for no definite remains of this early temple could be revealed by excavation.

Close to the temple of Artemis Nanaia our excavations of 1929–30 disclosed a second, slightly smaller, temple (xxviii. 1) of the same date, dedicated to that famous 'Syrian Goddess' (Dea Syria) of whom the Roman writers of imperial times speak so often, and whose temples were the rivals of those of Egyptian Isis and Anatolian 'Magna Mater' in Italy and in the Roman provinces. Her name was Atargatis and her divine consort was Hadad (xxx. 2). Her most famous temple in Syria was the splendid sanctuary in Hieropolis-Bambyce. To Atargatis and her consort were probably also dedicated the temples in Baalbek, while Palmyra and Damascus likewise had shrines in which they were worshipped.

The plans of both temples at Dura are exceedingly interesting, and many peculiarities of Christian Syrian church-architecture are explained by them. The temple was in its essence a large court surrounded by chambers ('oikoi', as the inscriptions term them), in

1. Temple of Atargatis

2. The Little Theatre

XXVIII. DURA
(for description see p. 217)

which were undoubtedly performed a number of ceremonies connected with the cult, such as holy repasts and incubations, i.e. dreams in which the god appeared to those who sought him. Part of these 'oikoi' could be used for the worship of those gods who were the companions of the chief deity. In the centre of the main courtyard stood a large altar, and sometimes a tank containing water, but the Holy of Holies was a small and modest building inside the courtyard or leaning against the back wall of the courtyard. The main part of the Holy of Holies was the little shrine (naos) which contained the cult-image of the deity. It was flanked on each side by two small rooms serving as the treasury of the god. So far the temples of Dura were of the regular Babylonian type. One essential feature, however, does not recur in Babylonia and seems to be closely connected with some Syrian cults. It is a small hall before the Holy of Holies with steps on both of its longer sides, a kind of tiny theatre. The seats in this theatre were the private property of definite people, in the same way as are particular pews in Catholic and Protestant churches to-day. In both temples the inscriptions on these steps indicate that women were the owners of the seats and it is obvious that, in these temples belonging to the great Syrian and Babylonian goddesses, men were not allowed to pass beyond the limits of the courtyard (XXXII. 2).

We discovered numerous dedications, altars, reliefs, and statues in both temples. These documents have disclosed to us many details in the history of the two temples, and the names of all those who added to their greatness. It is significant that the majority of the inscriptions are in Greek, though some are also in the

Semitic tongues, one, for instance, in ancient Syriac. One of the peculiar features of the temples is that they were richly painted, as was the temple dedicated to the Palmyrene gods of which we shall say more below. In this respect they are the forerunners of the early Christian churches. Unfortunately but little remains of these paintings; on one fragment from the temple of Atargatis the artist's signature alone survives, and thus his name has been immortalized, though his work has perished—so capricious is Fate. Our third report deals with these monuments and the reader must turn to it for further information on the subject.

In speaking about the temple of Artemis Nanaia I would like to point out that it served in the Roman period not only as a centre of religious but also of political life. It is known that, at some date in the Roman period, the temple, which was previously of the size of the neighbouring one of Atargatis, was enlarged and its disposition altered. A whole block of private houses was added to its court and the little 'women's theatre' was destroyed. In its place another theatre of larger dimensions was built at the back of the courtyard (xxviii. 1). The purpose of this theatre is a problem. One thing, however, is certain: it was a meeting-place not for women but for men. On its door-posts are carved lists of names, all names of men of the best families of Dura. Moreover, on one of the seats is scratched another name, and this man styles himself as a senator (bouleutes) of Dura. All these facts make me think that at some date in the Roman period the courtyard of the temple of Artemis Nanaia became a kind of substitute for the public square of the city, the agora. In this I am confirmed by the fact

The Ruins of Dura

that some inscriptions of a public character—dedications by the senate and the people and the 'chief coloni' (the leading men among those who were citizens of the Roman 'colony' of Europos)—were found in the temple-courtyard. Whether the temple at that time was still a centre of worship or not we do not know.

It is tempting to suggest that this change was connected with the establishment of the Romans in Dura. Last year's excavations have shown that a large part of the north-western half of the city was transformed in Roman times into a regular Roman military camp, with a praetorium, a temple dedicated to the cult of the emperor, a 'field of Mars' for military training, baths, barracks for the soldiers, houses for the officers, &c. Further excavations will yield more information about it. Since in all probability this part of the city originally contained the 'agora', the political centre of the city in Parthian times, it is natural to think that those emperors, who are responsible for the militarization of the city of Dura—I am thinking of Septimius Severus, Caracalla, and Alexander Severus—in taking away from the citizens of Dura, now a Roman colony, their agora, transferred the head-quarters of the colony to the enlarged and rebuilt temple of Artemis Nanaia.

In any case the militarization and thorough romanization of the north-western blocks of the city seem to me, after last season's excavations, to be established facts. This militarization completely changed the aspect of this part of the city, a fact which is again established by our last season's excavations. One of the most interesting results of the dig was the discovery of the third women's temple, which was built at the same time as the temples of Artemis Nanaia and Atargatis for the use of the residents of the north-western part of the city. It was found in a perfect state of preservation and was dedicated to a goddess whose Greek name was Artemis, but whom the Semites of Dura called Azzanathkona. Her cult-image looks almost exactly like that of Atargatis. The temple was of regular Babylonio-Syrian type with two naoi and a theatre-like building, owned by the women of the civic aristocracy. Now this temple was never destroyed and rebuilt as was that of Artemis Nanaia, but in the Roman times it was no longer a women's temple since no inscription later than A.D. 117 appears on the seats. If in the Roman period it was still a temple, it certainly no longer belonged to the women who lived in the north-western part of the city. The obvious explanation of this is that there were no longer any women in this part of the city. It had become the home of men—Roman soldiers, most of them of Syrian origin, who naturally continued to frequent the temple and to offer sacrifices to its great goddess.

Yet the real temple of the soldiers was the fourth well-preserved temple of Dura, the temple of the triad of Syro-Babylonian military gods (XXIX. 1). It stands in the north-western part of the town, in the north-western corner of the fortifications. The city wall is designed so carefully to enclose, surround, and protect this temple that there can be no doubt that it had to be taken into consideration when the wall was built. It was neither desirable nor possible either to destroy the sanctuary or to leave it unprotected outside the fortifications. If, as Cumont thinks, the city wall was built in early Seleucid times, then the temple must be even earlier in date, possibly of Persian or Assyrian origin. If, as I am inclined to think, the wall is of later date, the

1. Temple of the Palmyrene gods

2. Court of a sanctuary

XXIX. DURA

(*for description see p.* 217)

temple may also be later, that is to say of the Hellenistic or even Parthian period, and in that case it may have been built either by that section of the local population which had lived formerly at Dura or which had settled there after the establishment of the town as a Macedonian colony. In Roman times it was dedicated to the gods of Palmyra, to that Palmyrene trinity formed of Bel or Baal Samin and his two followers, Yarhibol and Aglibol. Whether, from its very foundation, the temple had been dedicated to this trinity, or whether in early times it was dedicated to the mighty Bel alone, is a fact which still remains to be established.

This temple of the Palmyrene gods proved a veritable treasury both for Cumont and for us. I shall speak later of the frescoes which were discovered in it and which have now been moved to the Damascus Museum, with the exception of two pictures which went to Yale. Here I may mention that numerous altars bearing inscriptions and hundreds of graffiti were found in the temple by Cumont and ourselves.

The plan of it is very unusual. Its earliest cella had at some period been transformed to serve as the base of one of the towers fortifying the city wall. It was not, however, in this tower, where the all-powerful god was worshipped in the form of a fetish, that stood the later Holy of Holies decorated with the frescoes which were discovered by Murphy and studied by Breasted and Cumont. This later double cella was built side by side with the tower leaning on its north wall in the western part of its area. Nevertheless it is probable that this addition of a new cella at the time when the temple was rebuilt from top to bottom (in the early first century A.D.) did not put out of use the earlier cella, now one of the towers of the city wall. Both cellas were probably in use, each having its god or gods.

In front of both of these cellas extended a courtyard adorned with columns, with an altar at its centre and rooms opening out all round it. A curious altar or naiscos of a deity stands close to the entry leading into one of these rooms, the nearest to the cella. The god of this altar or shrine was probably represented by a picture of a betyl, painted on the wall behind the altar or shrine. It is not surprising that no theatre-shaped hall was found. This was a temple for men and it is very likely that sacred theatres were connected with the cult of goddesses rather than with that of gods.

As regards the importance of this temple in Roman times, I may note two interesting facts. I have mentioned the great work carried out in the late Roman period to strengthen the city wall. A glacis of mud bricks was built and this glacis ruthlessly destroyed all the buildings adjacent to the city wall or the city towers. The only exception was the temple of the Palmyrene gods, to which no damage whatever was done during this work on the fortifications. The sanctuary played apparently an important part in the life of the masters of Dura of this period—the Romans. I am convinced that this temple of warrior-gods, gods who helped the soldiers to fight and to die for their country, and who were at the same time their own gods, of Syrian origin like the soldiers of the Roman Syrian army in the second and third centuries A.D., was *the* temple of the Roman garrison. This view is supported by the second fact which I wish to point out. The temple of the Palmyrene gods is famous for its frescoes. The painted decoration of it was not destroyed or

1. Artemis

2. Atargatis and Hadad

XXX. DURA. THE GODS
(*for description see p. 217*)

damaged by the builders of the glacis. After Dura had been evacuated, sand accumulated in large masses in this corner of the city and protected the frescoes from destruction by rain, sun, or wind. This painted decoration shows scenes of sacrifices by parishioners of the temple, donors of its mural decoration, to the gods of the temple. We have a set of them, both of Parthian and of Roman times. Now in the Parthian period the donors who are represented sacrificing are all civilians. We see magistrates and senators of the city, officers of the Parthian government, perhaps priests. With the coming of Rome the civilians disappear. The best preserved fresco of the cella, now in the Art Museum of Yale, shows a sacrifice performed by the new patrons of the sanctuary: the commander of the garrison Julius Terentius, the tribune, his eight officers, and a crowd of common soldiers (XXXIV).

I had long ago come to be of the opinion that this temple standing in the north-western corner of the fortifications would be balanced by a corresponding temple in the south-western corner, and our seasons of 1930–1 and 1931–2 have proved my surmise to be correct (XXIX. 2). This second temple was buried, at some date during Dura's last period of prosperity, under the heap of bricks forming the glacis to which I have already referred. The temple appears to have been a very complicated and ambitious construction. One part of it at least had two stories and the walls of both were painted. We found scores of fragments of this decoration on two levels, the ground level and that of the upper floor. Like the temple in the north-western corner our temple was built against the tower of the wall. It would take too much space to describe its architecture in detail. Such a description will be found in our fifth report. More important from our point of view is the question to whom the temple was dedicated.

During the last season of excavations Prof. Hopkins discovered in the area of the temple a curious little building: a chapel (oikos, according to the terminology of Dura) with a little shrine in its back wall (naos). In this shrine stood originally the cult-image of the deity before whom incense was burned on a small altar. This cult-image and a dedicatory inscription were found in a cachette, probably hidden by the worshippers when the sanctuary had to be sacrificed to the defence of the city. The god to whom the chapel was dedicated bears the name of Aphlad or Apalad, and is styled in the inscription of the cult-image the god of the village Anath (modern Anah to the south of Dura) on the Euphrates. The supporters of the shrine were members of a religious association. The shrine was built in A.D. 52. The figure of the god is very impressive: he is a warrior, and wears Hellenistic armour, yet Oriental dress, of Persian rather than Semitic appearance. He stands on two winged lions. On his neck he wears a torc, an ornament of a religious significance peculiar to the Iranians, on his bearded head is a tiara. The breastplate of his armour is adorned with the symbol of the sun and with crosses representing the stars. He leans on a curious sceptre, unique in its kind. Before him a priest is burning incense (XXXII. 1).

The sculpture is not easy to comment upon, although one is at once struck by some important peculiarities of the cult-statue. The god belongs, like Hadad and the Babylonio-Syrian warrior-gods of Palmyra and

Dura, to the large family of the Semitic Baals, who are the masters of heaven, gods of the sky and of the sun, the almighty rulers of the universe, and the great fighters against evil. In this, Aphlad is not different from his relatives of the Semitic world. Yet his sacred animal is not the bull, as is that of Hadad, but winged lions, fantastic animals peculiar to the Iranian world, though borrowed by the Iranians from the Babylonians and Assyrians. All the facts suggest that we have before us an Iranian version of the great Semitic god.

A curious, crude, and childish fresco painted on the wall near the naos shows a cult-scene which certainly refers to Aphlad: a priest is sacrificing to an eagle standing above the horns of an altar and crowned by a flying Victory. Hard by stands the man for whom the sacrifice is performed—a Parthian officer. It is well known that the eagle is the symbol of the great Sun-god of Syrian lands. This fresco recalls an altar found in the upper strata of the glacis in 1929–30. On this altar, which was described by Prof. Hopkins in our third report, we again see a Parthian officer performing a sacrifice, this time before a god who is fighting a lion—another motive borrowed from the Babylonians and Assyrians by the Persians.

To sum up. As far as our evidence now goes (the publication of the sanctuary by Prof. Hopkins in the fifth report may produce some new material which may contradict this theory) it seems as if the sanctuary or sanctuaries of the south-western corner were dedicated to gods worshipped, among others, by the Parthian soldiers and officers resident in the city. No wonder, then, that in the Roman period the sanctuary was neglected, fell into decay, and was finally buried under the mud bricks of the glacis. The Roman soldiers had no use for the gods of their enemies. They preferred the gods of their clients and friends the Palmyrenes. The two corner sanctuaries are real symbols of the double life of Dura: in the south-western corner the gods of the Parthian soldiers (XXXI. 1), in the north-western those of the Palmyrene caravaners, who were adopted in the last period of Durene life by the successors of the Parthian garrison, the soldiers of the Roman-Syrian army.

As a conclusion to this rapid survey of the city's temples I would like to add that in Dura, as in Palmyra, we discovered a series of temples dedicated to foreign and not to local divinities. I have already referred to Atargatis, Nanaia, Bel and his satellites, Aphlad, Artemis Azzanathkona, and later I will say a few words about Dura's Tyche and about a small military chapel standing at the gates of the citadel. As yet we have not come upon a single Greek temple, and we have no idea where the Greek and Macedonian inhabitants of Dura worshipped in early times; even at a later date we can only guess at these riddles. We must suppose that they probably used as their places of worship the temples which we have already excavated, although they belonged to Eastern gods.

In the Russian text of this book I closed this paragraph with the remark that not the slightest traces were found at Dura either of the Jewish religion or of Christianity. This fact surprised me considerably since one would expect to come upon Christian relics in the third century A.D. in most cities of the East, and especially at Dura which was in such easy reach of Edessa, one of the great centres of early Christianity.

The Ruins of Dura

Such was my statement a few months ago, and in such form it would have appeared in print were it not for our most sensational discovery of the season of 1931-2. It shows once more how careful one must be in drawing conclusions from negative evidence and how important it is never to leave an archaeological site alone before the place is completely excavated.

I cannot deal with this discovery at length since it is the privilege of our field-director, Prof. Hopkins, to illustrate his own find. A few words, however, must be said. In digging—somewhat reluctantly—in the chaos of walls between the main gate and the first tower to the south of it, walls belonging to a building destroyed by the mud-brick constructions of the aforesaid glacis, Professor Hopkins found two doors leading into a large room of the building. Great was his astonishment when he found that the walls of this room were painted and that the paintings illustrated famous episodes of the Old and New Testament, the centre of all this pictorial decoration being the apse or the naos of the back wall, showing the figure of the Good Shepherd. There was no doubt. The room had served as a Christian church at a date previous to the building of the wall-glacis. Since we know exactly when the glacis was built (between A.D. 232 and 256) we can date the church and its paintings with some accuracy: the latest date would be the decades before A.D. 250, but an earlier date is much more probable.

The most striking fresco of the church represents the Resurrection or rather the 'myrrhophores', the Three Marys bringing myrrh to the tomb of our Lord in the late hours of the night. The picture has not only a great interest from the point of view of the subject, but it is at the same time a piece of pathetic and forcible art with a beautiful display of colours.

A discovery of a Christian church with painted mural decoration which dates at the latest from the first half of the third century A.D. is beyond doubt a great find. It bears on various problems of the history of the New Testament, on the question of the influence of Syrian and Egyptian schools on early Christian art, and on the origin of this art—whether funeral or not. Let us, however, reserve the discussion of all such problems to the discoverer and go back to Dura.

While we have a large amount of information on its religious buildings, our evidence about its secular buildings, except the private houses, is very scanty. Every Greek city had a public square, an agora, in which its public life was centred. The same agora was used in most of the Greek cities as the main market-place, and almost always temples opened on to it. No such market-place has been brought to light in Dura. We are completely ignorant where the agora of the Seleucid city was situated, and whether or no the agora of the Parthian period was identical with that of the Seleucid. I suggested on p. 180 that this disappointing failure of our dig to find the agora might be explained by the hypothesis that, when the Romans transformed the north-western part of the city into their military camp, they incorporated the agora into it. Further excavations alone will permit us to judge whether my suggestion is right or wrong.

The private houses are uniform in appearance. Some are richer and larger than others, but all of them belong to a single type, which still exists in Mesopotamia to-day—Babylonian houses, dating back to the time of Ur of the Chaldees, with whose structure Mr. Woolley has made us familiar. A long corridor leading from the street turns at a right angle into the central (usually open) court of the house; one, two, or three large reception and business rooms surround this court, and there are stairs leading to the upper floor where the bedrooms and the living-rooms of the women were to be found. There was no aqueduct in the town, water being kept in enormous clay jars. Neither lavatories nor baths have been found in the houses.

How far the main type of a Durene house, of which the Babylonian origin is certain, conformed to that of the Macedonian or Greek house we do not yet know. An interesting feature of many such houses is their rich interior decoration, for the reception rooms of the better specimens are adorned, at the top of their walls, by plaster cornices richly ornamented with Greek Bacchic patterns with a certain admixture of Parthian elements. A set of these cornices was made, according to a frequently occurring inscription, by an Iranian called Orthonobazus. Wall-painting was extensively used, but its system is not Greek. Very common is a painted pattern imitative of a wall coated with square tiles painted red and black. In one room of a large and rich house of the Parthian period we found scores of painted tiles or bricks which without doubt covered originally the whole of the wall. Various figures and ornaments are painted on these bricks: human heads, animals, fruit, flowers. It is a very attractive suggestion of Professor Baur that some of these figures represent the Signs of the Zodiac. The general impression which such a wall, covered with painted tiles, produced on the visitor was no doubt that of a rich carpet. It is needless to say that this type of wall decoration can be traced back to Babylonia and Assyria.

Such is the general appearance of Dura and its outline is both interesting and unusual, for nowhere else do we find this combination of a fortress-city and a caravan town. The general plan was created by the Parthians, since we have already proved that all the more spectacular buildings were erected during the period of their rule and it is even probable that the fortifications were first outlined by them in the form in which they have come down to us. The Roman epoch, it appears, had a decisive influence on the general aspect of the city. While the south-western part, with the exception of some repairs and alterations, was left almost untouched, the north-western half was rebuilt from top to bottom. As I have said before, this part of the city, or one-half of it, was transformed into a regular Roman military camp. I will return to this topic later in the chapter.

But, apart from the Parthian buildings, what do we know of the culture of Dura during the most interesting and prosperous years of her existence? What materials have we with which to reconstruct the life of those days? Undoubtedly the first, and by far the most important, records are the frescoes of the first century A.D., which were discovered in the temple of the Palmyrene gods by Captain Murphy and by Cumont. The most important of them is the one (of the first century A.D.) which depicts Konon, a notable of Dura, his wife Bithnanaia and their children, at sacrifice in the temple of which they were all wealthy patrons. The sacrifice is being conducted by impressive-looking

1. Parthian god (?)

2. Nemesis

XXXI. DURA. THE GODS
(*for description see p. 217*)

1. The god Aphlad

2. Temple of Artemis-Azzanathkona

XXXII. DURA. THE GODS
(*for description see p.* 218)

priests, who wear tall, white, conical hats recalling those of the Persian magi or modern dervishes. Similar frescoes portray sacrifices by later benefactors of the temple. It is characteristic that one of these is an eunuch bearing an Iranian name, and another a senator of Dura, bearing a Semitic name (XXXIII).

No less interesting and significant are the objects discovered not only in the women's temples of Artemis Nanaia, Atargatis, and Artemis Azzanathkona, and in the men's temples at the two corners of the city, but also in private houses, some of which date back to Parthian times. Here the most important material consists of modest, often childish, drawings scratched on the plastered walls of the room, which show gods and goddesses, various buildings of the city (especially the walls), wild and domesticated animals, and, most interesting of all, men who lived in the city in Roman times and those who were her enemies, especially Parthian mounted and foot soldiers. One of them (fig. 3) shows an exact portrait of a Parthian or Sasanian *clibanarius*, a knight clothed in armour from head to foot, carrying in his hand a heavy spear and seated on a horse protected by chain-mail (fig. 3). Writers have

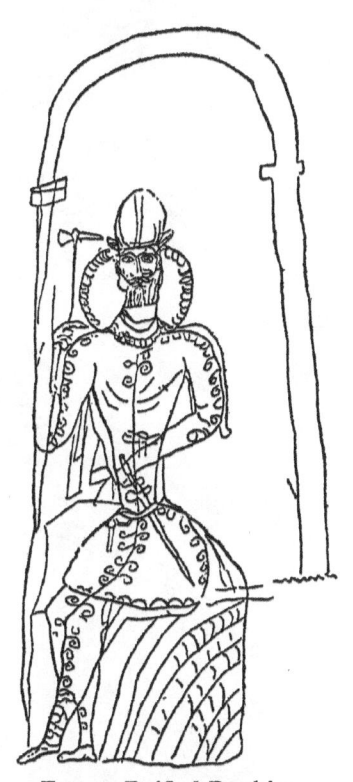

FIG. 1. Deified Parthian King. Graffito.

frequently referred to these Iranian knights, comparing them to statues, so immovably did they sit upon their mounts, but until these drawings came to light not a

Fig. 2. Parthian horseman shooting an arrow. Note the typical hairdress, the large arrow-case, and the elegant features of both the horse and the man. Graffito found in the house to the south-east of the temple of Artemis.

single picture of these early forerunners of the knights of the Middle Ages had come down to us. Now we know exactly what they and their Roman counterparts, the cataphractarii, looked like. We can compare them to their nearest relatives, the Sarmatian or Graeco-Sarmatian riders, dressed in coat of mail, who are depicted on Trajan's column and on the walls of some painted tombs of Graeco-Sarmatian Panticapaeum. No less interesting are the numerous figures of

FIG. 3. Parthian or Persian *clibanarius*, a heavy-armed horseman charging an enemy. He is clad from head to foot in heavy armour and is mounted on a horse which is protected by chain-mail. Graffito found in a house near the fortifications of Dura.

mounted archers, which we see on the walls of Durene houses (fig. 2). These are the Parthian bowmen whom even the Romans feared, the very men who overwhelmed Crassus' troops with showers of arrows. By their sides on the same walls a number of still more important figures appear: Parthian kings, great feudal barons of the Parthian kingdom, and governors of Dura (fig. 1).

These Parthians appear again in a most interesting parchment document which was recently published by myself and my pupil Prof. B. C. Welles. It is a contract of loan between Phraates, a noble Parthian, feudal lord of the village Paliga lying near to Dura, and an Arab, Barlaas by name, a man of humble origin. Instead of the interest on the loan, Barlaas agrees to give his own services, to live with Phraates and to do whatever he is bidden to do. The contract is dated by the name of the Parthian king and the two eras—the Parthian and the Seleucid—in the year A.D. 121, i.e. soon after Trajan's great campaign and the restoration by Hadrian of Mesopotamia to the Parthians. It is, by the way, a proof that Dura, after its capture by Trajan, was restored by Hadrian with the rest of Mesopotamia to the Parthians. The document gives an interesting picture of late Parthian life and throws much light on its feudal aspect, its Graeco-Parthian hierarchy, and its peculiar social and economic customs.

These recent discoveries give us such a definite impression of the peculiar, varied, and complicated life of this Parthian fort, that we can see it clearly before us to-day, with its garrison quartered high up on the citadel-cliff and its commander residing in the fortress-palace (a veritable eagle's nest) set between the Euphrates and the caravan road. Opposite, on the summit of the redoubt, the civil governor and his staff probably lived, in a large and handsome palace. Hundreds of suppliants came to him, and he would listen to their requests, seated in his great courtyard in front of the gates of his residence. In time of peace the Parthian governors would spend their days in much the same way as do their modern French successors, feasting in the palace or racing across the desert on thoroughbred horses in pursuit of lions, boars, deer, gazelles, hares, and other game, with swift dogs beside them. Such were the pastimes of these minor persons in the hierarchy of the Parthian state, as residents of Dura and neighbouring villages. The greater notables but rarely visited the town, and the Durenes but seldom caught a glimpse of their king's fair countenance. Yet the Parthians of Dura differed but little from their rulers, sharing the same interests and devoting their lives to the same pleasures and occupations.

Their neighbours in the city were members of the old Graeco-Macedonian colony who had retained their original names, many of their old traditions, and their own tongue and legal code. These had originally been landowners, but now they became merchants as well. Caravan trade enriched them and they were soon able to adorn their wives with heavy jewellery and to clothe themselves in the richly coloured garments and turbans so popular in the East. They built and decorated for themselves and their wives temples of Eastern type, in which they made offerings of vessels of gold, silver, or copper and gave other rich gifts. Regardless of the language that they spoke, they ceased to be Greek, and became typical Levantines. Their wives were Semites; their children semi-Semites; their deities those of the great Parthian empire, some of them of Eastern origin, some Semitic gods of the north, some

Arab gods of the south, and others Iranian. They gave them Greek names, but failed to make them Greek, while their own deities, Zeus, Apollo, and Artemis, were permitted almost to fall into complete oblivion.

We do not know if they were allowed much in the form of self-government. It is probable that, like the other Macedonian colonies of the Parthian kingdom, for instance Seleucia on the Eulaios, the ancient Elamite Susa, so carefully and successfully excavated by the French government, they retained a certain amount of autonomy, with their own constitution, their own magistrates, their own Senate. No doubt these would be strictly confined to dealing with their own petty local affairs and this under the watchful eye of the Parthian military governor. Nevertheless they cared little for these encroachments on their 'liberty', and in general were well satisfied with their life. The main point was that the Parthians did not wholly monopolize their privileges of 'ruling class' but shared with them the social and economic mastery over the Semitic section of the population, composed principally of farm labourers who tilled the fields belonging to the Macedonians, of shepherds who guarded their flocks, of artisans occupied in Macedonian workshops, or of camel drivers employed on their caravans. These Macedonians thus lived in wealth and plenty, forgetful of their Greek homeland, and became loyal subjects of the Philhellene Parthian king, whose suzerainty they preferred to that of their western neighbours, the Romans.

Such was Parthian Dura. We must now inquire for what innovations the Romans were responsible in the town, for wherever a spade is put into the ground traces of these new masters come to light. I have already said that in Roman times the chief use of Dura was that of providing lodgings for a Roman garrison, as one of the military bases for frequent wars with Parthia. The first thing, therefore, that the Romans did in Dura was to get comfortably and firmly installed.

So, as I have already said, the Romans gradually transformed the larger part of the north-western half of the city into a military camp. The excavation of this part of the city is not yet complete and we cannot therefore say how the Romans achieved their purpose of installing a military camp in an existing city. It is probable that in the Parthian period the 'continua aedificia' of Dura did not extend to the walls on the north-west and the south, and that large empty spaces existed near the two ravines. Thus there may have been a more or less extensive unoccupied building-area. If so, the Romans were certainly not satisfied with it; for instance, they built a little temple, probably dedicated to the cult of the emperor, in what I suppose to be one of the most ancient parts of the city just opposite the north-western gate of the citadel. In the Latin dedication found in this temple the dedicants speak of having enlarged the 'field of Mars' of the military camp. The natural suggestion would be to look for this 'square for military training' in the neighbourhood of the temple, e.g. eastwards in the direction of the fortifications. Such a location, however, hardly suits the topographical features of this part of the city.

The heart of the Roman military camp was the praetorium discovered last season. It is a fine building typical of Roman camps. Scores of such buildings have been excavated along the armed frontiers of the Roman empire: along the British, the German, the Danubian, the Arabian, and the African 'limes'. A monumental entrance with four gates, a regular 'tetrapylon', leads into the court of the praetorium, exactly in the same way as a much more stately tetrapylon leads into the court of the praetorium of Lambaesis in Africa. The court is surrounded by three rows of columns. The eastern portico gives access to a set of rooms. From the court a monumental archway leads into a high hall. Over the door of this gate stood a long Latin inscription speaking of its erection in the time of Caracalla, to be precise, in A.D. 211. On both sides of the hall are platforms with stairs leading up to them. From here the officers addressed the soldiers, here they sat as judges, here in all probability hearing was given by the generals to foreign embassies. Opposite the main entrance is a fine large room. There is a Latin inscription on the massive pillar to the left of the entrance in honour of Caracalla's brother Geta, a few months or perhaps days before his murder by that very brother. The inscription remained, but the statue in the niche above it was removed, and the name of Geta was erased. The central room of the hall was no doubt the shrine of the praetorium, where were worshipped the military gods, the emperors, and the standards (signa).[1] The two rooms on the right and left of this shrine may have belonged to the higher officers, while the two suites in the corners of the building were bureaux of the military administra-

---

[1] A recently discovered graffito seems to represent this sanctuary with two gladiators; it is perhaps a reminiscence of gladiatorial games given by the officers at the dedication of the praetorium.

1

2

XXXIII. THE ARISTOCRACY OF DURA IN THE
PARTHIAN PERIOD
(*for description see p.* 218)

XXXIV. DURA. WALL-PAINTING OF JULIUS TERENTIUS THE TRIBUNE
(*for description see p. 219*)

tion. In one of these suites was found a curious painted inscription in large letters: the sacred formula S.P.Q.R., standing for 'senatus populusque Romanus'. Inside the Q were good wishes for promotion extended to a freedman of the Empress Julia Domna and to five *adiutores* (military officials), probably accountants. In the building many carved, painted, and scratched inscriptions were found, which show that many a legion passed through Dura on its way to Parthia, and that many detachments succeeded each other as garrisons.

The future will show how the Roman soldiers of the garrison were housed, whether in special barracks or in private houses. We know definitely, however, that one of the first things which were done by the government for the soldiers was to build baths for them. One of these was excavated by us not far from the praetorium, another stood near the main gate, a third has been recently located by Prof. Hopkins. When one considers the district in which these were built, they seem to be exceedingly luxurious, since they were fitted with all the latest Roman appliances and with hot and cold water, with central heating, with the floors set upon pilasters, and the walls faced with clay pipes through which hot air could circulate. The room for undressing, which was probably also used as Dura's military club room, was decorated with frescoes, but unfortunately few fragments of them survived. All of these bore human heads. One cannot help marvelling at this quiet confidence of the Roman army, which, while neglecting all but the most essential repairs to the fortifications, built itself really fine bathrooms. And whence did men obtain water to fill the baths? Was it drawn by hand from the Euphrates in pails, or did they build themselves a conduit? Even more extraordinary is the manner in which they succeeded in maintaining the necessary supply of fuel. Wood was obviously used for heating the bath, for there are mounds of wood ashes close to the building; and in this connexion we may note the large quantity of wood which was also used for building purposes. Whence did they get this wood? Was it brought to Dura from the forests of the upper Euphrates, or did trees once grow in this now barren land?

The main duty of the Roman garrison was to protect the caravan routes and the strategic roads passing through Dura. The main point in the scheme of fortification for the protection of the Euphrates road was probably in and around the half-ruined citadel, whilst that for the protection of the Palmyra road was certainly situated at the main gate—a fine monumental structure which we examined in detail (XXVI). These gates are in themselves strong and impressive, consisting as they do of two double towers, two massive wooden doors, and an interior courtyard. Low doors connected the central courtyard of the interior with the towers, and there can be no doubt that in Roman times this courtyard was roofed. It is a most curious construction. A row of altars lines its walls and similar groups of altars stand by the gates connecting it with the town. Many of the altars bear inscriptions in Latin, Greek, and Palmyrene. Some reliefs were also found here, most of them representing Hercules (XXXI. 2).

Hundreds more inscriptions were found on the walls of the gates, covering all the lower parts of the walls, especially the northern. Most of these are cut or scratched on the stone; a few are painted or scratched on the plaster. Most are in Greek, a few in Latin, Palmyrene, or Safaitic Arabic. All are very short. The oldest contain the name and patronymic of the worshipper and sometimes the name of his country of origin. Many are names of local Europeans settled at Dura, many are Semitic. Later inscriptions bear in addition to the author's name the formula 'mnesthe', which means 'remember', placed before the name and date, and this same formula occurs in hundreds of Arabic inscriptions at Petra, at Hegra, at El-Ela, and in Sinai. 'Mnesthe' is without doubt the Greek translation of a Semitic formula. Another Semitic formula is translated by means of the Greek verb 'eucharisto' meaning 'I thank thee', coupled with the name of the goddess Tyche.

The fact that the majority of these inscriptions on the altars and the walls mention Tyche, the Fate or Fortuna of Dura, and that all the short inscriptions on the walls are undoubtedly religious in character, indicates that the main courtyard was a holy place, something in the nature of a temple dedicated to 'The City's Fortuna'. This deity was well known to the Iranians, who called her Hvareno, and to the Semites, who knew her by the name of Gad.

The religious character of the central arch of the gateway is also made clear by the fact that in Roman times at least the whole upper part of the walls was covered with paintings. These end at the level of a man's head, so that they would be out of reach of worshippers wishing to write up their names; the lower part of the walls was left bare for this purpose. Unfortunately very few of the paintings have survived, but the little which has remained—the legs of the standing figures only—proves that there were depicted here, as in the temple of the Palmyrene gods, sacrifices to the divine patroness of the city. Other deities may have been represented by her side, and in this connexion it is interesting to compare the frescoes in the temple of the Palmyrene gods, where the tribune and his soldiers are represented bringing sacrifices to the Palmyrene triad. At the feet of the deities are represented two Tyches—that of Dura and that of Palmyra. If this admirably preserved fresco dates from the third century A.D. (as is probable) it throws considerable light on the last Durene period of life, when the city became a part of the Palmyrene empire.

Then where, one asks, stood the temple of the Durene Tyche herself? Like all the inhabitants of the city she must have entered it by the gates, but where was her house? Was it one of the towers which flank the gates. We carefully examined both of them. In the northern one, whose walls bore no trace of painting, we found certain objects which may have once decorated such a temple. One is a small door bearing a coloured drawing of a figure of a Victory in purely Parthian style. She faces towards the right; in her hands she holds a palm branch and a crown, and she stands on a globe. This painted door was obviously once a part of a small wooden chapel, naos, aedicula, or tiny sanctuary with a double door. Inside it there stood either a small statue or a painted figure of the main deity. The building must have been similar to an Egyptian naos, or a triptych-chapel of the Middle Ages, and if it stood within the gates of the Holy of Holies, then its central figure and deity must most certainly have been that of Tyche, the empress of the world, depicted as being crowned by two Victories. It would be an apt symbol to find in a military sanctuary.

Another interesting object which we discovered in the tower was a wooden board bearing a Latin inscription, in which the subalterns of the cohort quartered there express their devotion to Septimius Lysias, a strategus of Dura, and to his family: they confide the portraits of this man, his wife and children (some of whom have Iranian, some Greek, and some Semitic names) to the care of the goddess. The portraits were undoubtedly painted on or inserted into (if painted on wood) the temple walls, in the naos belonging to her.

In spite of these discoveries, the nature of the towers does not suggest that the goddess' temple stood there, for they flank the gates in a military and not in a religious manner as they do also in the other defensive towers. Consequently the goddess' abode must be sought near the gates, but not necessarily inside them, and I think that she must have owned the small temple close to them which we discovered in our dig of 1929–30. In Roman times there stood opposite it, on the other side of the road, a small but very elegant bath, dedicated to the 'Great Tyche of the baths', as an inscription in mosaic found on the floor of the tepidarium told us. Moreover the greatest hoard of coins and jewels found in Dura was discovered in a small house standing close to what I suppose to be Tyche's temple. It is not impossible that the house belonged to priests of the temple and that the treasure was sacred to the goddess.

A careful study of the inscriptions on the walls of

the city gate, especially those of Roman date, reveals an interesting picture of Durian life. It becomes apparent that the soldiers of the Roman garrison ruled the town, and that the sanctuary at the gates belonged to them. It is the subalterns of the garrison who have expressed their devotion to the goddess in the most ornate of phrases; they are the beneficiaries and 'stators', the officers of the field gendarmerie. Since the time of Caracalla all had become Roman citizens, and each proudly adds his new name Aurelius to his Greek or Semitic name. All are placed under a tribune, the commander of the garrison, and this must be the man living in the palace on the redoubt whom we see sacrificing to the Palmyrene gods and to Tyche on the frescoes in their temple. He was certainly a Roman, not a Levantine, in origin as well as in name, and as such he was an infinitely greater personage than the semi-Greeks of Mesopotamia and Syria or the Aramaeans and Arabs who served under him in the army and composed Dura's civil population. Like many French officers of the present day, this Roman probably never came in contact with the local population, but lived the isolated life of a great man.

On the other hand the subalterns, his immediate inferiors, lived the same life as the local aristocrats, senators, magistrates, and other sons of rich and distinguished parents. Like their Parthian forerunners, these aristocrats were typical Levantines. When Septimius Severus raised Dura to the rank of a colony many of them became Roman citizens (as did their Palmyrene companions) and assumed the name of Septimius. But they were neither true Romans nor true Greeks, although their ancestors had certainly been Graeco-

Macedonian colonists. Their nationality is impossible to determine and, in one and the same family, the father will bear a Greek name, the wife a Semitic, and the children Greek, Iranian, or Semitic names.

A curious discovery which we made in 1930–1 throws some light on the problem of the occupations of these aristocrats. In a house standing on the main street, and close to the Roman triumphal arch which adorns it, we cleared a very interesting room. In this room there was a cupboard let into the most convenient side of the wall. It was definitely intended for books and papers. A series of shelves nailed to the walls, and a couple of niches, served a similar purpose. All the walls were carefully whitewashed and were found covered with inscriptions scratched in Greek. A special space amongst them was devoted to horoscopes, six of which all belonged to the same person—the fascination of astrology at this period must have been enormous. Interesting as these horoscopes are, the other texts are even more so, for they are the business diary of the owner of the house, a man named Nebuchelos, who lived in the third century A.D. In it are recorded all the transactions that he undertook. His occupations were varied: he was a land-agent, a moneylender, and a merchant. He was a ready purchaser of clothes and materials and the list of his acquisitions adorns his office walls. His son was called Abduchelos, but his son-in-law, to whom the horoscopes belong, proudly called himself Alexander the Macedonian. The third and fourth members of this company were Phraates, the Iranian, and Marabel, the Semite, both of them partners who had invested their capital in Nebuchelos' business enterprises.

A number of similar inscriptions were also found on the walls of other houses, all of them belonging to the later period of Dura. Not one of these contains any reference to the caravans and goods coming from or going to Parthia. All the business carried on by these merchants in the third century appears to have been in local transactions between themselves, often between small firms rather than individuals. This form of business is as characteristic of the ancient as of the modern East. The turnover involved was almost negligible, for the third century A.D. was a period of wars and general depression. Yet the houses in which these graffiti were found were large and rich; they were those of the aristocracy, half-Semitic, half-Macedonian, whose ancestors had lived in Parthian times and were much richer; rich enough, indeed, to have the walls of their temples decorated with frescoes; to have constructed 'oikoi' in many of these temples; to have bought therein seats of honour for their wives and to have made offerings of silver and of golden vessels to the divinities whom they worshipped.

The aristocracy remained the same, but it became poorer and less grand, and several families now came to live together in some rich but partially deserted house. They earned their living penny by penny and often they could not afford to buy paper, so that the transactions of Nebuchelos and his partners had to be entered (by the director of the company) on the plastered walls of his house. Obviously, hard times had set in, the only explanation for which is that caravan trade had ceased to enrich Dura. Its route must have been diverted some time in the third century, when the downfall of the Roman empire had

The Ruins of Dura

set in, and when Syria, after the death of Alexander Severus, lived in constant dread of a Persian invasion. We have already seen how the final Persian capture of Dura was the beginning of her end.

But one must not exaggerate; although Dura had ceased to be a rich caravan city, occasional caravans must still have visited her, for one can hardly suppose that all the names written on the gates are those of her inhabitants. Some of them are those of foreigners, probably camel drivers, who have gained immortality by writing up their names in Safaitic letters. In order to deal with these caravans and with the local import and export trade, 'tax-collectors', of whom we read in the Bible, sat at the gates. Inscriptions have made us familiar with all the members of one family of the third century, for the profession—not greatly esteemed in the East—was hereditary. They collected customs-dues which are called in the inscriptions by the hybrid name of 'telos portas', that is to say 'gate tax', and were ardent worshippers of the local Tyche, on whom depended the direction of trade and of caravans towards the city gates. They were assisted in their work by some kind of porters, 'pyloroi', who, it appears, levied a tax from all those who passed through. The police at the gates were also kept busy by travellers and caravans, for it must have been they who called themselves 'beneficiaries' and 'stators' in the inscriptions and so rendered themselves immortal. If the tax-collectors and the porters were the first to clean the pockets of travellers entering the town, the police came next. They certainly did not hold their hands whilst they cross-questioned each visitor 'who he was or whence and why he came'. Philostratus, the biographer of Apollonius of Tyana, magician and saint, has described them to us and told us of the miseries travellers had to endure at their hands before they were allowed to enter a Parthian town.

At the close of the third century Dura's new masters, the Persians, the successors of the Parthians, appear for a short time. We have already stated that they did not stay there long—for some two or three years only. Nevertheless, we found a most interesting testimony of their visit in one of the houses which we excavated.

Whilst working on a private house my pupil, Mr. Alan Little, found traces of a large painting on the end wall of a vast reception room. A thorough study revealed that it was part of a large composition which had once almost covered the entire wall and which probably reproduced a woven carpet on which was depicted a battle. In accordance with the principles of Persian warfare, as we see it depicted in art and literature, this battle is represented as a series of isolated combats and the inscriptions written in Pahlevi at the side of the figures tell us who the victorious heroes are (xxxv). One of them is called Ormuzd, the son, another Ardashir, while a third bears the title characteristic of members of the reigning house of Sasanian Persia.[1] In the painting the battle is being watched by a number of figures seated on couches placed in the centre of the picture, who represent either gods or ancestors of the fighting warriors. If we assume that this picture dates from the third century, it must certainly represent one

---

[1] These inscriptions were deciphered by experts in the Iranian tongues, Professor Pagliaro of the University of Rome, Professor Benveniste of the Sorbonne, and Professor Torrey of Yale.

FIG. 4. General view of the early Sasanian fresco showing a battle between Persians and Romans, the Persians being victorious.

of the great battles of the time of Ardashir or Shapur, very probably that fought at Edessa, in the course of which Shapur captured Valerian. It is extraordinary that such a document should have been discovered in an unimportant house at Dura.

Here I shall say nothing of the importance of this fresco in the study of Sasanian painting nor shall I

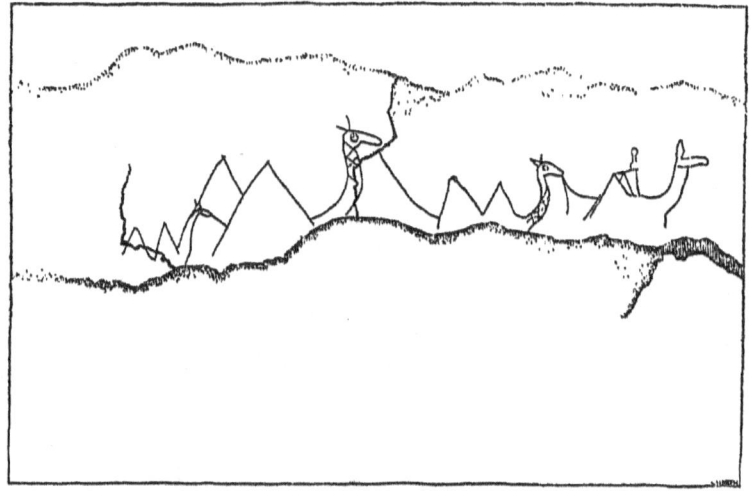

Fig. 5. Graffito showing a caravan in Dura.

speak of the significance of Dura in a study of Parthian and Sasanian art, though much material, not only relative to architecture and painting but also to other art, has been brought to light by our excavations. The curtain which has obscured so much of the history and principles of Parthian art is at last rising and our knowledge of the Sasanian period is becoming gradually more complete. Though we cannot attempt to give a general picture of Parthian art here, we may note the first thing which our recent work has taught us, namely that it is entirely wrong to consider Parthian art as a mere barbarian copy of Greek.

I will draw the attention of the reader to one point only. The most striking feature in the artistic life of Dura is without doubt the role which painting and drawing played in the life of the city. All the temples were painted. The frescoes represent gods and goddesses, mythological scenes, and scenes of sacrifice per-

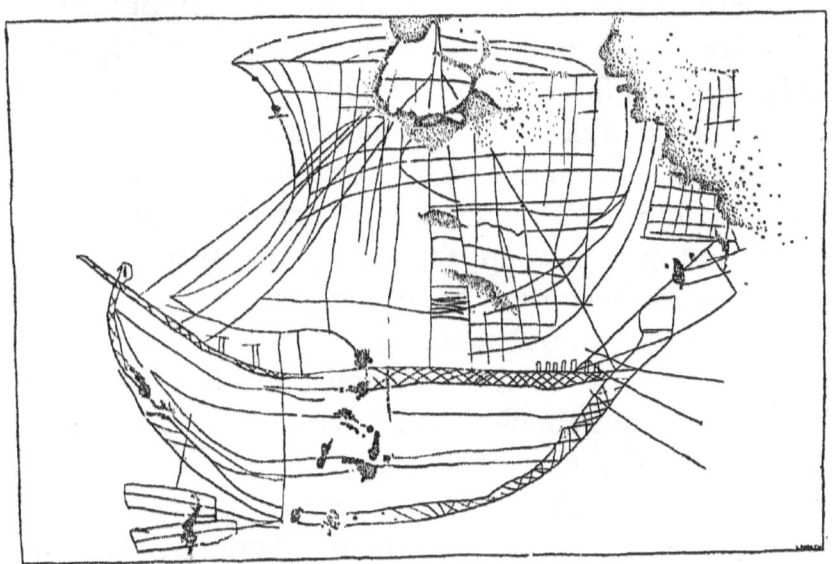

FIG. 6. Graffito showing a Euphrates ship. Such ships were probably used for transporting both goods and soldiers for the Roman armies.

formed by their donors. There were at Dura some painters who had the reputation of being great artists. They themselves expected to be remembered by many future generations, for they never failed to sign their pictures with their full names. This obviously had a religious motive. They wanted the god or the goddess whom or whose worshippers they painted to remember them for ever. Yet this is only one part of the picture; there is a great pride in these names, boldly written in large letters under the artists' works in a spirit very similar to that of the Renaissance painters.

Alongside the temples, the private houses shone with gay colours. Sometimes the walls were painted, sometimes they were covered with painted bricks or tiles, and often perhaps hung with fine rugs and carpets which often would not limit themselves to geometric, floral, or animal patterns, but would represent scenes of divine and human life. And those anonymous artists who drew with ink, or scratched with the help of a knife, various figures, objects, and scenes on the walls of houses, temples, and public buildings, were also under the influence both of the temple- and of the house-painters. Their reflected art deserves careful study and examination, for it may reveal to us many a trait in the history of art of the period which would otherwise remain unknown.

The products of the 'pictores Durani' or of the painters of the 'school of Dura' have never been made the object of serious study by any specialist in the history of art. Both Breasted and Cumont devoted very instructive articles to them. They pointed out the obvious derivation of much Byzantine painting from this source. But there is another question. Does the Mesopotamian school of painting, religious or secular, derive from Semitic, Babylonian, Assyrian, or Phoenician sources, or from the otherwise unknown Syrian and Anatolian pictorial art, or from the painting which made the Iranian people famous but of which we know very little during the interval between the Achaemenids and the Sasanians.

This is not the place to discuss such a problem at length. I must, however, draw attention to one point. In the secular art of Dura there is a great amount of life and movement. While the religious scenes are

1

2

XXXV. DURA: PARTS OF A SASANIAN WALL-PAINTING
Discovered in a private house (the House of the Frescoes) in Dura

stiff and 'ritual', the figures of galloping horsemen, of hunting riders, of running animals, are dynamic and more full of life than similar figures in Assyrian art. A favourite motive of the painters of Dura is the flying gallop. Now the flying gallop occurs for a short period in Aegean art, only to disappear completely from the later Greek horizon. Yet the same motive seems to have existed in all the periods of development of Persian, and in general of Iranian, art. We see it in full vigour under the Sasanians and much earlier, as a new motive, certainly of foreign origin, in the Chinese art of the Han period. Dura fills the gap between China and Sasanian Persia and shows that the Parthians cultivated this motive and made full use of it. Contemporaneously the same motive was well known to Sarmatian artists both in Siberia and in South Russia.

If therefore the religious art of Dura remains for a while a problem, its secular art seems to owe its existence to Iranian inspiration, and to have the right to be called a branch of the Iranian art of the Parthian period, just as another contemporary branch of the same art is known to us in South Russia and Siberia.

Let me now sum up my remarks on the city of Dura. Seven years of excavation at Dura have paved the way for anybody who wishes to see and learn something new and not to graft a new world on to old patterns. If we are able to continue digging there for another two or three years, Dura's contribution to the picture of this new world will be complete (although obviously not the picture itself!). By a new world I mean the world which was the cradle of the great new civilizations growing up in the Near East after the disintegration of the Roman Empire: that of

Sasanian Persia and the still more important Mohammedan Arabs, both of which civilizations so powerfully influenced medieval Eastern and Western Europe. Further excavations in Mesopotamia, Syria, and the Iranian lands will probably replace the poor provincial monuments of Dura by a richer and more perfect series, but they can hardly yield anything entirely new and unexpected. Her 'Tyche' gave Dura the luck to be the first Mesopotamian city of the Hellenistic, Parthian, and Roman times to be discovered, and the privilege of drawing the attention of the learned world to many problems hitherto unrealized and unformulated. And this, together with the contribution which each well-conducted excavation yields towards enlarging our knowledge of the ancient world in general, is her greatest bequest to history.

DESCRIPTION OF PLATES XXVI–XXXIV

XXVI. DURA. THE MAIN GATE

1. The main gate seen from the desert.
2. The main gate and the main street of Dura. To the left stairs leading to the late glacis. On the left side of the street are the remains of columns which formed a portico before the entrance into a bath dedicated, according to an inscription in mosaic, to the 'Fortune of the Bath'. To the right remains of a small temple probably dedicated to the 'Fortune of Dura'.

XXVII. DURA

1. The main street in the centre of the city. In the foreground foundations of a triumphal arch. To the left a base which bore a statue of a high Roman official of Syria. To the left towards the Euphrates the entrance into the house of the Archives.
2. Central court of the palace-fortress of the citadel. The court was surrounded by stone columns. The walls were built of large square stones.

XXVIII. DURA

1. Ruins of the temple of Atargatis. In the foreground the main entrance. In the centre the temple-court with a large altar in the middle. Behind the altar the entrance into the theatre-like square room with seats on both sides, each of which was owned by a prominent lady of the city. In front of the entrance into this room are altars and a column. Behind the stepped room the real sanctuary with the cult-image.

2. The little theatre in the back of the court of the temple of Artemis Nanaia. Perhaps the meeting-place of the 'boulé' (municipal council) of Dura.

XXIX. DURA

1. General view of the temple of the Palmyrene gods. In the foreground the temple-court with the altar in the centre. To the left a large throne-like seat or altar. Behind the central altar of the court the main entrance into the 'sancta sanctorum' which was richly adorned with frescoes (see Pls. XXXIII and XXXIV). To the left a tower of the fortifications built on the foundations of the early sanctuary.

2. Court of the corresponding sanctuary in the SW. corner of the fortifications. In the foreground five altars. In the background the late glacis which covered the rest of the sanctuary.

XXX. DURA. THE GODS

1. Fragment of a plaster statue of Artemis (Graeco-Parthian style).

2. Atargatis and Hadad. Bas-relief found in the ruins of the temple of Atargatis. The divine couple are shown seated on chairs in a little shrine, the columns of which are adorned with the heads of Hadad's sacred animal—the bull. Hadad is shown in a richly embroidered dress with the tiara or calathos on his head and holding a thunderbolt in his right hand. Atargatis, who is represented as bigger than Hadad, is seated between lions, her sacred animals. In her right hand she holds flowers (?). In the background, between the two gods, is a standard which may be that of the gods or a Roman military standard.

XXXI. DURA. THE GODS

1. Parthian god (?). Fragment of a bas-relief. The god is shown wearing the Parthian head-dress, armed with a sword and a spear.

2. Nemesis. Bas-relief found in the main gate at Dura. A man is shown burning incense on an altar before the goddess Nemesis with her symbols—the griffon and the wheel. In Greece Nemesis was the

goddess of Justice and Vengeance. Between the man and the goddess is shown the bust of the great sun-god who sees all and knows all. The dedication (in Greek and Palmyrene) states that the dedicant was one of the great merchants of Palmyra, Julius Aurelius Malochas. The date is A.D. 228.

XXXII. DURA. THE GODS

1. Stele showing front view of the god Aphlad standing on the backs of two winged lions, each with a bell on its neck. He wears a calathos on his head, a torc on his neck, high boots, a Hellenistic cuirass and under the cuirass a chiton and trousers. The centre of the cuirass is adorned with a star surrounded by crosses. He is leaning on a peculiar sceptre and holds in his right hand a thunderbolt. The inscription states that the god is 'the god called Aphlad of the village Anath on the Euphrates' (the modern Anah). A priest is performing an incense sacrifice to the god over a thymiaterium. The stele was found in a shrine in the temple in the SW. corner of the fortification. An inscription found near the chapel speaks of a religious association of which the dedicant was a member and is dated A.D. 54.

2. One side of a theatre-like room in the temple of Artemis recently discovered at Dura. Near the entrance to this *salle aux gradins* (it is the third discovered at Dura, the other two being those of the temple of Artemis and the temple of Hadad and Atargatis) stands *in situ* a stele. On this stele Artemis is shown, seated in an arm-chair between two lions in a little shrine with a dove in the pediment. She wears an Oriental head-dress (a sort of Phrygian cap or better a bashlyk) and is being crowned by a priest. Before the stele is an altar and a thymiaterium. Each seat in the room bears the name of its owner, all of whom are women belonging to the most prominent families in Dura. The dates of the inscriptions cover the whole of the 1st cent. A.D., the latest being A.D. 102.

XXXIII. THE ARISTOCRACY OF DURA IN THE PARTHIAN PERIOD

1. Konon and two priests performing a sacrifice. Part of the fresco found in the temple of the Palmyrene gods. The rest of the fresco shows the Semitic wife of Konon, Bithnanaia, and their family.

2. Iabsymsos and his son (Semites), member of the municipal council of Dura, and Otes and his boy Gorsak (Parthian names) performing a sacrifice to the five great Palmyrene gods. Part of a fresco found by Cumont in the temple of the Palmyrene gods. The rest of the fresco shows the figures of the gods.

XXXIV

Julius Terentius the tribune and eight of the non-commissioned officers of his cohort, the donors of the fresco, sacrificing to the three Palmyrene gods (Bel in the centre, Yarhibol to the right, Aglibol to the left) and to the Tyche of Dura and the Tyche of Palmyra (the last with the lion of Atargatis). Note the standard-bearer of the cohort, the priest (behind the tribune), and the mass of the common soldiers.

BIBLIOGRAPHY

CHAPTER I

A. *History of Trade in Antiquity in General*

1. E. Speck, *Handelsgeschichte des Altertums*, i-iii (1900–6).
2. Art. 'Handel und Industrie', by Gummerus in Pauly-Wissowa-Kroll, *Realencyclopaedie der klassischen Wissenschaften*, ix, pp. 1454 ff.
3. Art. 'Mercatura', by R. Cagnat et M. Besnier in Daremberg et Saglio, *Dictionnaire des antiquités grecques et romaines*, iii, 2, pp. 1772 ff.
4. H. Schaal, *Vom Tauschhandel zum Welthandel*, 1931.

B. *The Caravan Trade, the Caravan and Modern Arabia*

1. C. M. Doughty, *Travels in Arabia Deserta*, i–ii (originally published in 1888); cf. C. J. Kraemer, Jr., 'Light from Arabia on Classical Things', *The Classical Weekly*, xxii (1929), pp. 113 ff.
2. P. H. Lammens, 'La Mecque à la veille de l'Hégire', *Mélanges de l'Université Saint-Joseph de Beyrouth*, ix. 3 (1924).
3. P. Huvelin, *Essai historique sur les droits des marchés et des foires*, 1897.

C. *Caravan Trade in Various Epochs*

(a) *Early Babylonia and Assyria*
1. C. L. Woolley, *The Sumerians*, 1928.
2. Sydney Smith, *Early History of Assyria*, 1928.

(b) *Later Babylonia and Assyria*
3. B. Meissner, *Babylonien und Assyrien*, i, 1920; ii, 1925.

(c) *Early Cappadocia*
4. J. Lewy, article 'Kappadokische Tontafeln' in M. Ebert, *Reallexikon der Vorgeschichte*, vol. vi (1926), pp. 212 ff.; cf. A. T. Clay, *Letters and Transactions from Cappadocia*, 1927 (fine specimens of Cappadocian business documents).

(d) *Early India*
5. Sir John Marshall, *Mohenjo-daro and the Indus Civilization*, i–iii, 1931.

(e) *Early Arabia*
6. D. Nielsen, *Handbuch der altarabischen Altertumskunde, I. Die altarabische Kultur*, 1927.

7. Inscriptions of Ancient Arabia: *Corpus Inscriptionum Semiticarum*, pars quarta, tom. i–iii, and *Répertoire d'épigraphie sémitique*, vols. i–v.
8. Coins of Ancient Arabia: G. F. Hill, British Museum, *Catalogue of the Greek Coins of Arabia, Mesopotamia, and Persia*, 1922, pp. xliv ff., and pp. 45 ff.

(*f*) *Persia*
9. E. Meyer, *Geschichte des Altertums*, vol. iii, 1901; cf. vol. ii, 3 (second posthumous edition in preparation).

(*g*) *Syria and Palestine before Alexander*
10. A. T. Olmsted, *History of Palestine and Syria to the Macedonian Conquest*, 1931.

(*h*) *The Hellenistic period*
11. Summary and bibliography: M. Rostovtzeff, 'The Spread of Hellenistic Commerce', *Cambridge Ancient History*, viii, pp. 651 ff.; cf. pp. 561 ff. (Pergamum), pp. 619 ff. (Rhodes and Delos), and vii, pp. 109 ff. (Egypt), and pp. 155 ff. (Syria and the East, with map of the trade-routes by W. W. Tarn); cf. M. Rostovtzeff, 'Foreign Commerce in Ptolemaic Egypt', *Journal of Economic and Business History*, 1932.

(*i*) *The Roman times*
12. Tenney Frank, *An Economic History of Rome*, 2nd ed., 1927.
13. M. Rostovtzeff, *Social and Economic History of the Roman Empire*, 1926 (German edition under the title *Gesellschaft und Wirtschaft im römischen Kaiserreich*, 1930; Italian in course of publication).

(*k*) *History of Syria in Roman times*
14. J. Dobiaš, *Histoire de la province romaine de Syrie*, Part I: *Jusqu'à la séparation de la Judée*, 1924 (in Czecho-Slovakian with French résumé, a French edition of the whole work in four volumes in preparation).

CHAPTER II. PETRA

A. *Inscriptions*

1. *Corpus Inscriptionum Semiticarum*, pars secunda, tom. i, fasc. iii (here on pp. 305 ff. a bibliography to the year 1889 and on pp. 181 ff. sketch of the history of Petra and the Nabataeans).
2. *Répertoire d'épigraphie sémitique* (*passim*).

3. J. Cantineau, *Le Nabatéen. I. Notions générales—écriture—grammaire*, 1930 (continuation in preparation).
4. Du Mesnil du Buisson et R. Mouterde, 'Inscriptions grecques de Beyrouth. I. Dedicace à la Tyche de Petra', *Mélanges de la Faculté Orientale, Université Saint-Joseph (Beyrouth)*, vii (1921), pp 382 ff.

B. Coins

1. R. Dussaud, *Journal asiatique*, 1904, pp. 189–238 ff.
2. G. F. Hill, British Museum, *Catalogue of the Greek Coins of Arabia, Mesopotamia, and Persia*, 1922, pp. xii ff. and pp. xxxvii ff., pp. 1 ff., and pp. 34 ff.

C. Ruins and History

1. H. Vincent, 'Les Nabatéens', *Revue biblique*, vii (1898), pp. 567 ff.
2. R. Brünnow und A. von Domaszewski, *Die Provincia Arabia*, i–iii, 1904–7, esp. I, Abschnitt III.
3. Libbey and Hoskins, *The Jordan Valley and Petra*, 1905.
4. M. Khvostov, *History of the Oriental Trade of Graeco-Roman Egypt*, 1907, pp. 248 ff. (in Russian).
5. E. Schürer, *Geschichte des jüdischen Volkes im Zeitalter Jesu Christi*, 4th ed., i, pp. 726 ff.
6. A. Musil, *Arabia Petraea*, i–iii, 1907.
7. G. Dalman, *Petra und seine Felsheiligtümer*, 1908.
8. H. Kohl, *Kasr Firaun in Petra*, 1910.
9. RR. PP. Jaussen et Savignac, *Mission archéologique en Arabie. I. De Jérusalem au Hedjaz, Medain Salah*, 1909; *II. El-Ela, d'Hegra à Teima, Harrah de Tebouk*, 1914.
10. H. Thiersch, *An den Rändern des römischen Reiches*, 1911.
11. G. Dalman, *Neue Petra-Forschungen und der Heilige Fels von Jerusalem*, 1912.
12. H. Guthe, 'Die griechisch-römischen Städte des Ostjordanlandes' (*Das Land der Bibel*, ii. 5, 1918).
13. W. Bachmann, C. Watzinger, Th. Wiegand, *Petra*, 1921.
14. Sir Alexander B. W. Kennedy, *Petra, its History and Monuments*, 1925.
15. A. Kammerer, *Pétra et la Nabatène. L'Arabie Pétrée et les Arabes du nord dans leurs rapports avec la Syrie et la Palestine jusqu'à l'Islam*, 1929–30.
16. W. W. Tarn, 'Ptolemy II and Arabia', *Journal of Egyptian Archaeology*, xv, 1929, pp. 9 ff.

17. R. L. Robinson, *The Sarcophagus of an Ancient Civilization: Petra, Edom, and the Edomites*, 1930.
18. G. Horsfield and Agnes Conway, 'Historical and Topographical Notes on Edom; with an account of the First Excavations at Petra', *The Geographical Journal*, lxxvi. 5, 1930, pp. 369 ff.
19. G. Dalman, *The Khazneh at Petra*. Palestine Exploration Fund. Annual 1911.
20. J. H. Mordtmann, 'Ein Nabatäer im Safäerlande', *Klio*, xxv, 1932, pp. 729 ff.
21. Clermont-Ganneau, 'Les Nabatéens en Égypte', *Rev. de l'histoire des religions*, viii (1919), pp. 1 ff.

CHAPTER III. JERASH

A. *Inscriptions*

1. H. Lucas, *Mittheilungen des Deutschen Palaestinavereins*, 1901.
2. R. Cagnat, *Inscriptiones Graecae ad res Romanas pertinentes*, iii, nos. 1341–77.
3. P. Perdrizet, *Revue biblique*, xiii (1900), pp. 432 ff.
4. Cheesman, *Journal of Roman Studies*, iv (1914), pp. 13 ff.
5. F. M. Abel, *Revue biblique*, xxxvi (1927), pp. 249 ff.; xxxvii (1928), pp. 257 ff.; cf. xxii (1909), pp. 448 ff.
6. A. H. M. Jones, *Journal of Roman Studies*, xviii (1928), pp. 144 ff., and xx (1930), pp. 43 ff.

B. *Coins*

7. G. F. Hill, British Museum, *Catalogue of the Greek Coins of Arabia, Mesopotamia, and Persia*, 1922, pp. xxxiii ff., and pp. 31 ff.

C. *Ruins and History*

8. Bibliography of the descriptions of the early voyages to Jerash in Guthe, *Gerasa*, p. 63, note 2.
9. Prince S. Abamelek-Lazarev, *Djerash*. Archaeological Research, 1897 (in Russian).
10. G. Schuhmacher, *Dscherasch*, 1902.
11. H. Guthe, *Gerasa* (*Das Land der Bibel*, iii. 1–2, 1919).
12. J. W. Crowfoot, *Churches at Jerash*, British School of Archaeology in Jerusalem, Suppl. Papers, iii. 1931.
13. Accounts on current excavations in *Quarterly Statements of the Palestine Exploration Fund* (to 1931), and in *Bulletin of the American Schools of Oriental Research* (from 1931).

Bibliography

CHAPTERS IV AND V. PALMYRA

A. *Inscriptions*

1. *Corpus Inscriptionum Semiticarum*, pars secunda, vol. ii, fasc. iii (cf. *Répertoire d'épigraphie sémitique, passim*).
2. J. B. Chabot, *Choix d'inscriptions de Palmyre*, 1922.
3. J. Cantineau, *Inventaire des inscriptions de Palmyre*, 1930 ff. (in course of publication, fasc. i–vii ready in 1931); cf. J. Cantineau, 'Fouilles de Palmyre', *Mélanges de l'Institut Français de Damas*, i, 1929.
4. The Greek inscriptions of Palmyra: Lebas-Waddington, *Inscriptions grecques et latines*, &c., *VI, Syrie*; W. Dittenberger, *Orientis Graeci Inscriptiones Selectae*, nos. 629–51; R. Cagnat, *Inscriptiones Graecae ad res Romanas pertinentes*, iii, nos. 1026–56.
5. RR. PP. A. Poidebard et R. Mouterde, *Comptes rendus de l'Académie des Inscriptions*, 1930, pp. 183 ff., and 'La Voie antique des caravanes entre Palmyre et Hit au second siècle ap. J.-C.', in *Syria*, xii (1931), pp. 101 ff.
6. J. Cantineau, 'Textes palmyréniens provenant de la fouille du temple de Bel', *Syria*, xii (1931), pp. 116 ff.

B. *Topography and Physical Conditions*

7. A. Musil, American Geographical Society: Oriental Explorations and Studies, no. 3, *The Middle Euphrates*; No. 4, *Palmyrena*, 1927–8 (cf. E. Honigmann, 'Neue Forschungen über den syrischen Limes', *Klio*, xxv (1932), pp. 132 ff.).
8. E. Huntington, *Palestine and its Transformation*, 1911.
9. J. Partsch, 'Palmyra, eine historisch-klimatische Studie', *Berichte und Verhandlungen der Sächsischen Akademie der Wissenschaften, Phil.-hist. Kl.*, lxxiv (1922), pp. 1 ff.
10. G. Carle, 'De l'alimentation en eau de Palmyre dans les temps actuels et anciens', *La Géographie*, xl (1923), pp. 153 ff.
11. R. Dussaud, *Topographie historique de la Syrie antique et médiévale*, 1927.

C. *Ruins and History*

12. On the early reproductions of the monuments of Palmyra F. von Duhn, *Jahrbuch des Deutschen Archaeologischen Instituts, Archaeologischer Anzeiger*, 1894, pp. 110 ff. (oil-painting of

Palmyra of 1693 by G. Hofsted in the University of Amsterdam, cf. the drawings published in *Philosophical Transactions*, xix (1695–7), pp. 83 ff.), and W. Anderson, *Stralsunder Tageblatt*, 17. 3, 1927 (on the drawings of Cornelius Loos).
13. R. Wood, *The Ruins of Palmyra*, 1753.
14. Prince S. Abamelek-Lazarev, *Palmyra*. Archaeological Research, 1884 (in Russian).
15. Th. Mommsen, *Römische Geschichte*, v, pp. 413 ff.
16. L. Piccolo, 'L'ascesa politica di Palmira', *Rivista di Storia Antica*, x (1905), pp. 75 ff.
17. S. B. Murray, *Hellenistic Architecture in Syria*, 1921.
18. Ch. Clermont-Ganneau, 'Odeinat et Vaballat, rois de Palmyre, et leur titre romain de corrector', *Revue biblique*, xxix (1920), pp. 382 ff.
19. J. B. Chabot (see No. 2).
20. P. Dhorme, 'Palmyre dans les textes assyriens', *Revue biblique*, xxxiii (1924), pp. 106 ff.
21. A. Gabriel, 'Recherches archéologiques à Palmyre', *Syria*, vii (1926), pp. 71 ff.
22. J. G. Février, *Essai sur l'histoire politique et économique de Palmyre*, 1931.
23. J. G. Février, *La Religion des Palmyréniens*, 1931.[1]
24. Th. Wiegand, *Palmyra, Ergebnisse der deutschen Expeditionen von 1902 und 1917*, Berlin, Keller (in preparation).
25. M. Rostovtzeff, *Les Inscriptions caravanières de Palmyre*, Mélanges Glotz, 1932.
26. M. Rostovtzeff, 'The Caravan-gods of Palmyra', *Journal of Roman Studies*, xxii (1932).

D. Art

27. H. Ingholt, *Studier over Palmyrensk Skulptur*, 1928 (cf. idem, 'The oldest known grave-relief from Palmyra', *Acta Archaeologica*, i (1930), pp. 191 ff., and *Syria*, xi (1930), pp. 242 ff.).
28. J. Strzygowski, *Orient oder Rom*, 1901.
29. B. V. Farmakowsky, 'Painting in Palmyra', *Bulletin of the Russian Archaeological Institute in Constantinople*, viii. 3 (1903) (in Russian).

[1] The two books of M. Février came into my hands too late to be utilized in the text of my book.

CHAPTERS IV AND VI. DURA

A. *Inscriptions, Parchments, and Papyri* found at Dura are published in the books and articles quoted under B

B. *Ruins and History*

1. J. Breasted, *Oriental Forerunners of Byzantine Painting*, 1924.
2. F. Cumont, *Fouilles de Doura-Europos*, Text and Atlas, 1922-3.
3. P. V. C. Baur, M. I. Rostovtzeff, and A. R. Bellinger, *The Excavations at Dura Europos*, Preliminary Report, i, 1929; ii, 1931; iii, 1932.
4. M. Rostovtzeff, 'Les Inscriptions de Doura-Europos (Salihiyeh)', *Comptes rendus de l'Académie des Inscriptions*, 1928, pp. 232 ff.
5. M. Rostovtzeff, 'Yale's Work at Dura', *Bulletin of the Associates in Fine Arts at Yale University*, 1930, February.
6. H. T. Rowell, 'Inscriptions de Doura-Europos', *Comptes rendus de l'Académie des Inscriptions*, 1930, pp. 265 ff.
7. M. Rostovtzeff and C. B. Welles, 'A parchment contract of loan from Dura-Europos on the Euphrates', *Yale Classical Studies*, ii, 1931, pp. 3 ff.
8. J. Johnson, *Dura Studies*, University of Pennsylvania, 1932.
9. P. Koschaker, 'Ueber einige griechische Rechtsurkunden aus den östlichen Randgebieten des Hellenismus', *Abhandlungen der Phil.-hist. Kl. der Sächsischen Akademie der Wissenschaften*, xlii (1931), Nr. 1.
10. A. R. Bellinger, 'The Temples at Dura-Europos, and certain early churches', *Seminarium Kondakovianum*, iv (1931), pp. 173 ff.
11. A. R. Bellinger, 'Two Roman hoards from Dura-Europos', *Numismatic Notes and Monographs* (The American Numismatic Society), no. 49, 1931.
12. M. Rostovtzeff et C. B. Welles, 'La "Maison des Archives" à Doura-Europos', *Comptes rendus de l'Académie des Inscriptions*, 1931, pp. 162 ff.
13. M. Rostovtzeff et A. Little, 'La "Maison des Fresques" de Doura-Europos', *Mémoires de l'Académie des Inscriptions*, xliii.
14. C. Hopkins, 'The Palmyrene Gods at Dura-Europos', *Journal of American Oriental Society*, li (1931), pp. 119 ff.

INDEX

Abduchelos, 207.
Abgar, 99.
Abu Kemal, 153, 169.
Aelanitic Gulf, 33.
Afghanistan, 24.
Africa, 5 ff., 19, 25, 42, 47.
African goods, 13.
Aglibol, 137, 139, 141, 150, 155, 183, 219.
Ahuramazda, 141.
Aila, 27.
Akaba, 27, 65.
Akkad, 8, 10 f.
Aleppo, 14, 16, 21, 32, 91, 95, 159 ff.
Alexander the Great, 23 ff., 55, 93, 106, 156.
Alexander Jannaeus, 64.
Alexander Severus, 110 f., 113, 115, 119, 146, 181, 209.
Alexandria, 20, 24, 27, 56 f., 61, 67 f., 89, 146.
Allat, 44 f., 138, 151.
Amman, vi f., 31, 33 ff., 46, 72, 74 f., 130. *See also* Philadelphia.
Ammonite rulers, 58 ff.
Ammonites, 61.
Amorites, 19.
Anath, 106, 186, 218.
Anderson, Prof., 121.
Andrae, 97.
Andurain, Vicomtesse d', 147.
Angell, Prof. J. R., 158.
Anthony, 29, 98, 101 ff., 106.
Antigonus, the one-eyed, 24, 56.
Antioch, 25, 27, 94 f., 117, 161.
Antioch of the Gerasenes, *see* Jerash.
Antiochus I, 25.
Antiochus III, 25, 62, 64, 96, 99.
Antiochus IV, Epiphanes, 26, 62, 99.
Apalad, *see* Aphlad.
Apamea, 161.
Apamea-Zeugma, 95.
Aphlad, 106, 186 f., 218.
Apollo, 198.
Apollonius, 39 f.
Apollonius of Tyana, 210.
Arabia, 8, 12 f., 17 f., 20, 22 ff., 31, 33, 49.
—, climate of, 3.

Arabia, Felix, i, 12, 13, 27, 30.
—, geography of, 1.
—, South, 6, 13 f., 17, 55.
Arabian desert, 1, 5.
— trade, 21, 30.
Arabs, 6, 12, 30, 34.
Aradus, 16.
Aramaean language, 133.
Aramaeans, 22, 51, 61, 134.
architecture at Petra, 44 f.
Ardashir, 116, 212.
Armenia, 24.
Arsacids, 65, 115.
Arsinoe, 59.
Arsu, 112, 131, 138 ff., 150 f.
Artaxerxes Ochus, 22.
Artemis, 198, 217.
Artemis, temple of, at Dura, 82, 173, 178, 180 f., 193, 218.
Artemis, temple of, at Jerash, 70, 78 ff., 88.
Artemis Azzanathkona, 106, 154, 182, 193.
Artemis Nanaia, 105, 178, 180 f., 182, 193, 217.
Asclepius, 138.
Ashur, 97.
Ashurbanipal, 17.
Asia Minor, 1, 6 ff., 20.
Assyria, 10, 14 ff., 22.
Assyrian empire, 15 ff., 21.
— legal code, 9.
— ornament, 44.
Astarte, 137 f.
Astrabad, 7.
Atargatis, 78, 105, 131, 138, 151, 182, 217 f.
Atargatis, temple of, at Dura, 173, 178, 180, 193, 218.
Athtar-Dhû-Gabdim, 22.
Attalus, 102.
Augustus, 29 f., 32, 50, 66, 102 f., 127.
Augustus, policy of, in the Near East, 106 f.
Aurelian, 35, 118 f.
Avidius Cassius, 110.
Azizu, 112, 131, 138 ff., 151.
Azzanathkona, *see* Artemis Azzanathkona.

Index

Baalbek, 100, 178. *See also* Heliopolis.
Baal Samin, 131, 137, 183.
Bab-el-Mandeb, 12.
Bab-es-Sik, at Petra, 47.
Babylon, 109.
Babylonia, 6 ff., 15, 134.
Babylonian gods, at Palmyra, 138 ff.
Babylonians, 53, 55.
Bacon, Prof., 72.
Bactria, 24.
Baghdad, 17.
Balkan peninsula, 177.
Barlaas, contract of, 196.
barter, 4, 9 f.
Baur, Prof., 191.
Bedouin, 7, 12, 39, 42, 45, 52.
Bel, 127, 136 f., 140 f., 150, 155, 183.
Bell, Gertrude, 155.
Bender, 121.
Bene Komara, 135.
Bene Mattabol, 135.
Benveniste, Prof., 210.
Beragish, 22.
Berenice, 59.
Bet-shur, 59.
Bible, 18.
Bithynia, 24.
Black Sea, 19 f.
Blake, R. P., 35.
Bosra, 29, 31, 33 ff., 51, 64 f.
Breasted, Prof. J., 155, 183, 214.
Bulla Regia, 47.
Byblos, 10, 16.
byssos, 57.
Byzantine caravan trade, 70.
— period, 35, 48.

Caligula, 32.
Cambridge, Fitzwilliam Museum, 41.
Canatha, 31, 86.
Cappadocia, 6, 9, 13, 24.
—, mines of, 10.
Caracalla, 110 ff., 181, 200, 206.
Carchemish, 148.
Carrhae, 101.
Caspian Sea, 7.
Cassius, Dio, 98, 101.
Catabania, 13 f.
Caucasus, 22.
Chaî al Qaum, 138.

Chaldaeans, 22.
Chalkis, 28.
— (Lebanon), 100.
Charax, 27, 65, 109, 143, 145.
Charles XII of Sweden, 121.
China, 19.
Chinese art at Dura, 215.
Chrysorrous, 63 f., 82.
Cilicia, mines of, 10.
Cimmerian Bosphorus, 24.
Circassians, 39.
Claudius, 32.
Colonnaded courts, origin of, 132.
Commagene, 99, 148.
Commodus, 69.
Constantine, 40.
Conway, Miss A., 40, 47.
Crassus, 98, 102, 130, 190.
Crete, 15.
Crowfoot, 72, 89.
Ctesiphon, 114, 140.
Cumont, Prof. F., 114, 155, 157 ff., 167, 169, 171, 174 f., 178, 182 f., 192, 214, 218.
Cyprus, 15.
Cyrene, 102.

Dacia, 109, 139.
Damascus, 11 f., 14, 16 f., 21, 28, 31 f., 61, 65 f., 68, 91 ff., 100, 134, 143, 146, 159 f.
Damascus Museum, 183.
Darius, 19, 21, 23.
Dawkins, 122.
'Dea Syria', 178.
Deir es Zor, 153, 160, 163, 169.
Delos, 62, 131.
Demetrius, 24, 56.
Dessau, Prof., 122.
Diocletian, 35.
Diodorus, 48.
Dioscuri, 44, 139.
Domitian, 67.
Don, 20.
Dura, 32, 74, 91 ff.
—, Christian church at, 189 f.
—, frescoes of, 128.
—, private houses of, 190.
Dusares, 45, 88, n. 1, 138.
Dushara, *see* Dusares.

Index

Edessa, 28, 95, 99, 117, 188, 212.
Edomites, 18 f., 22 f.
Egypt, 5 ff., 12 ff., 18 ff., 22, 24 f., 28, 55 f., 109.
Egyptian trade, 28, 30.
Elan, 27, 65.
El-Ela, 22, 33, 57, 203.
El Habis, 47.
El Hegra, 50.
El Khasne, at Petra, 64, 139.
El Mu'eisra, 47.
Emesa, *see* Homs.
English merchants at Palmyra, 121.
Epiphanius, Bishop of Cyprus, 87.
Eshmun, 138.
Es Siyagh, 47.
Eudoxus of Cnidus, 28.
Euergetes I, 58.
Euphrates, i, 4 ff., 10, 12, 17, 23, 29, 32, 34, 65, 92, 167, 177.
Europe, 20.
Europos, *see* Dura.

Farmakovsky, 122.
Fayum, 57.
Fisher, Dr. C., vi, 83.
Flavians, 32, 67 f.
'fondouqs' of Palmyra, 143 f.
Forath, 143.
Fortuna, *see* Tyche.

Gabriel, 129.
Gad, 43, 203.
Gallienus, 117.
Garian, 47.
Garstang, Prof., 72.
Gaul, 109.
Gaza, 22, 61.
Gazara, 59.
Gennaes, 145.
Gerasa, 31, 61 ff. *See also* Jerash.
Gerrha, 12, 19, 27, 65.
Gerrhaeans, 13 f.
Geta, 200.
Gilead, 18.
Gordian III, 115.
Greece, 5, 11, 19.
Greek architects in East, 44.
— law, 9.
— states in East, 23, 30.
Guidi, 41.

Hadad, 78, 105 f., 131, 138, 151, 178, 186, 217.
Hadramaut, 13 f.
Hadrian, 68, 107, 144 ff., 196.
Halifax, William, 121.
Hama, 21, 32, 91, 93, 95, 143.
Hamath, *see* Hama.
Hammurabi, 9, 11, 14 f.
Han period, 19.
Harappa, 7.
Hašaš, 135.
Hatra, 97, 171.
Hegra, 203.
Helena, 40.
Heliogabalus, 110.
Heliopolis, 100.
Hellenism and Parthia, 98 ff.
Hellenistic culture, 24, 28 f.
— period, 48.
— period at Petra, 50.
— tombs at Petra, 45.
Hellenization, policy of, 59, 62.
Hercules, 202.
Herod the Great, 67.
Herzfeld, Prof., 97.
Hieropolis-Bambyce, 178.
Hipparchus, 28.
Hittite art, 148.
— law, 9.
— power, 14.
Hofsted, 121.
Homs, 21, 28, 32, 91, 93, 95, 100, 143, 159 f.
Hopkins, Prof. Clark, vi, 159, 167, 186, 189, 201.
Horsfield, 40, 47, 72, 78, 80.
Huntington, Elsworth, 3.
Hvareno, 43, 203.
Hyksos, 14.

India, 5 ff., 13, 19, 24 ff., 28, 30, 49.
Indian trade, 12, 30.
Ingholt, Prof., 145.
Iran, 1, 5 ff., 96 ff.
Iranian plateau, 12, 23, 26, 32.
— religion, 139 ff.
Ishmaelite caravan, 18.
Ishtar-Astarte, 131, 137.
Isis, temple of, at Petra, 43.
Italy, 5, 19, 50.
Ituraean dynasty, 100.

Index

Jaussen, RP., 49, 123.
Jerash, vi, 31, 33, 37, 39 ff., 46, 52, 65 f., 125, 129 f., 132.
—, Arab period at, 71.
—, Christian period at, 69, 73, 86 ff.
—, topography of, 74 ff.
Jerusalem, 32, 63, 71.
Jews, 39, 48, 55, 64.
Jewish trade, 22.
Jordan, 1.
Judaea, 28.
Julia Domna, 111, 201.
Julia Maesa, 111.
Julia Mammaea, 111.
Julia Soaemisas, 111.
Julian, 119.
Justinian, 70, 87 f.

Kasr Firaun, at Petra, 48.
Kertch, 104.
Khabur, 1, 17.
Kish, 7.
Konon, 192, 218.
Kul Tepe, 9.
Kushan kingdom, 140.

Lambaesis, 200.
Lammens, RP., 35.
Laodicea, 25.
Latysheff, 122.
Lazareff, Prince A., 122.
Lebanon, 1.
Leptis, 86.
Leuce Come, 27, 65.
Lihyian kingdom, 55, 57.
'limes' (Roman), 200.
Lisams, 134.
Little, A., 210.
Loo Collection, 19.
Loos, Cornelius, 121, 123.
Lucius Verus, 110.
Lydia, 20.
Lysias, Septimius, 205.

Maan, 39.
Maccabees, 64, 67.
Macedon, 24, 30.
Macedonian colonies, in East, 59, 61, 97, 104, 156.
— colony at Dura, 188, 197.

Macrinus, 115.
Main, 22.
Maiumas (Semitic), 70, 84.
Malakbel, 137.
Maps, early, 16, 177.
Marcus Aurelius, 69, 108, 100.
Maresha, 59.
Mariba, 17.
Mazaka, 10.
Mearists, 33, 39, 51.
Mecca, 35, 46, 52.
Medians, 22.
Mediterranean, 8, 19, 29.
Memphis, 89.
Mesopotamia, 1, 4, 10, 12, 20, 25 f., 62, 96.
Mesopotamian painting, 214.
Michigan expedition, 97.
Miletus, 20.
Mina (silver), 11.
Minaean kingdom, 55, 57.
Minaeans, 13 f., 17, 21 f.
Mithridates the Great, 97, 101.
Mohammed, 52.
Mohenjo Daro, 7.
Mond, H., 40.
Monikos, 100.
Monimos, 138.
Murphy, Capt., 153, 155, 183, 192.

Nabataean kings, 50, 55, 100.
— period at Petra, 48.
— texts, 43.
— trade, 64.
Nabataeans, 18, 22 f., 28, 30, 32 f., 51 f., 56 ff., 65, 113.
Nabonidus, 18 f.
Nanaea, 137. *See also* Artemis Nanaia.
Naram-sin, 8.
Naukratis, 20.
Nebuchelos, 207 f.
Nejd, 28.
Nemesis, 217.
Neo-Babylonian empire, 18 f., 23.
Nergal, 137.
Nero, 32, 66, 73.
Nicanor, 93.
Nicephorium, 95.
Nile, 5 f., 57.
Nimrud-Dagh, 99, 148.
Niniveh, 17.

Index

Nippur, 22.
Nubia, 24.

Odenath, 115, 117 f.
Ogelos, 145.
Omar II, 70.
Orontes, 1, 25, 161.
Orthonobazus, 191.
Osrhoene, 99.

Pagliaro, Prof., 210, n. 1.
Palace-court, at Dura, 172 ff.
Palestine, 1, 5, 8, 25 ff., 37, 39, 56, 58 ff., 68, 134.
Palmyra, 17 f., 28 ff., 42, 46, 52, 85, 91 ff., 120 ff., 177.
—, art of, 147 ff.
—, political constitution of, 141.
—, Trajan's policy at, 107.
Palmyrene gods, temple of, at Dura, 183 f., 204.
— tariff, 122, 142.
Panticapaeum, 20, 104, 195.
Parthia, 23, 26 ff., 34, 52, 65, 96.
—, importance of, 97 ff.
—, importance of, at Dura, 156 ff., 170 ff.
Parthian art, 147 ff., 191, 193 ff., 212 ff.
Paul, St., 32.
Perdiccas, 56.
Pergamum, 24, 102.
Persia, 15, 19, 23 f., 34, 210.
Persian Gulf, 1, 12, 26.
— period, 22, 50.
— trade, 19 ff.
Petra, vii, 23 f., 26 ff., 55 ff., 68, 85, 101, 109, 120, 125, 129, 132, 134, 146, 203.
Petraea, 18.
Philadelphia, 31, 41, 59 ff. *See also* Amman.
philhellene kings, 52.
Philip, 86.
Philip the Arab, 115.
Philostratus, 210.
Philotereia, 59.
Phoenicia, 1, 5, 8, 10, 14, 16, 19, 20, 25 ff., 32, 50, 56, 68, 95 f.
Phraates, contract of, 196.
Phrygia, 20.
Pieria, 25.

Pillet, M., vi, 159.
Poidebard, R. P., 145.
Pompeian wall-painting, 43 f.
Pompeius Trogus, 97.
Pompey, 29 f., 32, 66, 98, 100 f.
Pontus, 24.
Procopius, St., Church of, at Jerash, 79.
Ptolemies, 25 ff., 30, 56 ff., 61 f., 96.
Ptolemy, son of Mennaeus, 100.
Ptolemy II, Philadelphus, 26 f., 57 f.
Ptolemy VII, Euergetes II, 102.
Puteoli, 50.

Rabbath Ammon, 60.
Red Sea, 1, 5, 13, 19, 22 f., 25, 27, 57.
Renard, 171.
Rome, Palmyrene settlements in, 109.
— and Parthia, 100 ff.
Roman law, 9.
— period, 48.
— policy in the Near East, 66.
— power, 28 ff., 34 f.
Roudha, 138.
Russia, South, 20.

Sabaean kingdom, 55.
— stelae, 36.
Sabaeans, 13 f., 17 f., 22 f.
Safaitic Arabs, 134.
Sampsigeramos, 100.
Šamš, 138.
Sargon, 8 f., 17.
Sarmatian warriors, 194 ff., 215.
Sarre, F., 97.
Sasanian art, 212 ff.
— period, 34, 41, 69, 97, 115.
Satrapes, 140.
Savignac, Père, 49, 123.
Seistan, 7.
Seleucia, 25, 65, 91 f., 94, 97, 161.
— in Pieria, 25.
— on the Eulaios, 198.
Seleucid period, routes of, 161.
— power at Dura, 170.
Seleucids, 25 ff., 30, 56, 58, 62, 65, 94, 96, 98, 100.
Seleucus I, 25, 93, 98.
Semitic cities, 21.
— elements at Jerash, 85.
— elements at Palmyra, 110, 133.
Sendjirli, 148.

Index

Severi, policy of, in Mesopotamia, 110 f.
Severus, dynasty of, 69.
Severus, Alexander, 181.
Severus, Septimius, 86, 110 ff., 181, 206.
Seyrig, H., vi, 127.
Shamash, 137 ff.
Shapur I, 116, 119, 174, 212.
shekel, 11.
Sicily, 19.
Sidon, 50, 58.
Simeon, St., Monastery of, 162.
Sinai peninsula, 13, 103.
Skythopolis, 31.
Soados, 145.
Solomon, 18.
Spain, 5, 109.
Spasinu Charax, *see* Charax.
Stadium, at Jerash, 74.
Stein, Sir Aurel, 97.
Strabo, 48.
Suez Canal, 19.
—, Isthmus of, 5.
Sumer, 7, 9, 10, 21.
Sumerian culture, 11, 53.
— language, 9.
Susa, 198.
Syria, 1, 5 ff., 13 f., 18, 21 ff., 55, 62 f., 68, 91.
Syro-Arabian Empire, 48.

Tacitus, 98.
Tadmor, *see* Palmyra.
Taurus, 1.
Tell Halaf, 148.
Tema, 13, 19.
theatre at Palmyra, 129 f.
Theodore Stratilates, St., Church of, at Jerash, 70, 79, 87 f.
Thothmes III, 15.
Thrace, 24.
Thughra, at Petra, 47.
Tiberius, 32, 103.
Tiglath-pileser I, 17.
Tiglath-pileser III, 17.
Tigris, 1, 4 ff., 12, 25, 27, 92.
Torrey, Prof., 210, n. 1.
Trade, earliest history of, 4 ff.

Trajan, 32 ff., 49 ff., 68, 144, 196.
Trajan, policy of, in Near East, 106 f., 110.
Transjordania, 25, 30 f., 39, 55 ff.
Transjordanian legion, 39.
Tripoli, 47.
Tubias, 60.
Tunisia, 47.
Turkestan, 7, 20.
Turkmaniye, at Petra, 47.
Tyche, 43.
Tyche, at Jerash, 79.
Tyche, at Dura, 188, 203 ff., 209, 219.
Tyche, at Palmyra, 151, 219.
Tyre, 16, 58.

Upsala, University Library, 121.
Ur of the Chaldees, 7 f., 11, 191.
— —, third dynasty of, 8 f.
Ur-Nammu, 8.
Uspensky, 122.

Vaballath, 117 f.
Valerian, 115, 117, 212.
Vespasian, 67, 73.
Vogüé, Marquis de, 122.
Vologesia, 109, 143 ff.
Vorodes, Julius Aurelius Septimius, 117, 130.

Wady Musa, 48.
Welles, B. C., 196.
Wiegand, T., 46.
Wood, 122 f.

Yale expedition to Dura, 107, 157 f., 167.
— Museum, 183, 185.
Yarhibol, 137, 141, 150, 155, 183, 219.
Yarhibol-Malakbel, 139.
Yathil, 22.

Zebida, 134.
Zenobia, 35, 118 f., 123, 125.
Zenon, archives of, 59 ff.
Zeus, 198.
Zeus, Temple of, at Jerash, 74 ff.
Zoroastrian religion, 140.